IAN.
Toombes.

JOHN WARE'S COW COUNTRY

by

Grant MacEwan

ACKNOWLEDGMENT

Western Producer Book Service wishes to acknowledge the contribution of William Clarence Richards, who as president of the Institute of Applied Art Ltd. (Edmonton) made the creation of this book possible through his personal desire to have the history of Western Canada recorded while the people who made that history were still alive. **John Ware's Cow Country** was first published by the Institute in 1960.

WESTERN PRODUCER PRAIRIE BOOKS
Saskatoon, Saskatchewan

Copyright © 1973 by Grant MacEwan
Western Producer Prairie Books
Saskatoon, Saskatchewan

First softcover edition 1976
Second softcover printing 1979

ISBN 0-919306-77-2

Canadian Shared Cataloguing in Publication Data

MacEwan, John W. Grant, 1902-
John Ware's cow country

ISBN 0-919306-43-8
ISBN 0-919306-77-2 pa.

1. Ware, John, 1845-1905. 2. Cattle
trade - Alberta. I. Title.
FC3217.1.W37M32   971.2'02
F1060.9.W

Printed and bound in Canada
by
Modern Press

Saskatoon, Saskatchewan

FOREWORD

Three main reasons motivated this work. First, there was a sincere admiration for the Negro rancher who so completely captured the pioneer hearts. Then there was a hope that the story of John Ware's career, clearly a success story, might carry the bigger one about ranching on the western range during his lifetime. And, finally, the author would wish to proclaim a conviction that present-day society, with some silly and shameful prejudices, needs the story surrounding the big, powerful, skilful and generous colored cowboy It is to the everlasting credit of the early West that John Ware could win success and such unstinted respect.

Being illiterate, John Ware left no personal records to help a biographer. Fortunately, the part of the book dealing with the rise of the ranching industry on Western Canadian soil can be supported reasonably well by records; but for the principal part of the narrative of John Ware, the author was obliged to go directly to the people who knew him. Fortunately, the pioneers still with us have good memories.

Grant MacEwan.

CONTENTS

John Ware cabin near Duchess. Photo taken in 1958.

John Ware cabin in its new location at Steveville. Photo taken in 1964.

Mildred   Robert   Nettie   John

CHAPTER I

THE SLAVE

"John Ware, ex-slave from the South and for 25 years a rancher and cowhand in the West, owner of a thousand head of the finest range cattle on the Red Deer River, was killed today by a horse stumbling and falling on him, killing him instantly. Deceased was 60 years old and leaves a family."

Thus the Calgary *Daily Herald* of September 12, 1905, carried news from "Brooks, North West Territories," informing a saddened frontier of the passing of a familiar personality. Feelingly, the pioneers whispered, "John is dead! He was a great soul." Even fifty years later, when men of the Old Range gathered at Calgary's Palliser Hotel for the Annual Rangemen's Dinner, one of the patriarchs proclaimed softly: "John Ware? Bless his Negro heart. He was the finest gentleman I ever knew."

What was it about this man to command such respect and even affection from the thousands who knew him? Was it the Samson-like strength by which he could wrestle a two-year-old steer to the ground, or was it his unsurpassed skill with horses? Would success in overcoming crushing handicaps like slavery, poverty and total lack of education account for the esteem in which he was held? Could it be that his complete triumph over false stigmas associated with race and color brought him distinctiveness, or was it inherent friendliness and good humor that accounted for the place of honor John Ware gained in the hearts and memories of the men and women who knew him?

Whatever the answer, John Ware's story — a tribute to himself and to the fellow pioneers who acknowledged his manly qualities without prejudice — is one to be shared.

When the Civil War ended and the southern slaves found themselves with freedom and power they didn't know how to use, this colored boy was twenty years of age. He was big and powerful and awkward; he couldn't read or write, and he had never traveled beyond the swamps less than an hour's walk from the low-roofed Ware cabin on the South Carolina plantation. As for Canada, this big fellow with tattered clothes and a ragged crop of adolescent whiskers had never heard of it — at least not until a fellow slave was said to have been helped to escape to that place. It might be north, south, east or west — for all the slaves on that cotton plantation close to Georgetown knew or cared.

For at least three generations John Ware's people lived like plantation work-mules, assured only of food, clothing, and toil. Like the same draft animals they were bought and sold — usually at slightly higher than mule prices. Sometimes their owners and masters were considerate people; just as often they were brutal.

The first slaves in the English-American colonies were twenty African Negroes brought to Jamestown, Virginia, in 1619, and sold to the highest bidders. Colonists could use cheap labor, and the shippers who enticed or kidnaped natives from the west coast of Africa soon found the piratical trade to be both exciting and profitable.

Of course, there were voices being raised against trafficking in human cargoes, but they were scarcely heard above the tinkle of profits in high places. Queen Anne of England was said to be a prominent shareholder in the evil operations, and even Christian churches in the South did little or nothing to oppose the trade. In some instances, prizes were offered for the best sermons on "free trade" in Negroes, and ministers with flexible standards of morals proclaimed righteously that pirating of heathen natives in Africa and selling them into North American slavery was a practical means of bringing them to Christianity — and immortality to their souls. It was salve for the conscience to say that bringing Negroes, even by force, to Christianity would do as much for their eternal welfare as taking the faith to them in Africa. "If you take slaves with the intent of conducting them to Christ," said one churchman, "the action will not be a sin." Bondage and threat of whiplash here below should be a small price to pay for the assurance of eternity in Heaven.

So went the reasoning of those who coveted the benefits of slavery. And laws were no better. The British Parliament in 1750 legalized trade in Negro slaves between Africa and the English-American colonies. Although one State Legislature moved in 1761 to place an import tax on slaves, the bill was vetoed in London and the Governor of Virginia was instructed by King George III to "assent to no law by which importation of slaves should in any way be prohibited or obstructed."

John Ware's birth on the South Carolina cotton plantation was an event of small consequence, except to keep his mother away from cotton work for a few days. He was just one more curly-haired pickaninny in a community where people were restrained in everything except propagation.

The idea of attending school was so remote that nobody entertained it. Educating a boy wouldn't make him a better slave; and the masters, speaking with aristocratic English accents, knew it. At the age of eight John Ware was picking cotton alongside adults; and life, as far as anybody could imagine, held little else. Cotton picking began at the first of August and, as new bolls broke open to enliven the fields with specks of white, it continued until nearly Christmas. In the remaining part of the year were other chores related to cotton — cultivation of fields and so on.

The only release from labor was on Sundays when the slave owner, with pious concern for souls, demanded that all Negroes attend services for Christian instruction. There the adventures of Jonah and Daniel were related, and all present repeated to memorize selected portions of scripture, mainly promises of reward in the Next World. "In my Father's House are many mansions," the Negro people intoned solemnly. It was quite legitimate to whip slaves on week days as long as the appropriate saving grace was administered on Sabbath.

But the subjected people entered willingly into the spirit of religious services, showing more faith than those who were the teachers. Sacred song brought comfort at any time, and when men and women at work sang spirituals, the melodies echoed back from magnolia groves to fill the fields with enchantment.

Rarely did anybody, at the end of a day's work, feel like indulging in pastimes more laborious than singing spirituals; but when slaves did turn to sport, the boy John Ware, with muscles like those of a plantation mule and a smile as continuous as toil, could outrun and outjump all others. And when there was provocation he could outfight any Negro of his age.

It was quite common for Negroes to fight Negroes. White masters striding majestically about in high boots and long coats encouraged barefisted combat for their personal amusement. Bloody noses and swollen faces made the entertainment that much better. But no slave dared strike a white person — not even in self-defense. It was the law, just as it was law in some states that a runaway slave could be shot.

Young Ware was an even-tempered fellow and pleasant — as Canadian ranchers discovered in later years; but he was no coward, and when he struck, he struck hard. As he recalled youthful adventures to his rancher friend, Sam Howe, two fights stood out in his memory. One could have been considered a triumph, but the other he paid for painfully.

Concerning the first of those fisticuff episodes, John Ware laughed heartily in the telling. The South Carolina slave owner had guests — noble males and stylish females. It was not sufficient to provide wine and the finest foods like roast snipe and quail in that land noted for hospitality. Desiring to entertain his company, he invited them to witness a battle royal among his slave boys.

The willingness of the boys to participate was not considered. The ring was roped off and comfortable chairs were placed in the shade for the guests. When all was ready, twelve Negro boys about twelve to fifteen years of age were placed in the enclosure, much as fighting cocks would be placed in a pit. As for rules, there was only one: when a boy was knocked down he was required to remain down. It was a free-for-all; and the last boy standing would be the winner and qualify for the prize, a pair of shoes.

The boys weren't angry at each other. There was no ill-feeling among them, but compliance was the master's command. Moreover, there was an element of sport about it; and everyone of them, accustomed to going in bare feet, would wish to own a pair of shoes.

With bare hands, bare feet and bodies bare above the waists, the boys entered the ring. John Ware was among them. Tall and handsome Mr. Chauncey called, "Are you ready? Start."

For a moment or two there were only gentle jabs by laughing punchers. Then the blows became heavier. One boy went down and then another and another. Some who fell crawled out of the ring; others remained insensible on the ground. As still-active participants became fewer, genteel white spectators applauded with dignified caution.

"You really have some splendid physical specimens, Mr. Chauncey," visitors remarked to their host. "Do you have any discipline troubles with your slaves?"

"Discipline? No. No trouble; but I would have if I were not firm, even severe. They've all felt the whiplash, you know, and they understand what it means. Oh, there's another one out! Just the two left now. That one with the big smile we call John and the other is Mose. But it's all over now. John's as strong as a bull. Mose has been sick a lot in his life — hardly worth keeping."

But John didn't finish Mose in one blow. He missed his opponent, missed every time he struck. It was a strange performance and spectators asked, "What's wrong with that John fellow?"

Before the question was answered, John Ware went down from what seemed a light but direct blow and Mose was the winner. As the shoes were handed to Mose, John Ware, still prostrate on the ground, was peering attentively and smiling more than ever. Mose understood. He went to John, helped him to his feet and said gratefully, "Yo ol' scamp, yo could a had those shoes. I know yo wanted me t' have em. Now didn yo?"

John laughed at the smaller fellow and wiped a mixture of sweat and blood from his face. "Dem shoes'll go on yo feet, Mose; ma feet were neva in shoes in ah ma life an' I don imagine any shoes'd be big 'nough. Besides, Mose, yo mammy was awfu good to my mammy when she was sick."

The other fight, bred in anger, was nothing to laugh about. Mr. Chauncey was a hard master — harder than most slave owners. Never did he go outside of his house without his black-handled whip with six-foot lash. Carrying it may have been from cowardly fear of attack, but in any case he did not hesitate to use the cruel thing on the backs of inoffensive slaves.

To strike back would insure painful punishment, and John Ware proved it. Mr. Chauncey was in an ugly mood that day when he came into the field where his people were hoeing. It was the first year of the Civil War. Perhaps reports about Confederate reverses made him more irritable than usual. Maybe he had lost money at whist or possibly he had a hangover from too much gaiety. Anyway, the hoes were moving too slowly to suit him, and as he shouted a curse for all to hear, his whiplash fell across the back of a man becoming feeble from old age. Every able-bodied slave knew exactly what retaliation he would like to take against this master whose high station in life was due to inheritance rather than skill or achievement of his own. But reprisals had always led to cruel punishment, and it was better to take the indignity of a casual cut from the master's lash then be publicly whipped, stroke after stroke.

But this day, Mr. Chauncey went too far. He struck a Mammy taking time out to nurse her baby, and then he struck a girl — John Ware's sister. John's anger boiled and all sense of caution left him. He walked directly and fearlessly toward the master, muttering, "She's ma sistah. Don yo do it again."

The master was shocked. He scowled, stepped back, swung the whip about his head and brought it down on John Ware's shoulders, shouting, "Slave! You don't tell me what I shall do. Take that."

John forgot all about prudence, forgot the plantation rule that any slave hitting back was asking for a flogging. He sprang forward like a cat and seized the lapels of the white man's coat. "Yo can kill me if yo likes, Boss," John was saying, "but yo not whippin any mo slaves today. Give me that whip."

Furious at the very idea of such disrespect — a slave telling him to give up his whip — Mr. Chauncey struck John Ware in the face, struck with all the might he possessed. The big youth could restrain himself no longer, and his powerful right hand came down upon the master, knocking him violently to the ground.

As Mr. Chauncey lay motionless on the freshly hoed soil, Negro men whispered admiringly about young Ware, but women wept, knowing that this would be the beginning of trouble.

The embarrassed white man recovered consciousness, raised himself slowly to his feet and made his way to his house. Later in the day, his left eye black and swollen and two pistols hanging from his belt, he appeared before the slaves to announce that John Ware must present himself to be tied to the whipping tree. "Until he has been scourged for his crime there will be no rations for any slaves."

John expected it. He knew he wouldn't be shot or hung, because a living slave was worth much more than a dead one. He was ready for the ordeal. Unless he submitted at once, all the slaves would suffer. And so, while mother and sisters sobbed, he came forward, stood with his face to the chestnut tree in the courtyard, and allowed himself to be tied with a heavy leather strap at the level of his waist. Now all the slaves were commanded to witness and be duly impressed by white authority and plantation justice.

Mr. Chauncey was a showman as well as an autocrat, and before proceeding to chastise the slave who would dare to question his tactics, he cracked the long whip ceremoniously. What he was going to do pleased him. The smirk of satisfaction on his swollen face made that fact plain. With long and deliberate strides he came to his position about eight feet from the tree, swung the whip and brought it down on the slave's bare back. The victim flinched, groaned, and gritted his teeth as each of ten painful blows fell, and blood oozed from welts and bruises.

Oh, to meet the brute on equal terms, thought John Ware. At that moment he would have given up the little of joy that life held for a slave, to square off with this sadist and bully holding the whip handle. The fact remained, however, that fighting back had never yet achieved anything except added suffering for the slaves.

Punishment completed, fellow slaves unfastened John Ware and aided him to the family cabin, a log structure beside the swamp, where his mother washed her boy's back tenderly and applied pork grease to the bloody bruises.

Next day John Ware was at work as usual. There could be no holiday because of whip welts. But with new intenseness he was thinking; how were his people to overcome the yoke of·slavery? What chance was there of some day meeting a contemptible wretch like Mr. Chauncey on common fighting ground?

From time to time there was whispered talk of insurrection. Abolitionists Benjamin Lundy, John Brown who was hanged in 1859, and others had spoken courageously about the evil of slavery, but not much was achieved. John's father remembered secret meetings among the Negroes along the South Carolina coast to plan rebellion to coincide with the landing of Admiral Cockburn who would proclaim freedom for the slaves. But nothing came of the scheme.

But for John Ware and others who yearned to demonstrate that they could be at least as good as the average white men, the chance was coming — even though South Carolina was the chief champion of slavery, the first state to secede because of the controversy and the first to witness the clash of arms marking the beginning of the War of Secession.

When Abraham Lincoln was elected to the Presidency of the United States in 1860, the North was wrathfully conscious of the injustice of slavery, just as the South, with four million slaves worth a thousand dollars each on the market, was conscious of financial benefits. "This nation," said Lincoln, "cannot endure half-slave and half-free." Showdown was imminent. Northerners were known to have aided Negroes to escape to free territory, and Southerners vowed to resist with force any interference with their affairs.

The Ordinance of Secession passed by a convention held at Charleston, just over fifty miles from John Ware's Georgetown, December 20, 1860, was the first step toward separate government and, indeed, toward war. The declaration was clear: "That the Union now subsisting between South Carolina and other States, under the name of the United States of America, is hereby dissolved."

Mississippi, Florida, Alabama, Georgia, Louisiana, Texas, Virginia, Arkansas, North Carolina, and Tennessee followed the South Carolina example, and on February 18, 1861, the Confederacy had its birth. Jefferson Davis became the President and the city of Richmond, in Virginia, the Capital. Shots fired from South Carolina guns in Charleston Harbour precipitated the crisis, and both North and South prepared for a long war.

The turning point in the North's favor came at Gettysburg on July 3, 1863, when General Lee's Confederate troops were soundly defeated. April, 1865, saw General Grant capturing Petersburg and Lee surrendering his Confederate army at Appomattox Court House. Five days after that surrender President Abraham Lincoln was shot; but he had already issued his emancipation order to free all the slaves in the United States.

Half a million lives were lost as a result of the war; and property damage, especially in the South, was terrific. The Negroes, unable to participate actively in the war, were now free men and women and, for a time, they ran wild. The South was torn by chaos, hatred and violence; and federal troops were needed to maintain a semblance of order. It was a bad time for the South. Commercial depression followed war, and reconstruction was further impeded by "carpetbaggers" from the North who benefitted by Negro votes. People were upset and tense. Masked night riders, generally lawless whites, played upon superstitions and filled the countryside with fear.

The Negroes, of course, had some quite legitimate accounts to settle with certain brutish whites, and nobody about Georgetown was more uneasy than Mr. Chauncey. With no further excuse for carrying the whip, he quite wisely remained at home after nightfall. Just as the sun was setting one evening, however, he came face to face with John Ware, now six feet tall and strapping in build. The Negro opened the conversation as he blocked the white man's path, saying he might be leaving Georgetown and had something important to talk about before going. Taking the frightened Mr. Chauncey by the hand, John led him to the edge of the grove and stood him against a big tree — the old whipping tree.

"Now don twy t' wun away, Mistah Chauncey, cause ah can ketch yo an yo might get awfu hu't when ah dwagged yo back."

John raised his shirt and pointed to scars over his ribs. "Oce those Mistah Chauncey? Yo membah the day ah got em? This was the twee. Yo membah a wight."

Mr. Chauncey, trembling and pale, said nothing. He could wish he didn't remember.

"What yo think ah should do bout it now, Mistah Chauncey? You know, ah figahs ah'm a betta man than yo and therah's seve'al things ah could do. It's gettin pwetty da'k now an ah could easy hang you t' dat t'ee wherah yo whipped me, and yo fwiends'd find yo long body danglin fwom a bwanch in the monin. O' ah could tie yo up an do a bit o whippin myself. Do you know, Mistah Chauncey, ah could punch yo till yo wouldn wecognize yo own face. Yo dese'ves em all an yo knows it. Ah 'v ben thinkin a lot bout this time when yo an me'd meet an have this little talk, an ah always figahed ah 'd sta't punchin an give yo a chance to punch back if yo had any man in yo. But ah'm leavin ol Ca'olina t'mo'ow, Mistah Chauncey—goin t' Texas an ah'v decided what ah'l do t' you. Ah'm just goin t' do nothin to' yo, Mistah Chauncey— just t' show you that an ol slave can have mo man about him than you evah had. See, Mistah Chauncey? Yo can go home now, but don fo'get, mo man than yo evah had. Go-bye Mistah Chauncey."

CHAPTER 2

TEXAS

John Ware wasn't sure why he was going to Texas, except that it was "out West" and likely to offer more freedom and opportunity than released slaves would find in old Carolina. Wearing a pair of ill-fitting shoes left by a Northern soldier, and an expression of sorrow at leaving members of his family — father, mother, and ten brothers and sisters — he was on his way.

After five months of working more than traveling, he stopped at a rural home on the outskirts of Fort Worth, Texas, and inquired if he might perform some labor in return for food.

The elderly man of the place looked John over the way he'd study a race horse before making a trade and said: "You're right big enough to do a day's work. What you good for? Had any experience with hosses?"

"No, sah," John replied with characteristic honesty, "but ah knows about feedin mules an ah figahs ah ken still wide a buckin jackass."

His thoughts went back to those times in boyhood when, to amuse guests, Mr. Chauncey would throw the Negro boys, one at a time, on the back of the orneriest donkey on the plantation. The ass would buck furiously, and without benefit of saddle or bridle, a boy had little chance to remain long before crashing to the ground. When a boy fell spectators laughed heartily, but John Ware's legs were long and he alone could grip the animal's body to hang on while Mr. Chauncey cracked the whip to keep the donkey performing.

"Wall," said the tall Texan with white goatee, "if you know anything about mules I reckin you could help with horses. You can stay and work a day for your keep, and if you're any good I might give you some wages after that. You can sleep in the empty stall next to the stud colt. Go hang your coat on a harness hook. Hain't much of a coat — looks like the squirrels been camping in it — but hang the thing up anyway. Then get the scythe and start cutting hay. Nobody eats around here till the work's done. If you're still around tomorrow, you can take the long-handled rake and gather your hay into bunches."

John had never used a scythe and was as awkward as a bachelor holding a neighbor's baby. But when he had had some instruction and practice his swaths became wide and clean. The old man, watching from the shade of a tree, mumbled, "If the boy can keep that up we'll hang on to him."

"You said your name is John?" the old man inquired when he went to report that supper was ready in the big kitchen. "My name's Murphy Blandon. Folks here call me Old Murph and call my boy Young Murph. The young fellow's away hunting the hosses. When he gets back we'll have some breaking to do. Dozen three-year-olds never had a halter on yet. If I know anything about race hosses some of 'em have speed in 'em. Couldn't live without a few race hosses! Awright, wash your face and we'll see what ma's ben a'cookin' for supper."

Next day John cut and piled as much hay as Old Murph would have expected from two men. "Look you," the elder said at the end of the day, "better decide to stay with us. You can move into a room in the attic. There'll be lots of work here with the hosses and cattle and, damn it, you act like you might be a good man."

John smiled. He found Mrs. Blandon friendly, and a good cook; sure, he wanted to stay and help with the horses and cattle.

After an absence of nearly a week Young Murph returned with most of the family horses — sixty of them with good withers, clean limbs, and evidence of breeding. He was saddle sore and his gray gelding was tired, but Young Murph had a lot to tell, mostly about the wild cattle he saw. "Millions of 'em," he said. "Some branded, some not. No wonder we can't sell our own cattle for more'n three dollars with all those wild ones on the range. They'd be worth forty dollars if they were in Chicago, I suppose. Why don't we get in on the gathering and driving of those critters to New Orleans or somewhere?"

But his father's mind was not on cattle. "Afore you start galavantin' with longhorns, Son," he said, "don't forget you got some hosses to break."

Young Murph chuckled. "I understand. You'll be laying awake at nights till you know how many racers you've got in the bunch. Unless they's got some fast hosses in Heaven, they'll never hold you inside the fence."

Haying ceased when horse breaking started. John's instructions were to stand by and hang onto ropes when his unskilled strength might help. Young Murph took command, corralled the horses and then released all but the three-year-olds. Admiringly, John watched him twirl a lariat and drop the loop over the head of a brown colt. Snubbed to a post, the young horse was haltered and then tied by the shank. Old Murph insisted that his horse be taught to tie and lead before being introduced to saddle and harness.

To John Ware it was all so new. He couldn't rope a tree stump, had never even seen a Mexican saddle before. But a strong man can be a useful man around livestock, and it was after a colt was haltered that he found a special task for himself, teaching the young horses to lead. Once John's big hands were on the rope, a colt could rear and plunge but couldn't get away. Laughing all the while, John would play with an obstreperous horse the way a fisherman would play with a trout on his line. Here was something he could do better than his experienced boss, and one by one the colts were educated to lead. Conceding that John had a natural "way with horses," Old Murph observed the halter breaking to be the best he had seen.

John was happy. He discovered a fondness for horses and, for the first time in his life, a purpose worth pursuing. He wanted to ride and rope like Young Murph. There was a new reason for living.

When the day's work was done he tried throwing the lariat over a post in the pole fence, and before the horse-breaking chores were completed he asked, "Boss, das yo 'spose ah could twy widing one o dem hosses?"

"You know, you could get hurt, but go to it."

The colt was bridled but not saddled when John leaped on — almost as a cat would pounce on a mouse — and the half-broken horse's inclination was to buck or run. It did both — bucked first and then dashed madly toward the logs forming the corral fence, bounded into space like a deer taking a deadfall, cleared the wall and galloped out across the plain. And John, miraculously, was still riding, still clutching the animal's mane and pressing his untrained heels irritatingly against the pony's sensitive rear flanks. The Murphys, completely unable to intervene, watched with astonishment. They expected to witness mishap — probably a mangled human body. For Old Murph, fear mingled with surprise and admiration — fear for the safety of a boy he was growing to like, surprise that John had not fallen, and admiration for the little bay gelding showing almost unbelievable speed.

Horse and rider, still streaking away in the general direction of Mexico, dropped from sight as they entered a dry ravine, came back into view on the other side and, finally, disappeared in the belt of trees near the river.

As the young horse grew tired and John was able to collect his thoughts, he became conscious of the loose rawhide reins he was holding and discovered a use for them. With his pull on the right leather the bay yielded, circled in that direction, and continued to run at only slightly slackened pace in the direction of the corral so recently left in mad flight.

For John there was the sensation of triumph. Fear departed. He was still on the horse and now, with a rein held firmly in each hand, he was in control.

Halfway back to the corral he met Young Murph on the gray gelding, anxiously on his way to rescue or find the terrified young horse and a Negro boy making his first ride.

"Are you all right?" Young Murph asked while scanning the panting colt to make sure there was no outward injury.

With a broad grin betraying the satisfaction of mastery, John replied, "Ah'm fine, Boss, but ah was afea'in ah'd neva see yo again. We seemed to be leavin Texas in a big huwy."

"Don't know how you managed to stay on when you jumped that fence. It's a four-foot fence. Holy Jerusalem, that thing can jump — and run. Do you want me to lead him back for you?"

"Ah'll wide him, Boss. Ah knows how t' do it now. Ah found how t' make a hoss tu'n."

Returning to the corral the two riders were met by Old Murph, on foot, excited and shouting. "Gosha' mighty, man, can that thing go! Why, there ain't a nag in Texas to catch him. Wonder you didn't kill yourself though, John. Nobody hurt, I guess. Say, that colt's going like a broke horse now. That's one horse that's not for sale. No sir! If he can run that fast, he can trot too. We've got to get harness on that fellow. I'll train him myself. What're we going to call him? John, got any ideas?"

John was now standing beside the gelding, rubbing foamy sweat from the animal's steaming hide. "Call 'im Jack Wabbit o' Hound Dog," John replied, half in fun.

"All right. He's Hound Dog."

John Ware's next experience was to ride in a saddle, and in the days to follow he was on a horse whenever there was opportunity, sometimes working young horses, sometimes riding with Young Murph.

Under the intent supervision of Old Murph, Hound Dog was introduced to harness and the two-wheel breaking cart. Thereafter, as regularly as breakfast, the bay was hitched and driven. As a trotter his stride was long and straight, but his natural inclination was to run rather than trot, and Hound Dog's disposition was that of a fighter. But Old Murph was determined he'd have a blue ribbon race horse at the local racing day in September.

Fort Worth had fewer than 500 inhabitants, but every adult loved a race and everybody attended on that day when the best horses in eastern Texas came together to settle local disputes about speed. The first contest of the program was for three-year-old trotters hitched to buggies or sulkies. If brief but intense training would do it, Hound Dog should be at his best. Old Murph, as always, insisted upon driving. Young Murph was absent in the South, but John Ware was now well able to groom the young racer and bring him, hitched, to the track. It being Hound Dog's first race, the strange surroundings and the hundreds of spectators made him nervous. Old Murph, with anxious hopes, was just a bit nervous too, but was trying to hide his feelings. He wanted so much to have a winner and he believed Hound Dog could be one.

The race was called and John led the bay to the track. Old Murph, a short whip in his right hand and chin whiskers trimmed with special care for the occasion, seated himself in the vehicle, braced his feet, measured his reins, and said, "How's he feeling, John?"

"Well, Boss, ah'd say Hound Dog feels lak me — so'ta wo'ied."

The three-year-olds were given their positions and started. It was a good start and all seven Texans were driving like men who loved a race. Hound Dog looked like an equine model but he was rattled and unhappy. The rattle of six other buggies was enough to confuse any young horse racing for the first time and Hound Dog broke from a trot to a gallop. That was his downfall, exactly what Old Murph feared most. There was just one thing to do, draw him in to recover the proper trotting pace. The colt resented the interference and was in no mood to settle back into an approved trot. Meanwhile, all six competitors drew past, leaving Hound Dog in seventh position. John Ware's heart was beating fast. He loved that colt and he wanted Old Murph's faith to be rewarded.

But nobody knew more about race course conduct than Old Murph. He didn't strike Hound Dog but talked to him, eased him into the proper gait, then relaxed the reins to let the horse set his own fast stride. Sure enough, the horse found it. It was magnificent. Hound Dog was closing the gap ahead of him. He drew abreast of one horse and passed, passed another and then another. Spectators were really seeing superior trotting action, bold and threatening. Old Murph was pressing skillfully, but it was too late. The race ended and Hound Dog was second. Old Murph was disappointed — terribly disappointed — but he knew he had a good horse; everybody knew Hound Dog could be a winner and John Ware threw his heavy arms around the colt's neck, saying, "Yo ol scamp; yo'll do it nothah day an ah wants to see yo do it."

The spectators and horsemen turned their attention to other races, and then the last event on the day's program was called — the free-for-all running race. John Ware was getting ready to take Hound Dog home when he had an idea: why not enter the colt in that contest? Anxiously, he looked about for Old Murph and rushed to him.

"Boss, will yo let Hound Dog go in this las wace? The scamp can wun. Will yo let him?"

Old Murph chuckled. "Don't think so John. He hasn't been trained to run."

"But Boss, yo saw him wun away wuf me — wufout twainin."

"I know, he ran that day, but we haven't got a saddle and I'm too old to ride in a race like that. And Young Murph isn't here."

"Ah'll wide 'im Boss," John gasped. "Ah'll wide 'im wufout a saddle. Ol Hound Dog laks to wun."

Old Murph was showing interest. "Damn it, do as you like. You're too heavy to win a race, John, but go do as you like."

In an instant John had a riding bridle on Hound Dog and was bringing him into line with fifteen other contestants. Some of the best runners in Texas were there in the field, all saddled and conditioned for a full mile.

Again Hound Dog became excited, kicked wickedly at the horse standing alongside and tossed his head rebelliously. John's broad smile obscured his own nervousness. After a brief moment of fidgeting the starter shouted, "Go!"

The trained runners started at a gallop. Confused, Hound Dog started to trot and once again was at the rear of the field. John didn't know what to do, but the circumstances of the day the colt bolted with him from the corral flashed back upon his mind. On the former occasion he hadn't used the reins at all, just grabbed the colt's mane and clung with his long powerful legs, digging heels into the flank. At once, John loosened the reins, pressed heels against the tender flank and pleaded, "Wun yo scamp; wun away again."

Instantly Hound Dog lit into a gallop — that sort of gallop John remembered from that first wild ride. It was the gallop of a horse giving its best, its frenzied best. "Come on yo scamp," John was mumbling, and the colt was gaining at a spectacular rate. All human eyes were upon Hound Dog and the awkward rider. Old Murph was showing symptoms of madness, shouting and tugging nervously at his goatee.

Even with a loose rein Hound Dog seemed to know what he was supposed to do. John was using his heels but not his whip. At the three-quarter mark the young horse was threatening, and at the finish line Hound Dog was the first over — the winner by a good half length to spare.

The horse-loving Texans yelled with surprised pleasure, and above all the voices was that of Old Murph, forgetting his seventy-odd years and shouting like an intoxicated Comanche. John Ware tightened the reins and gee'd the three-year-old around to meet the Boss.

"What a race! By ginger, what a race!" Old Murph was proclaiming in a gasping voice. "Never in all my days did I see the beat of it. Nearly had heart failure. I don't know now which of you two hounds I love the most — man or hoss. John, damn it, you're excited too. I know some gents who'll want to buy that hoss now, but don't fear, John, the little hound isn't for sale. You wouldn't want me to sell him? We didn't win at trotting, but we won the race of the day. Damn it, John, he's the best hoss on the field today — maybe the best in all Texas.''

That night, after the colt was rubbed down and bedded luxuriously in his box stall, Old Murph drank a brandy to the "best three-year-old in the South," and told John there was a job there for him as long as the Blandons were raising horses and cattle.

John smiled even more broadly than usual. "Boss," he said, "yo been good t' me and fo now ah wants t' stay wuf yo people and ol Hound Dog. Ah wants t' be as good a cowboy as Young Mu'ph and someday, Boss, ah might even have some hosses and cattle of ma own.''

CHAPTER 3

TRAIL TO THE NORTH

Old Murph was a horseman, first, last, and always. Young Murph, on the other hand, was attracted by cattle and the opportunities presenting themselves in the semi-wild critters multiplying on the Texas ranges, especially in the angle formed by the Rio Grande River and the Gulf coast. Longhorned, longlegged descendants of Spanish stock brought to Mexico many years before, they were neither handsome nor amiable. The Republic of Texas, existing prior to 1845, declared them to be public property; hence they belonged to anybody who could catch and brand them. But until they had a cash value there was no incentive to establish personal claims upon them.

For years tough Texans, conditioned by skirmishes with Indians, Mexicans, and Northerners, talked about rounding up herds of the wild things and trailing them to a market — somewhere; but not many drives were successful. A herd was delivered at New Orleans in 1842, and a Texas-to-Chicago drive was completed in 1856. But cattle multiplied faster than they were claimed, and if Texas had two million of them before the War, it had at least four million at War's end.

When hostilities ceased interest in exploiting unclaimed stock revived; and cattlemen saw the railroads, penetrating westward into Missouri and Kansas, as aids in carrying out their purpose. In the year 1866, a quarter of a million Texas cattle were driven to Sedalia in Missouri and Baxter Springs in Kansas, to be loaded on freight cars and sent to St. Louis. This marked the beginning of a new and exciting chapter in cattle history.

In the next year when the trails led mainly to a point on the Kansas Pacific Railroad, Young Murph rode away with a herd; and after two months of driving, sweating, swearing and fighting, the thousand-mile journey was terminated at the upstart town of Abilene, created for cattle and cattlemen by the McCoy Brothers from Springfield, Illinois. Within weeks after getting the idea, the McCoys built stockyards for 3,000 cattle, weighing facilities, office, and a three-story hotel, and dispatched riders to intercept and invite cattlemen then on the trail. The response was immediate; herds headed for Abilene, and so did frontier gamblers, traders, thugs, and prostitutes.

John Ware watched Young Murph ride away and was filled with envy. His dream was to do the same, but none but seasoned and experienced cowboys were wanted for these expeditions made dangerous by warlike Indians, heavily armed bandits, and irritated settlers. But John wasn't unhappy. He was totally responsible for the care of Old Murph's race horses and for training them at times. Gradually he was gaining recognition as an expert horseman, although not necessarily in a cowboy sense.

John's chance to ride with a big trail herd came in 1879, came at a time when most cattle trails originating in Texas led to Dodge City. Age was telling upon the elder Blandon, and though reluctant to see John leave, he wished him success and presented him with a saddle and his old favorite, Hound Dog, now retired from racing, but still able to do a good day's service in working cattle.

"When you come back from the drive, John," said the old man, "you'll still have a home here."

It was a big year in cattle trailing. At least 160 herds were taken northward, and well over a thousand Texas cowboys saw **Dodge City,** the unchallenged cowboy capital of the world at the time.

The herd with which John rode, however, was going beyond, going to Montana where new ranges were being stocked. Nelson Storey took Texas cattle to western Montana and sold the beef to miners and prospectors around Virginia City thirteen years before, but not until 1877 was it considered a safe gamble to release breeding stock on that grass where Sioux and Blackfoot Indians had been in a vengeful mood for years.

Now, twelve cowboys including John, a foreman, horse wrangler, cook and remuda of some eighty horses were starting for what everybody considered the "Far North." Nothing less in men and horses would be adequate to insure delivery of 2,400 unco-operative, bawling, ill-tempered Texas cows — largely horns, legs, and tails.

The first day out was full of difficulties; it was bound to be. The cattle, contrary at any time, were excited and confused. They wanted to turn back to familiar surroundings and would fight to have their way. Cattlemen aimed to drive hard for the first day — twice as far as on an ordinary day, to make the cattle more amenable to handling and tired enough to settle down at night. It was a matter of "trail breaking," as the Texans called it.

Even with precautions, the first night on the trail involved special risks, and none of the cowboys was likely to get much time in his blankets. But sleep or no sleep, the new day's work began at sunrise. While men breakfasted on beef hash and morning atmosphere, the wrangler was bringing in the remuda of saddle horses It then became the duty of each cowboy to rope a fresh horse for the day's toil. Frequently there was a bit of honest bucking before the saddled horses settled down, giving point to the saying that "any Texas horse will buck and any Texas man will shoot."

But riders seemed to welcome the early morning high jinks as a means of demonstrating their qualifications for places in the outfit. Actually, the rough riding was competitive to a greater extent than anybody admitted, and to be bucked off was as much a reflection upon cowboy character as being caught in the act of brushing one's hair.

John Ware's ability to ride the rough ones had to be proven. He had acquired lots of riding experience while working with Old Murph, but it wasn't with the hard-bucking horses and he had some misgivings. Eagerly he wanted to prove an equality with fellow riders. But John possessed a natural skill in staying on a bad actor, and the crushing force of his muscles furnished added advantage. From the beginning of the long journey, he was able to master every horse that struggled to dump him.

As the cattle accepted the necessity of travel, cowboys took allocated positions. Monty, the foreman, rode at the front when his authority wasn't needed elsewhere. Otherwise, the oldest men or those having the most influence occupied the favored positions close to the forward end or "point" of the herd. New and inexperienced men rode at the rear or "drag" where they were required to prod lazy cattle and suffer in clouds of dust. Riders worked in pairs, members of each pair occupying opposite sides of the plodding herd.

John Ware was a "dragman," breathing dust and biting sand loosened from the dry trail by thousands of sharp feet. Sometimes the dust was so thick he could hardly see the cattle in front of him. But somebody had to ride in that most unenviable position. As the only Negro in the outfit he could expect nothing better than the dustiest post, and he knew he must do far more than his mathematical share of the work in order to command recognition as a cowboy equal.

Therein was injustice. It was universal in the South. But still, he knew he was lucky to have gained even a lowly position of a drive which had rarely taken Negro riders. Without Old Murph's influence he wouldn't have been accepted at all and he recalled the old man's advice: "John, if there's a God, He thinks you're as good a man as any of us, but a lot of white men reckon they know better. You're going to find 'em hard to convince but, by ginger, you can do it. You're stronger than any white man in Texas, and you can teach most of 'em something about being a gentleman. Remember that, even when critters are kicking dust in your face."

And so, with the good nature for which he was to become famous, John Ware accepted the silty sand, heat, and long days — sunrise to sunset; and men who had resented his inclusion at the beginning of the journey, found themselves attracted to him. Moreover, here was a sense of humor at first unsuspected. Abraham Lincoln was the name John gave to the unhandsome longhorn winning the first trail-side bull fight for herd supremacy; the vanquished he called General Lee.

But there were trail trials for everybody. One of the earliest was the necessity of driving through dry country — a "dry drive" they called it. Before they were out of southern Texas there was a spell of nearly three days without water for either cattle or horses. By the third day the animals were almost unmanageable; they seemed to lose all sense of fear of humans; they tried to turn back, and thirsty horses exhausted themselves as they blocked the passionate bovine determination. It was awful; and inexperienced men, not knowing the exact distance to water, had visions of the entire herd being lost. Thousands of longhorn skulls and whitened bones lying among cactus plants beside the eroded trail told of the fate of cattle which had failed to survive the terrible test in previous drives.

Hardy cowboys as well as their mounts were near the point of collapse when the Concho River came into view, and cattle with fevered tongues hanging pitifully from open mouths galloped recklessly into the stream, stopping only at belly depth to gorge themselves with water.

This was only one of many streams across which the cattle would have to be forced, but after the suffering of these dry days in the cactus country, the outfit halted to make a night camp beside the reassuring water. Cattle were ready to graze and settle down for the night. And John Ware and others exposed to days of trail dust indulged in the luxury of a wash.

The Concho was low and crossing was not difficult. Other rivers flowing south and east were deeper and more swollen. The Texas River was in flood, but herd movement couldn't be delayed and horses and cattle had to swim it.

Dodge City in Kansas was just halfway between San Antonio and the Montana destination. It was a town to which the Texans brought their own brands of vice and lawlessness, and cowboy celebrations were made rowdy by liquor and gunfire. John Ware could celebrate too, but was never one to carry his fun to extremes; and while other cowboys visited the Dodge City dance halls, gambling joints and saloons, it was he who assumed the main responsibility for supervision of the big herd.

The farther north the cattle were driven, the greater were the dangers. There were more rivers to cross — North Platte, Tongue, Yellowstone, Musselshell, and a score of little ones; and Indian risks increased. The tribesmen were supposed to be under control by this time but they were still fighting back, though less openly than formerly.

When the outfit was thought to be progressing peacefully, Sioux Indians appeared and halted their horses directly in front of the herd. The cattle stopped. The sour, silent natives blocking the trail outnumbered the cowboys. Only the experienced trail riders knew what the intruders wanted. Foreman Monty, an old hand in the Indian country, understood this trick which the Sioux always chose to play at a spot where the prairies were impressively littered with whitened buffalo bones. Without an utterance, the Indians were demanding payment for the privilege of passing through what they still regarded as their country, so recently deprived of buffalo.

It would be easier to give them something than to argue and encounter the risk of violence. Monty pointed to a dry cow and the Indians nodded in agreement. At once the cow was cut away from the herd and dropped in her tracks by a bullet from Monty's revolver. Almost before she quit kicking, the hungry Indians were on the ground, skinning and cutting. The cattlemen had no desire to linger, and without more delay whips cracked and the herd was moving again.

The next encounter with Indians revealed them in their most cunning light. The cattlemen were now on the plains of central Montana, three long months away from their starting point. John Ware was taking his turn at night herding and riding Hound Dog. The old horse offered a special sort of companionship at times when it would be easy to become lonely and sentimental. Night riding wasn't a nice assignment at any time. Generally the cattle remained quiet, but the hours of darkness seemed long as well as dreary and it was difficult to stay awake. A superstitious man would find it easy to see eerie forms flitting everywhere. John didn't deny seeing ghostly figures at times as he rode alone at night, but had never yielded to the temptation to fill them with revolver bullets.

It was common for cowboys to sing while waiting for sunrise to relieve them of their night shift. John Ware had a good singing voice. He loved to sing and he sang regularly when he was alone at night. There were advantages; singing helped a rider to stay awake and more important, it served to identify the cowboy's presence at all times with less chance of his movements frightening the cattle and causing a stampede.

A stampede in daylight when all helpers were on hand to check it was bad enough; but one at night, when a rider was alone or when two men at most were on duty, was infinitely more to be feared.

A bolt of lightning or clap of thunder could send a herd into a frantic run; even a rifle shot or the sudden appearance of some strange object was known to do it.

Nothing but the words of a Negro spiritual broke the night silence as John and his reliable Hound Dog moved slowly around the herd resting quietly beside a Montana stream. Clouds were low and the night was darker than usual. John figured it was still two hours before sunrise, when suddenly he saw the outline of an animal form crawling from the riverbank trees toward the resting cattle. He didn't think of this being a ghost and reached for his revolver. Realizing in time that a shot in the dark might send the cattle into a panic, he returned the weapon to its holster. Instead of gun, he seized the lariat in his right hand and, swinging it widely, he spurred Hound Dog toward the object. To his astonishment, he could see the creature rise on its hind legs and scamper back into the trees. John couldn't be positive, but he thought the thing was running away like a man. Could it be that one of the cowboys was having a nightmare? Could it be a prank by one of his fellows? If so, no harm would come of this midnight drama; but it might be an Indian bent on mischief.

John was worried, knowing that it would be positively futile to pursue the search among the trees during hours of darkness. The big herd was becoming progressively more valuable with each mile it advanced northward, and John had no wish to take needless risk with it. He rode to the bed wagon around which cowboys were sleeping in blankets on the ground. He awakened the foreman and said, "Boss, I's sowy to waken yo but ah saw somethin; look awfu' lak a man cwawlin' up t' the cattle. He ran away, Boss, but maybe we should have 'nothah boy t' keep watch wuf me."

The foreman was too sleepy to be alarmed by what a rider thought he saw in the dead of night.

"Hell, boy," he said, showing his annoyance at being wakened, "you're probably dreaming. Leave me alone. If you can't tend things at night I'll get somebody who can."

But John wasn't dreaming. The thing was real; and instead of making a permanent retreat, it crawled back to the cattle. Just as the foreman was settling again in his blankets, a fiendish Indian scream from the river side of the bed ground cut the night air. Instantly, 2,400 cattle were on their feet and dashing to escape southward.

There it was, a night stampede — the devilish event experienced people talked of in terms of fear. John had never seen a real stampede, but he understood the dangers and recalled from stories told at campfires what one might hope to do to stop the mad run.

The foreman was on his feet in an instant and rousing the other cowboys. But they were without horses and were helpless. John Ware alone had a horse. At once he was in the saddle and spurring Hound Dog, racing to reach the cattle leaders. Only by reaching the leaders was there any hope of turning the herd. Left to themselves, the cattle would dash straight on with increasing fear; they'd run until exhausted and perhaps scattered. Galloping through the darkness was dangerous. John knew that. There were badger holes to trip a horse, and the clash of horns against horns showed how the cattle were running blindly. Unknowingly, they might stampede their way right over horse and rider, trampling both into the ground.

But John recognized his duty, as he did always, and urged Hound Dog to give the extra bit of speed which long ago had won the Fort Worth free-for-all and sent Old Murph into a frenzy of joy. The horse, despite his sixteen years, was doing fine; he seemed to understand, and was making his way to the point of the thundering column of beef. Near the front the danger was obviously greatest, because cattle refusing to turn would inevitably collide with horse and rider.

Pulling in close to the leading longhorns, John hoped to see them swing away from him to start the circle he was praying for at that moment. But the cattle could not see him in the darkness, or they ignored him. He swung his lariat and shouted, but still there was no response. The wave of cattle roared on and, momentarily at least, John felt helpless. What else could he do? He reached for his revolver, again reined Hound Dog in close to the left side of the leaders and fired at the indistinct outline of a horn close to him. His aim was good, even in the dark. The old cow whose left horn was shattered by the bullet turned sharply to the right. The gun sounded again as John drew near another cow; another horn was shattered. The line was bending and the herd was following the leading animals. John knew he must keep the leaders bearing away from him. Still riding dangerously close to the maze of long, sharp horns, John fired his revolver again and again until all six bullets were spent. But the procedure was working, even if it was one never used before. The leaders were finally pursuing the cattle at the rear of the column; 2,400 frantic cattle were running in a circle and their speed was slackening. A few panting cattle near the center of the ring stopped and others followed their example.

Daylight was returning when the foreman and eleven mounted cowboys, having caught a horse apiece where the animals were grazing, rode out to where John was sitting on the grass, beside Hound Dog, just watching the cattle, now satisfied to lie peacefully once again.

The foreman was talking loudly: "Damned Sioux. That's a favorite trick with them. Stampede a herd at night so's half the critters get lost and then they pick up the strays for weeks later. You beat 'im on that draw though, John. Damned if I don't think you've got the whole herd yet. Did you ever fight a stampede before? Don't know how you managed it — alone and in such short order. But never mind the story now. These boys'll watch the cattle. You go get some grub in you and have a sleep. But for all of you: better keep your guns handy; may be some shooting before we go far."

After four months and nearly 2,000 miles of trail travel, the trail-weary Texas cattle were delivered to their Montana owner in the Judith Basin and branded. The cowboys were paid off and separated to go their various ways. Some would return to the Rio Grande; some would seek fortunes in the gold diggings farther west, and one announced his intention of "taking a look at the grass up in Canada when we're so close to it."

"Close t' it?" John asked. "Wheah is Canada f'om heah?" He had no reason for more than casual interest. He intended to return to Texas and the Blandons, but Bill Moodie, his riding mate on the drag end of the trail herd, wanted to go on toward the Rocky Mountains and Virginia City made famous by a gold rush. John agreed to go too.

"Won't be many cattle back there," Bill allowed, "but I figure we can look after ourselves and, who knows, we might hit gold."

CHAPTER 4

TRAIL TO THE HIGHWOOD

John Ware and his former riding pal tried their hands at digging for Montana gold. There was little else to do, but the venture proved no more rewarding than hoeing plantation cotton for Mr. Chauncey. There was one important difference between hoeing and mining, however. In one case the worker was an oppressed slave, and in the other a free man, free to work, play and laugh as he chose.

Leaving Bill Moodie, John took to hunting in the mountains. Big game animals like deer, elk and mountain sheep were plentiful. There were bears of all shades and sizes, and he discovered what it was like to have arguments with hungry grizzlies. Throughout his life he was an able fellow with a gun — any kind of gun, but hunting brought no gain beyond that of adventure in the wilds. He was soon ready for another change; and after being followed to his tent by an orphan fawn whose mother had been shot by a hunter, John decided to seek some other livelihood immediately. About the same time, he lost the faithful horse which had come over the trail from Texas with him. It was like losing a close friend and John wanted to weep; but if there was a Heaven for horses, he reasoned, "ol Hound Dog" would be sure of an unfailing pasture with lots of good grass and clear water — and opportunity now and then for a race.

Now John Ware was on foot in a land where there were just two classes of people: those with horses and those without. Moreover, it was a land in which vice and lawlessness were rife and loaded guns were always within reach. Law enforcement was largely a matter of theory, but vigilante bands made up of ruthless citizens undertook to deal punishment to the worst of the rustlers and other scoundrels. Perhaps those self-appointed dispensers of rough justice believed they were serving a good purpose, but to John Ware their conduct was repulsive. Too often he saw the "hangman tree" bearing its grisly fruit, and he resolved to leave Montana, go back to Fort Worth. It would be good to see the Blandons again.

Before starting, however, he wanted to locate Bill Moodie who, after separating from John, had drifted to the grass country beside the Snake River in southeastern Idaho, an area which was seeded with Texas-type cattle introduced by way of Wyoming. The two men understood each other and Moodie, John reasoned, would help him to get a horse; perchance they would ride home to Texas together.

It was early in 1882 when John found his old friend, back in the saddle and doing well as an Idaho cowhand. The white man had a warm welcome for his former riding partner and was ready to consider the proposition, to go back over the long trail. But at this point a long, lean Canadian cattleman, all bone and muscle like a Texas steer, intervened and completely changed the shape of destiny for John Ware and for Canadian ranching. He was Tom Lynch, stockman extraordinary, who wore out his saddles faster than his boots.

Things were stirring in the North, where Canadian grass was attracting attention. The buffalo, whose millions had been so recently destroyed, had fancied the northern grazing as much as any other, and there was no reason to suppose that ranching opportunities ended at the international boundary.

Missouri-born and Montana-raised Tom Lynch, with the dust of many trails in his whiskers, was enthusiastic. In partnership with another High River worthy, George Emerson, he had driven cattle on to those expanses of grassland which would one day be known as Southern Alberta. The first Lynch and Emerson drive was a small one; starting in the Sun River section of Montana and terminating at Fort Macleod, where an uncertain market was created by the new Mounted Police post. The cattle were sold and the two men took their next herd to Fort Edmonton, where they found a few settlers eager to buy breeding stock — even the Texas kind with long horns and short tempers.

Returning southward from Fort Edmonton, the cattlemen halted to examine the good grass along the Highwood River. It was knee-high and there was water and shelter beside it. Tom Lynch was inspired by what he saw and, there and then, he and his partner resolved to try ranching on their own account.

While John Ware was on the trail leading to Judith Basin, Lynch and Emerson were driving a thousand cattle from Montana to the Highwood River and releasing them on the north side where the stream would be a deterrent to home-loving critters with ideas about returning to southern ranges.

It was an experiment, admittedly, and skeptics were ready to prophesy failure; winter would be too cold or meat-hungry Indians would be all too ready to kill. It wouldn't work, the cynics were sure.

But it did work. Indians shot a few cattle but that was no fault of grass or climate and, generally, the herd flourished. Lynch and Emerson built a log hut at a beautiful river site, a few miles west of "the Crossing," where the town of High River emerged, and their confidence grew.

Two years after Lynch and Emerson made their bold experiment, as reports about the ocean-like expanses of unoccupied grass were reaching Eastern Canada, the Land Act providing for twenty-one-year leases received Ottawa approval. Honorable M. H. Cochrane of Hillhurst, Quebec, came to see for himself. From Fort Benton, Montana, he drove a democrat and team of temperamental cayuses and, somewhere near the Old Man River, met John George Brown, better known as "Kootenai" Brown, who had been squatting beside the Waterton Lakes for thirteen years. The commanding Brown, former member of the Queen's Lifeguards but now wearing buckskin clothing, was the first white man to settle in what was to become Southern Alberta, and his stopping there beside the lakes was because he had seen nothing in his travels on four continents to rival the grandeur and beauty of these chosen surroundings.

With Oxford accent Brown talked convincingly: "Where buffalo thrived, cattle will do the same — but there'll be some hard winters."

The honorable gentleman acted quickly. Back in Montana, he bought 3,000 cattle and instructed men of the I. G. Baker Company to deliver them to his new ranch manager, James Walker, at the north side of the Bow River.

Three months later the few people living at and near Fort Calgary saw the Cochrane cattle splash their way across the Elbow and Bow rivers, to be handed over to Major Walker, recently retired from the Mounted Police. But there was trouble ahead — lots of it. The drive from Montana was made too rapidly. Cattle were thin, in the poorest possible condition to face the autumn storms which were particularly severe that year. Losses were high.

While the Cochrane cattle were plodding along the rutted Macleod Trail to Fort Calgary, plans were being made for another mighty ranching adventure, this one by the Allans of the Allan Steamship Company of Montreal. This venture marked the beginning of the famous Bar U Ranch, although it wasn't called by that name for a few years.

The Allans sent the heavy-set, loud-talking Fred Stimson to make a survey of foothills and prairie locations and saw him bound back in enthusiasm, recommending early action in securing and stocking a ranch — in the foothills. With the least possible delay a lease was obtained in the name of the North West Cattle Company, and Stimson was appointed ranch manager with authority to buy breeding stock.

Early in 1882, Stimson was on his way back to the West, traveling by Chicago and Fort Benton. Brandon was still the most westerly point served by the Canadian Pacific Railway, and the river boats splashing their way up the Missouri River to Fort Benton offered the best means of travel to foothills country. Halting briefly at Chicago, Stimson bought twenty-one bulls and hired a slim-waisted youth from a nearby Illinois farm to take charge of them. This nineteen-year-old who met Stimson rather by chance at the Chicago Stock Yards was Herb Miller, and in accepting a job as keeper of a bull herd until it was delivered at Fort Benton, he was hiring with a ranch outfit that owned no cows. His position might have seemed ridiculous, but it was the beginning of a fifty-two-year association with the Bar U Ranch.

Stimson's instructions, issued in a loud, clear voice that rose above the bellow of the new bulls, were to accompany the animals by rail to Bismark, North Dakota, and from there by river boat to Fort Benton. At the latter point the bulls were to be left to be trailed north with a herd of Cochrane bulls being brought from the East. Miller was to proceed from Benton to the ranch by any means available and help in the construction of log buildings for the new outfit.

After an uneventful upstream journey on the steamboat *Black Hills,* Herb Miller unloaded the twenty-one bulls, made arrangements for their care until the Cochrane stock arrived, and was granted a passenger's seat on an ox-powered freight wagon going to Fort Macleod and beyond. The "bull train," in which each freight unit consisted of three heavy wagons hooked together and hauled by sixteen oxen, moved no faster than a man with rheumatism would walk; but, as Miller was warned, traveling by "train" was safer than walking, especially for a stranger in the country.

For the first part of the journey the young fellow had nothing to do except study prairie scenery, and the hours dragged monotonously. At Fort Macleod, however, the I. G. Baker Company was faced with a transportation crisis, a shortage of bull skinners, and the train boss, turning to Miller, said, "Young man, you want to go to the Spitzie Crossing? We'll take you and your stuff that far if you'll drive a string of bulls. Otherwise, this is the end of the line."

Of course, he had never driven anything more complicated than a pair of quiet Illinois horses, but by this time Herb Miller was ready to try anything and replied, "Sure, I'll drive."

With help from men who knew something about freighting, the sixteen surly oxen were hitched, and the young man fresh from Chicago mounted the horse from which the big outfit was normally guided. He tried to crack a blacksnake whip but with little success. He shouted in terms he hoped the oxen would understand. And, somehow, he succeeded. In due course the "train" arrived at the Highwood River Crossing, from which place Miller walked west to that place where logs were being assembled for ranch buildings.

Meanwhile, the brash, two-fisted Fred Stimson had turned to Tom

Lynch, now the acknowledged "king" of the northern cattle trails, to bring in the main herd. Lynch advised going to Idaho for the foundation stock and Stimson replied: "All right, I'll meet you in Helena and we'll go together from there."

As planned, Stimson and Lynch met at that western Montana city already famous for mining prosperity and madness, rode south to cross the mountainous range marking the Idaho border, and on to the open country along Lost River in southeastern Idaho. Tom Lynch was right; cattle could be bought to better advantage there than in Montana. Stimson contracted for 3,000 head at nineteen dollars a head — six dollars cheaper than Montana men were asking; also seventy-five horses for the drive to Canada. From that point until the cattle were delivered beside the Highwood, responsibility rested with Lynch. And as everybody acknowl edged, trailing experience and a cattleman's skill could mean the difference between success and failure.

Lynch's first task was to assemble a crew of dependable cowboys. He'd need at least a dozen men who understood the ways of cattle and horses. He hired Ab Cotterell, a local cowboy, to be trail foreman; and then he tried to persuade Bill Moodie to join the group. Moodie was interested in seeing country on the Canadian side but did not wish to disappoint John Ware, now out of work and proposing to ride back to Texas. The cowboy thought a moment and replied, "I won't go on your drive unless you hire my friend John Ware to go too."

"Hire John Ware?" Lynch was cold to that idea. He needed especially good and able men for this expedition through mountains and remote regions known for their rustler bands. He couldn't afford to experiment with greenhorns and apprentices. Negroes, Lynch knew, had never distinguished themselves as horsemen and cowboys and, besides, this man Ware of whom Moodie was talking was on foot; perhaps he couldn't even saddle a horse, let alone ride one. The fact was that he didn't want Ware but there were Moodie's terms: "take both of us or neither," and Lynch wanted Moodie.

"All right," Lynch replied, annoyed to be capitulating to such demand. "We'll take your little colored friend too. He'll probably eat more than he's worth but, damn it, we'll take him. Can he hang on a horse?"

The Idaho cattle, with gawky faces and horns and rough frames revealing the Texas ancestry, were only perceptibly less ready to fight than parent stock which grazed beside the Rio Grande. Colors varied, mostly reds and yellows with patchy white markings. Most cows had calves, which didn't improve their dispositions. And, like all cattle of the longhorn strain, they were good on their feet. When they walked, they walked boldly; and when they ran, it took a better-than-average horse to catch them.

While the big herd was being rounded up in preparation for departure from the Lost River district, John Ware's job was that of peeling potatoes for the traditionally volatile fellow who ruled the chuck wagon, the camp cook.

All being ready, John was given a dilapidated saddle with rope for a stirrup, a debilitated horse, and informed of his job, that of night herding. It was the assignment nobody else wanted — sitting alone and singing through the long, eerie hours of darkness, but John hid his disappointment with a smile and said, "Them cows'll know all ma songs by the time we get t' Canada." But notwithstanding the despised task of keeping the sleepy herd company at night, John was glad to be earning "a dollar a day and grub", once again glad to be working close to Bill Moodie.

The route lay eastward along an old trail crossing Idaho from Oregon and then northward on the Madison-Gallatin Trail leading through rugged country, over the Monida Pass and into the state of Montana. But Tom Lynch — at home anywhere west of Chicago or Winnipeg — knew exactly where he was going. He had been over this route before when, as a youth, he had helped to drive cattle from Oregon to the mines in western Montana.

Mountain country, however, presented special problems in finding feed, and even night herding in such areas was enlivened by visits from bears and other nocturnal predators. With imagination such as usually accompanies superstition, it was easy to see bright and vicious eyes staring through the inter-mountain darkness. Not that John Ware had any fear of animals, domesticated or undomesticated, but anything with a ghostly shadow about it made him wish he wasn't there.

Weeks after departure, as the herd was resting between Virginia City and Helena, John mustered courage to make a request he had wanted to make ever since the trip began. "Boss," he said shyly, "ah was just awunde' in if yo 'd give me alil betta saddle an a lil wuss hoss, cause ah thinks ah can wide um, maybe."

Cowboys hearing the suggestion chuckled and thought they recognized an opportunity for some entertainment. They felt the need for something to break the monotony of the constant company with the longhorns. There was a single horse in the remuda which had taken the conceit out of more than one seasoned cowboy. If the night herder wanted a "wuss hoss," he might as well have one that would furnish some amusement. What John was given was this outlaw bronco, and all hands including the cook were present to see if the big fellow from the night herd would bounce when he hit the ground. Nobody except Moodie had any idea of what John might be capable of doing, and he said nothing.

With John seated insecurely in the saddle, the wicked horse was released. The white around its eyes disclosed its evil temper and, with ears back and mouth wide open, it leaped instantly to be rid of this human parasite; kicked, pitched, sunfished and did unnamed contortions in the air. As the horse groaned in its violent heaves, the rider gave forth some fiendish yells as though terribly worried. But he was not unseated and was not really worried.

Gradually the outlaw horse was giving up its fight, and members of the little audience standing beside a prairie water hole — old hands with horses — looked on with silent awe. Cowboys, forgetting their plot to create some fun at John Ware's expense, knew they were seeing an exhibition of rough riding such as to fill every one of them with admiration and, indeed, envy.

At the end of the ride, as the once-famous bucking horse stood in subdued quiet, and surprised cowboys struggled to find words of praise, the smiling night herder dismounted, saying apathetically, ''Thanks Boss. Ah'll keep this hoss — if it's ahwight with yo.''

''Keep that horse? You can sure keep him,'' the foreman was saying. ''Nobody else ever wanted him. If you can make a working horse out of him, he's sure your pony, John. That was a great ride. You've been fooling us, eh!''

From the moment of that notable demonstration, John Ware commanded a new measure of respect. One of the cowboys quit at Helena and John was promoted from night herding to day crew. His new position was near the point of the herd, and never again on that drive was he asked to take a night shift. Never again was there any doubt about his skill as a horseman.

The new position brought the satisfaction of achievement by dint of honest effort. Here was added reassurance that Old Murph was right, John was thinking. By trying he could succeed and do so without fighting with the people around him.

And so, on this new shift, John's day began at sunrise instead of sunset. After the morning routine of breakfast at the business end of the chuck wagon, and catching a saddle horse for the day, the crew allowed the cattle to graze in a northerly direction for a couple of hours. That period was followed by a steady drive until noon, a two- or three-hour break for rest and grazing and, finally, more driving until time to stop for the night. An average of twelve or thirteen miles a day was considered satisfactory progress.

Riding by day with the cowboys of acknowledged standing, John soon showed skill with a lariat and a general resourcefulness becoming to every good stockman. A demonstration that his colleagues did not forget was witnessed in the Marias River section, midway between Fort Benton and the Canadian border, where rustlers were reported to be at work. Lynch suspected that a few of his cattle had been cut out and whisked away. It was suggested to John that he might attempt to follow some tracks in the hope of learning something of the animals' fate. The tracks led into a draw a few miles to the west and there, sure enough, he came upon two men heating branding irons beside a crude corral holding what seemed to be the lost cattle.

The men, with all the appearance of desperados, let John ride up close to them and then drew their guns in the best Montana manner. They expected the intruder to retreat, and they would go on with their iniquitous work. John had his gun, but he neither drew it nor retreated. Without showing either fear or emotion, he addressed the gunmen asking, "Anywhere round here a thirsty man could get a drink of water?"

Before there was time for reply, John's spurs were pressed against his horse's belly and the animal leaped forward, completely upsetting both men. Just as quickly John was on the ground, seizing the two cocked revolvers and overpowering the rustlers with his giant hands. They tried to free themselves but without success. John had all the guns and he had the men.

Hours later cowboys with the main herd gazed westward to witness a strange spectacle — a mounted man approaching, driving the stolen cattle and leading at the end of his thirty-foot lariat two terror-stricken rustlers, terror-stricken because they knew very well the traditional Montana corrective for cattle thieving.

But there was no hanging. Nobody considered it seriously, least of all John Ware. The rustlers were given some appropriate advice and released, on foot and without their guns.

Early in September the herd crossed the border and continued on Canadian soil. "Just a little more than a hundred miles to go now," the foreman announced. "We'll be there in ten days."

The trail went by way of Fort Macleod where, only eight years earlier, Jerry Potts had pointed out a good place to build the far-western post from which men of the new force hoped to put down the sale of whisky to Indians and bring order to an area rapidly becoming notable for lawlessness. The town, still located on "the Island," consisted of the police quarters, some shabby shacks and little else. All local paths led to the unimposing edifice known as Hotel Fort Macleod, where short and plump Harry "Kamoose" Taylor dispensed meals, beds, and beverages, and where, as it happened, Fred Stimson was stopping to see his herd come in from the South. Kamoose was an Isle of Wight man who had sailed around the Horn of South America to qualify as a "49er" in the California gold fields and he was one of the first to be arrested by the Mounted Police for selling liquor to the Indians — two cupfuls of stuff, more accurately described as "fire water" than as whisky, for one buffalo robe. Now the inimitable Kamoose was a fairly respectable citizen, operating the most unorthodox hotel in the world, with house rules demanding that boots and spurs be removed before patrons retired for the night, no dogs be allowed to sleep in the hotel beds, patrons to pay extra for soap, customers to take their baths down at the river, guests to rise at 6 a.m. when bed sheets were needed for table cloths, and so on.

It was in this hotel, two years later, that nearby cattlemen formed the South West Cattle Association, first organization of ranchers in Canada. "The Cow Country Cathedral," was the name Taylor liked to give it as he pointed with pride at the bullet holes in its cottonwood logs.

For years all cattle drivers halted near Fort Macleod to let trail-weary cowboys spend an evening of merriment at Kamoose's, and when John Ware and his friends stopped for their few hours, jovial Fred Stimson acted as host. He had reason to be pleased with the condition of the cattle, and around Kamoose's bar that night nobody made more noise.

Next morning the herd was moving again, but Stimson remained at Fort Macleod for another day or two to transact company business. Then, with a new man hired to work at the ranch, he was starting by team and wagon, intending to overtake the herd and be at the Highwood ahead of it. The new man was German-born Phil Weinard — bull driver, cowboy, scholar, and riverman on the Missouri when the main cargo out of Fort Benton was salted buffalo tongue in barrels. As the High River community of later years knew him, there were added distinctions: connoisseur of art and friend of artist Charlie Russell and actor Will Rogers.

Indian summer dignified the countryside as Tom Lynch and his men continued their course on or close to the Macleod Trail, that life line linking Fort Macleod and Fort Calgary. The mountains, with fresh snow on their peaks, stood out like polished monuments. Deer and antelope were numerous and screaming hawks glided overhead, but the hand of man was not much in evidence. The dozen cattlemen and their cattle seemed to have the trail to themselves, except here and there. At the Leavings of Willow Creek a stage coach drawn by four horses and directed by a joyful driver waving a bottle, circled widely to escape the herd.

A little farther along, an I. G. Baker bull train returning from Fort Calgary held rigidly to the trail and temporarily split the immigrant herd. A few curious Blackfoot Indians came to watch in silence as the cattle went by but neither barbed wire nor cultivated land, nor human habitation more permanent than a teepee was seen between Willow Creek and the Crossing at Highwood.

As though knowing they were nearing their destination, the cattle quickened their pace to fifteen miles a day, forded the Highwood River without urging, and settled down for the night of September 25, 1882, beside the new log cabin built for the company by John Meinsinger from Montana and Herb Miller who, by this time, was reunited with the twenty-one bulls he had accompanied out of Chicago and left at Benton. The cabin was still without windows and such conveniences as tables, chairs and beds, but nights were becoming cold and John Ware and his friends were glad to sleep under a roof for a change.

For the cowpokes, it was "the end of the trail," roughly 700 miles from the Lost River range. Tom Lynch assured his men they'd be paid their wages in a day or two, or as soon as Fred Stimson got back from Fort Macleod. The fact was that Stimson and Weinard encountered a Cochrane herd on the trail — part of 4,000 cattle in the second drive to the Calgary range — and the two men reached the Highwood a full day behind Lynch and his boys. "We arrived at the ranch near supper time," Weinard recalled, "and John Ware and Al Deeves took charge of the horses." The evening turned quite cold, Weinard added, and "John Ware and I doubled up our beds for the night."

Next day, while Lynch was paying off his riders and saying farewell to each one, Stimson whispered a question: "By the way, Tom, any boys here that I should keep for the ranch work?"

"Yes," was the answer. "Maybe several. You'll be a fool if you don't hang onto the colored lad. I almost didn't bring him, but I'll be hanged if he didn't turn out to be the best man in the crew."

Straightaway, Fred Stimson turned to John Ware and made an offer; "How about you staying to work for me? I'll give you twenty-five a month."

Secretly John had hoped this might happen. He was captivated by what he saw of this new country and he wanted to stay and help with the Double Circle cattle he had come to understand so well. The frontier spirit, as he sensed it, convinced him that this country would give a fellow like himself an honest chance to be a man.

But John was smart and wasn't ready to admit the full extent of his desires. In a voice loud enough for Tom Lynch to be sure to hear, John replied, "Wall Boss, ah neva thought ah'd be so fa fom ol Ca'oline an Texas, but ah so't a likes this heah country. Tell yo what ah'll do; ah'll take yo job on a condition: that yo hiah my fwiend Bill Moodie too.''

Tom Lynch heard the words all right and, snickering, recalled the day he had engaged Moodie. And Fred Stimson, looking a little puzzled at the gleam in John's eyes, replied, ''All right John; it's a deal.''

CHAPTER 5

AT WAR WITH THE WEATHER

Trail's end brought reward in various ways. The late September sky was clear and warm and the cattle, no longer prodded to do twelve miles a day, gorged on the generous grass and ruminated contentedly. For men who rode in with the herd there was lure in the frontier surroundings and the few colorful people already residing thereabout: big-framed George Emerson with honey-colored whiskers; the Irish Quirks; the cavalier partners, Smith and French, operating the stopping place on the south side at the Crossing; and the other Smith — poker-playing "Buck" Smith with one eye and a handy revolver.

George Emerson, partner with Tom Lynch in bringing the first cattle to the river, was already as much a part of the community as the nearby Medicine Tree with its double trunks united mysteriously a few feet above the ground, inviting mystically minded Indians to come with gifts as bribes for the Great Spirit. Unlike the swashbuckling Fred Stimson, Quebec-born Emerson was a quiet fellow, but nobody commanded more local respect. His cow-country judgment was unchallenged and even in the art of making flapjacks he was the acknowledged master. At the time of his death in 1909, George Emerson was described as the "Father of High River."

The Quirks, with a small herd of cattle, also fresh from Montana, were building a house close to the Crossing and glad to be settling down. Mrs. Quirk, first white woman in the High River district, could tell of unusual marital trials. After being married in Ireland, John Quirk crossed the ocean to seek fortune. There was nothing so unusual about that; but months passed and, having received no message from her husband, the lonely bride became restless and resolved to follow. Skillfully she traced him to Detroit and overtook him in Montana where he and a partner, John Sullivan, were digging with no particular success for gold.

"Enough of that," the Irish wife ruled; "we'll try something else." The Quirks then gathered together a few cattle; and when Fred Stimson's herd was on the trail, the Quirks were driving their little band from Missoula to the Highwood.

John Ware received an early welcome at the incompleted Quirk cabin, marking the beginning of long and loyal friendships. Often thereafter, the two Johns met to talk and laugh at the Smith and French store, while Mrs. Quirk was mending John Ware's socks or knitting him a pair of mittens.

Oliver Hawkins Smith and Lafayette French were the typical traders, cold, shrewd and ruthless, with a combined trading post and stopping place on the Highwood and a trading post close to the Blackfoot Indians. The latter store, beside the Bow River, was there by special sanction from Chief Crowfoot whose life the versatile and wiry French had once saved by knocking a gun from the hand of a would-be assassin. The chief did not forget his debt. Moreover, Smith and French had a few cattle, kept mainly to furnish beef for the meat-hungry travelers stopping at unexpected hours at the Crossing.

These were the people John Ware and Phil Weinard and other newcomers saw and hoped to know better. But work on the ranch left limited time for visiting neighbors. Phil Weinard was put to work at once hauling firewood, while John Ware and Bill Moodie were instructed to ride herd along the Macleod Trail to prevent the Double Circle cattle from wandering eastward and mingling with the Cochrane herd still on the trail.

If Fred Stimson's cattle chose to graze and fraternize with Quirk's few animals branded Q, or Smith and French cattle marked OH, no harm could come of it, because both herds were now at home on that grass. But it wouldn't do to let the North West Company cattle get mixed up with a trail herd that was fifty miles from its destination at Big Hill, west of Calgary.

What John Ware and his riding partner saw in the grassland billowing gracefully toward mountains in one direction and leveling off into endless prairie in the other brought flights of speculation. "It's hard to believe," Moodie noted. "Here we are more'n two thousand miles from San Antonio and in the most inviting cow country we've seen. Doesn't seem to be any limit."

John agreed. "Gollyme, Bill, ah didn't think it would be lak this. If ol Adam saw this he'd wanta sell the Ga'den of Eden. The way ah feels now, ah don think ah'll evah want t' go back south. Ah might just stay heah till the Good Lo'd sends fo me. Do yo spose an ol slave boy f'om Ca'oline could evah have a few cows of his own up heah?"

"John, you devil, you've come a long way from old Carolina and I guess you can go some more. You've got the cow savvy and you've got the guts. By gad, it seems to me you're in the right place if you want to be in cows for yourself. The business is just starting in these parts."

While they relaxed in their saddles, the Poindexter and Orr crew from Dillon, Montana, went by, driving the mile-long Cochrane herd. The significance was unmistakable. Like a mighty tidal wave hurdling obstacles such as boundaries, cattle ranching was rolling in from the South, bringing with it the Rio Grande breed of longhorns, Texas-type saddles and traditions, and even a cowboy lingo with crisp new words like "bronco," "remuda," and "maverick."

"Yes, it looks like a good bet," Bill repeated as the two men made their way back to headquarters at sundown, bending among the huge cottonwoods bordering the river. "But damn it, we better not judge too soon. We're only here a few days, and every cow country can be cussed at times."

Sure enough, the new range was capable of tricks, some of them harsh and cruel. The newcomers saw four days of sunshine and then with dramatic suddenness, Nature's temper changed. After a day of rain, wet snow began falling slightly faster than it melted. The riders were out as usual to keep the immigrant cattle within reasonable bounds while becoming accustomed to their new home range; and George Emerson, who could look back upon nearly a dozen years in the country, was confident the snow wouldn't amount to much. "It'll disappear completely in a few hours. Snow at this time never stays long."

Only a Blackfoot Indian displayed the least premonition of an early winter. At the Medicine Tree he caught the Great Spirit's counsel: "Lay in a supply of wood and meat because weather will be bad for hunting." The native hurried on.

The Indian hunch was a good one. A northerly wind gave the falling snow a wintry sting and unacclimatized cattle humped their narrow backs, turned their long heads toward Texas and drifted. The river, low at that season, offered slight resistance in the retreat and, after crossing, the animals continued to travel with bony rumps to the wind. Stimson's men tried to turn them; but the longhorns, acting with blind fearlessness like cattle overfeeding on loco weed, were unmanageable; they refused to face a Canadian storm.

As night fell and the wind continued to howl, beaten riders, one by one, made their way back to the shelter and warmth of the log cabin. The will to indulge in conversation was gone; their efforts of that trying day had proven futile. Nothing could be done to hold the crazed cattle. The men would just have to wait for the storm to end and then gather the herd and drive it back to the north side of the river.

But one cowboy didn't return. John Ware was still missing when the others were ready to retire for the night, and Stimson speculated about where he had gone for shelter. When last seen, John was trying to hold a herd in the trees on the south side of the river but not meeting with much success. Nobody at the camp could overlook the possibility of accident, however: his horse falling on him, horse and rider traveling through blinding snow and tumbling over a cutbank, or simply his becoming hopelessly lost. Even oldtimers in the country had told about losing all sense of direction in a blizzard and wandering aimlessly. But the most probable explanation, men spreading their blankets on the dirt floor of the log structure chose to think, was that John Ware had found shelter for the night in the unchinked hut at the upper camp six miles west, where hay had been stacked in the previous weeks, mainly for the purebred bulls. Then too, had he wandered eastward through the storm, he might have reached shelter at the Smith and French place or at John Quirk's. If he wasn't at one of those places, nothing could be done about it anyway —certainly not until the storm abated. More worried than they admitted, Fred Stimson, Bill Moodie, Herb Miller and the others retired to their bedrolls, hoping prayerfully that the sky would be clear in the morning.

Stimson and his men had their troubles; but no more than Poindexter and Orr, whose 4,000 Cochrane cattle were overtaken by the storm a few miles south of Fish Creek. With all helpers including the night herders and horse wrangler in saddles before the snow became heavy, the cattle were forced to the shelter of trees at the creek and held there.

Crushing the hopes of cattlemen, the storm continued with no less fury through the second day and then the third. When the sun finally shone feebly on the fourth day, two feet of soft snow covered the ranges, making the landscape appear more like that of Christmas than early October. The Cochrane cattle were still together, however, and Poindexter thought it better to let them remain there a while longer, rustling feed from branches and bushes along the creek, rather than force them through the snow to Calgary and Big Hill. With this proposal, he was setting out toward the Cochrane headquarters.

Back on the Highwood, the anxiety for the company's scattered cattle assets was equaled only by continued fears for John Ware's safety. He wasn't at the hay camp; he wasn't at the crossing; and without food and shelter through those three days and three nights of unceasing blizzard, no man could survive. If John's horse and saddle were discovered, it would seem certain his big body was frozen somewhere beneath the heavy snow. It was sad to contemplate. But cowboys controlled their emotions, said little more than, "John was an awfully good fellow."

As soon as the weather permitted, all available men set out to reconnoiter. Travel was slow and difficult. The Macleod Trail was deserted. Saddle horses plunged with difficulty through drifts in the trackless expanses. But where were most of the cattle? Here and there were small groups huddled in bluffs and ravines, bellies contracted from hunger and ice clinging to the sad bovine faces. Calves separated from their mothers bawled pitifully. But even a full day of riding revealed only a small fraction of the animals. A large part of the herd was probably together — but where?

After a night in which Fred Stimson and his men tried to sleep in blankets spread on spruce bows, they continued to scour the country southward. It was good to see the sun shining, but after one clear day the snow was falling again.

Bill Moodie encountered the stage coach from Macleod, bucking the drifts. "Snow's not as deep in the South," the driver reported, "but damned wintry all the way."

"Seen any cattle along the trail?" Moodie asked him.

"No, not a hoof. But say, down at the Leavings I heard 'em talking about cattle seen moving south — and somebody on horseback with them."

"Somebody on horseback with them?" That seemed strange, Moodie was thinking. Could it be that a cattle rustler was taking advantage of a storm to whisk a big cut of company cattle into his lair? Moodie was puzzled, but one thing was clear — regardless of the explanation, the mounted man and cattle would have to be pursued.

Moodie rode west and intercepted Fred Stimson. "Sure sounds like cattle thieves," the forthright Stimson said after listening to Moodie repeat what he heard. "By God, we got to find out."

Two weary men turned up their coat collars to protect ears from the cold and turned their horses toward the Old Man River, near which they hoped to overtake that mysterious "somebody" riding with a lot of cattle.

"This is going to be a hard trip, Moodie, damned hard," Stimson warned, "But time's important and we'll not be keeping regular meal hours today. Wiggle your toes if you feel them getting cold. Believe there is less snow here than back at our river; but judging from drifts, the wind was just as rough."

"Yes, less snow down here toward the Old Man. That's what the stage driver said," Moodie replied. "By the way, do you want me to ride with you or will I take a course farther west?"

"Let's stay together until we're closer to the Leavings, anyway. Then we might separate and keep our eyes skinned for cattle and that rascal with them."

From a hilltop, late in the afternoon, Moodie saw a curl of smoke and thought he distinguished cattle against a background of what might be trees growing in a river valley. His first thought, in keeping with the fears of large-scale rustling, was that the smoke came from a branding fire. He rode hard to report to the boss, and together they prepared to take the occupant of the fire by surprise. There were still two miles to ride but they estimated they could be there before darkness settled down. They assured themselves their guns were ready and rode away, taking a devious course so they would be unobserved until quite close.

Here the snow was shallow with grass extending above it. Here too, for the first time during the day's travel, were the tracks of cattle. Whatever cattle these might be, it was evident they had feed.

The moments became increasingly tense for the two men on tired horses. Drawing closer to the fire beside the trees, Stimson and Moodie could see the indistinct figure of a bareheaded man, squatting close to the heat, his horse tied with a lariat nearby. While thoughts of a gun battle persisted, the man arose and faced the riders. He too was fingering for reassurance in his holster. Nobody spoke. Even the horses became nervous and wanted to turn. But finally, through the deepening dusk, the lone figure appeared unmistakable; it was that of John Ware, and at close range the broad smile on his frostbitten face became as conspicuous as his big frame.

"Well bless my soul, John!" Stimson gasped. "What's the meaning of all this? Did you chase the cattle down here or did you follow them? Hell, man, we decided you were dead."

"Chase 'em, Boss? What yo mean, chase 'em? Those cwittahs we'e bound t' go wuf the stohm an ah thought ah betta come too cause maybe ah could save em f'om goin wheah they shouldn go. Ah didn think it was right t' let 'em stway away alone an get 'emselves lost. So ah says to maself, 'John, this aint goin t' be lak a fwied chicken picnic but if yo wide along yo might keep 'em cow cwittahs togethah an yo might keep 'em alive!' A don know Boss, but most of em ah heah and they been feedin good."

Stimson, normally noisy, was almost speechless. But after listening for a moment, he bounded from his saddle and grabbed Ware's hand. "God, John, that's wonderful. Have you had anything to eat?"

"Eat? Ah ben a'wight since ah shot that buck deah yeste'day. Befo he came ma way, though, ma stomach an testines din't have much t' do fo a few days."

Moodie was all smiles. "You old beggar," he was saying admiringly, remembering his own part in bringing John Ware to the country. "But say, the boss and I could do with some food if you have any to spare."

While Tom and Fred ate greedily from the deer meat, John told his story. To turn the cattle and hold them that day when the blizzard came down upon them was obviously impossible. The more he tried to check them, the more they were inclined to disperse. He might have abandoned the effort, but it occurred to him that by riding with the cattle he might keep them together; he might guide them away from cutbanks and be with them when the storm ended. Once he embarked upon that course of action, however, there was nothing to do but stay with it to its conclusion.

Cold? He was never so cold in his life as during that first night when the cattle walked or trotted continuously and he was never out of the saddle. Ice formed as tears trickled from his eyes; snow filled his curly hair after his hat blew away in the semi-darkness, and as for his stiff fingers in summer gloves, John was afraid to use them in case they would break off like icicles.

Again he tried to hold the cattle in a draw to give them and his fatigued horse some rest, but the cattle wouldn't stop and the general retreat before the north wind continued. Late in the second day out, there came a lull in the storm and the cattle bunched and most of them lay down — until the wind and snow resumed their savage pounding. Again, the cattle were trying to escape.

Not until the fourth night did John Ware attempt to sleep in the blankets tied to his saddle. Fortunately, he had matches and a fire was possible for that hour when he bedded down. But not until that fourth day when the buck providentially crossed his path did he have any food. Thereafter, with the wind going down and enough grass protruding through the snow to let the cattle eat, John felt safe, even though he didn't know where he was. It could be Montana for all he knew and there was nobody near to tell him.

But John didn't forget Old Murph's advice to smile no matter how much trouble he had, and John was smiling. "If that ol sto'm kep up a few mo days, ah might a ben eatin Missus Blandon's co'n bwead bout now."

While Fred Stimson was inspecting the cattle as they fed and rested on the north side of the Old Man next morning, Herb Miller rode up to the campfire and asked the same questions about how so many of the cattle happened to be there and how John had managed to escape being starved and frozen. He had taken a more westerly course in search for the lost cattle.

"An amazing fellow," Stimson said to Miller when they were alone and recounting John Ware's feat. "There isn't another man who would do it or could do it. And even before he's thoroughly warmed up after that awful chill, by cracky, he's as cheerful as a woman with a new hat. I sure hope we can keep him."

Miller agreed and then asked Stimson what he proposed to do with these cattle now more than fifty miles from the home place.

"No use taking them back until we get a chinook and lose the snow up there," Stimson drawled. "I think we might leave Moodie and Deeves to set up a tent and stay here for a while — all winter if necessary. We'll take John Ware back with us. He's worth taking care of."

A few days later, Stimson arrived back at the Highwood, happy in the thought that nearly the entire herd of company cattle was accounted for. The losses, if any, would be small, and John Ware was promised an increase of five dollars a month.

But the cold and wintry weather persisted and most of the cattle remained on the Old Man River range where grazing continued to be possible. Less fortunate were the Cochrane herds, especially the one which was partly stormbound at Fish Creek. As soon as the blizzard ended, Poindexter rode on to Big Hill, proposing to Manager James Walker that the immigrant cattle be kept at the creek until the Cochrane range lost its two feet of snow. Walker, who was shortly to resign from the company, simply recited the terms of the contract, making it plain that the cattle must be brought to their destination without further delay.

The Montana cattleman recognized such insistence upon delivery as a major mistake, but he had no choice but to comply. Back at Fish Creek he borrowed some native steers from John Glenn, who was farming beside the stream, and used them to break a trail through the deep snow. The big herd was then forced forward toward Fort Calgary and on to the snow-blanketed range at Big Hill.

"Here are your cattle according to contract," Poindexter said. "Better count them today, for this time next month a lot of them will be dead."

No winter feed had been provided and the cattle were already weakened from hunger. Even the longhorn will to fight was gone. They were ready to drift with the slightest chill wind.

The chinook for which the Cochrane people waited and hoped came near the end of October, but cold air moved in too quickly, leaving an icy crust on the snow. The cattle were now worse off than ever. The best fare they could find was in the ends of branches from trees along the Bow River. All grass was sealed beneath a firm cover of ice. Although the footing was treacherous, some of the starving beasts wandered eastward as far as Fort Calgary and tried to feed upon the hay stacked for Mounted Police horses.

By spring the country along the Bow was stinking from the bodies of dead cattle. The loss, said to be $100,000, would have been enough to drag most ranches to ruin.

And for the men at Highwood, some of them seeing a Canadian winter for the first time, there was almost complete isolation. Travelers came no closer than the Crossing and ranch workers were too busy for needless journeys. Jim Miensinger, now pardoned for shooting one of the company's purebred bulls when meat supplies were low in the previous summer, was taking out logs for a stable; Cal Morton was helping him; Phil Weinard was cutting fence rails for "Buck" Smith at the Crossing; Herb Miller was filling that despotic role of camp cook, and John Ware was driving three yoke of oxen and hauling hay for the herd bulls. Just like whackers on the Macleod Trail, John directed his string of oxen from a position on horseback. This was already the spirit of the ranch country: any self-respecting cowboy was loath to accept a job he couldn't perform from the seat of a saddle. One of Fred Stimson's men refused to skin a dead cow because the operation couldn't be performed from a cowboy's throne on a saddle horse.

Along about Christmas, Phil Weinard relieved John Ware of his ox-driving duties for a spell, but there were unforeseen technical difficulties: Weinard's language was so different from John's that the oxen had to be re-educated.

It was a long and severe winter, to say the least, and men with less than the George Emerson experience and faith found it easy to conclude that this section of the continent was overrated. It would take a critter all summer to gain back what it lost in the winter, they said. "No sir, it'll never rank with Montana and Wyoming."

The North West Cattle Company fared much better than the Cochrane outfit, but it too had its cattle losses; and John Ware, who was so infatuated by the Canadian range as it appeared in September, had some serious second thoughts. Recollections of Texas seemed especially sweet when he was rubbing snow on a frostbitten nose, and Moodie chose such a moment to inquire, "Do you still think you want to stay here forever?"

CHAPTER 6

THE RAILS REACHED CALGARY THAT SUMMER

Nothing dispels memories of frost and snow more quickly than a foothills spring. This was most apparent in April, 1883. Floods, robins, ducks, and new calves came together, and Fred Stimson ordered an early season roundup, mainly to consolidate the herd and make a count. With not more than a few dozen brands on the entire Canadian range at that time, and only one other big herd, there was no need for a general roundup such as cattlemen inaugurated in the next year

But even though this roundup rated no higher than a private gathering, the riders who followed Fred Stimson on this occasion made up the most notable group of rangeland personalities ever assembled around a Canadian chuck wagon: George Emerson, Tom Lynch, John Ware, John Quirk, Herb Miller, Phil Weinard, Duncan Cameron, Ab Cotterell, Bill Moodie, and a newcomer, Fred Ings.

On more than one occasion the ranch of the North West Cattle Company was described as a "training school" for cattlemen. Indeed, the men who rode out together in that month of May looked like the "school's" most distinguished class of "graduates."

The country between the Highwood and Old Man rivers witnessed most of the roundup activity that year. The landscape was strangely different from what John Ware had seen as he traveled the same countryside in the storm a few months before. Instead of snow there were wild flowers imparting the character of a garden, and wild animals were about as conspicuous as cattle. Soil and grass beckoned with a motherly gentleness.

On the roundup, John Ware was in his element. He liked a hard bed; he preferred tough meat to tender, and he fancied a horse that began the day with a bit of bucking. Moreover, he could give-and-take in the good-natured teasing which went on around the chuck wagon — at least, up to the point where somebody dragged a snake, dead or alive, across his path. He was never tired, never ill, and rarely disgruntled. At the end of a long day he was ready to gather wood for the cook or indulge in some friendly wrestling. Gradually, this man with big frame and matching smile was becoming a source of special interest. Clearly, he was versatile; and as a horseman, more and more of his fellows were seeing him as a showpiece.

With "green" horses in the roundup band, every morning brought opportunities for men to test their skill and tenacity on rough ones. One young Easterner whose ambition to be a cowboy exceeded his experience was having trouble with a black gelding known as Mustard. The horse, magnificent in appearance, was a deception; in the corral, he was the only animal inviting human attention. With the disposition of an old work horse, he liked to be patted; but, when saddled, the black became a rebel. Worst of all, this gelding was a "blind bucker."

Nobody admitted objection to a certain amount of spirited morning bucking; usually it was the mark of a good horse, but a "blind bucker" held added dangers for its rider. In one of the recent bucking tantrums, Mustard crashed into the dispensing end of the chuck wagon, trampled a pot of coffee into the ground, upset all the pancake flour on that side of Fort Macleod and incurred the unpardoning wrath of the cook. With loud and profane oratory the master of the chuck wagon threatened to shoot the big horse.

The roundup wagon was situated on the north side of the Old Man, within stone-throwing distance of a twenty-foot cutbank dropping abruptly to the river. Proximity to water was extremely important in locating a camp, and this ideal spot offered wood for fuel and a sweep of picturesque scenery in addition. Any special hazards had been overlooked.

After being thrown ungraciously by the black horse on one of those May mornings, the disgusted youth turned to John Ware, saying, "That devil is getting the best of me nearly every time I get on him. How about you trying him. Maybe you can teach him something he'll remember."

Ever ready to help, John replied: "Sho; yo sna'e 'im again an ah'll be wight theah."

As usual, Mustard was easy to catch—tame as an orphan lamb when nobody was on his back. John, with shapeless hat resting insecurely on the back of his head and goatskin chaps flapping like shirts on an outdoor clothesline, strode fearlessly to the horse. With a giant's heave which made Mustard flinch, John tightened the cinch, then drew himself into the saddle and shouted, "Out o the way ev'ybody what doesn wan t' get wun over."

For an instant Mustard stood motionless, as though trying to analyze this new plot and the extra weight on his back. Then, with all the fury he possessed, the horse leaped into the air, groaning bronco determination as he kicked. To the boys who gathered to watch, the black gelding seemed to have been saving his mightiest efforts for this test. With head hanging low, mouth open, nostrils distended, and back arched, he was showing the real demon in him. Landing hard on his feet, he would plunge upward and forward with increasing vigor, doing it all blindly as was his manner of bucking.

John seemed to be sitting at times on a high and precarious pinnacle, but he wasn't worried, not even when the "blind bucker" ran head on into another horse and almost upset himself. But after a few entertaining moments, the situation took a more serious turn as the animal circled and pounded his aimless way toward the river.

"Gosh a'mighty," Fred Stimson shouted. "That fool horse won't stop for a cutbank. Head him off boys. Move fast."

Men sprinted to turn the horse, waved their arms and shouted, but with no success. The brute was totally insensitive, and as cowboys scattered to avoid being knocked down, Mustard jolted his blind course toward the precipice, John raking the horse with his spurs in the hope of getting all the evil notions out of him at one time, seemed equally unconscious of the hazard presented by the sheer cliff, closer at every jump.

"Get off him, John!" Stimson shouted as Mustard approached the brink. "Pile off, you fool."

But John didn't hear and, anyway, it was too late. It looked like disaster, and horrible visions of the horse falling on John and crushing him came to every onlooker.

Instead of falling off the cliff, however, the animal leaped clear of the bank and was descending in a perfectly horizontal position, John still in the saddle. So level was the horse's body that all four feet struck the water together. Fortunately for both horse and rider, the river was deep at that point. Had the landing been on the shore or in shallow water, the impact would have broken bones most certainly. As it was, the water eased the fall; and horse, saddle and big cowboy went completely under.

The frenzied cook and the cowboys, not sure that John could swim, scrambled down the bank in the hope of being of assistance, at least being as near as possible to the point of disaster. But before they reached the water's edge, John's head appeared a few rods downstream, and then the head of the horse. John was still in the saddle. Without trying to hide their surprise, men watched as he guided his horse out of the river, still spurring the beaten and dejected Mustard.

"You all right, John?" Tom Lynch shouted. "I thought you were going to be killed for sure that time."

"Me? Oh ahm ahwight," John replied cheerfully, at the same time coughing river water from his lungs. "A lil damp, ah guess. That watah's pwetty wet yo know. Do yo think ol Mustahd'll behave lak a genelman hoss now?"

John dismounted, stroked the horse's wet face gently and passed the reins to the young rider, saying: "He should be ahwight now. Yo got a good hoss theah. 'Taint eve'y hoss that can buck and swim at the same time lak that fellah."

As fear for John's safety passed, Tom and Fred and others began to chuckle at what they had witnessed — horse and rider taking what looked like a death plunge, coming out of it all without even a bruise and the amazing John Ware still in the saddle as though he were glued to it.

Nonchalantly, John emptied the water from his boots, wrung the free water from his socks, and pulled the same wet things back on his feet. Stimson inquired if he had dry trousers and shirt and the reply was, "No, but it doesn matta, Boss. Ah'll be dwy by noon an ah know yo wants t' get those cows a'movin. Jus as soon's ah catches ma hoss, ah'll be weady t'go."

Cowboys turned again to saddling up for the work ahead. Mustard gave no more trouble, but whenever two or more cowboys were together later that day, conversation turned to events of early morning. "If I live to be as old as Methuselah," Fred Stimson told Herb Miller, "I'll never forget that spectacle. Damn it, I didn't think it could happen — man and horse sticking together through it all. And the star performer is going about his work as if there was nothing more unusual than spilling his tea. Most amazing man I've ever worked with."

Of course he was an amazing fellow. Neither a killer horse, an infuriated longhorn, nor a pack of painted Indians could cause him to flinch. But with a snake the situation was quite different, and one of these crawly things would make John want to scream. The haunting fear was deeply ingrained, probably a carryover from early years when, as a young slave, he had been whipped in the cotton field with a dead snake in the hands of his white master.

The fear became evident to John's new associates during the days of that roundup. Some of the boys, not knowing how intense was the sense of horror, made the mistake of carrying their teasing too far. They were not in rattlesnake country, but there was talk about snakes and some of the smaller kinds were seen at times. A dead garter snake was knotted around the horn of John's saddle one morning and the Negro's usual good nature failed. It wasn't funny; as John saw it, there was nothing humorous about a snake and his friends should have understood. But they didn't properly comprehend, and a couple of evenings later their pranks were carried to an ill-considered length.

Fred Stimson and George Emerson enjoyed the luxury of a tent over their bedding. John and others spread their blankets on the open prairie, each man having a tarpaulin doubling under and over the bedding. For a pillow, each cowboy used a grain bag in which he kept his personal belongings. Depending on what it contained, the thing didn't add much to sleeping comfort, but usually it was somewhat softer than a package of nails.

The sun had set after a long day in the heat and the boys were preparing for bed. John's blankets were laid out and ready, but while he was temporarily occupied elsewhere, mischievous hands pushed a couple of coils of lariat between the blankets and the lower half of the tarpaulin, with the free end of the rope extending to and under the flap of the tent.

In the deepening darkness, the rope could scarcely be seen and, lying on ground that was rough at the best of times, the bed's occupant wasn't likely to feel the part beneath him.

"G-night, all yo pokes," John called as he settled into his bed. "Keep yo dweams clean."

The countryside was still, except for an occasional nighthawk and the bellowing of a calf separated from its mother. John was ready for sleep and daylight would come soon enough. He had just closed his eyes when there was the movement of something under his bed. In awakened fear he raised his head, paused, listened attentively. Sure enough, it moved again — a long, narrow thing. Horrified, he sprang to his feet, crying, "Snake!"

To escape from this "reptile" in his bed, he dashed madly away, but in so doing, he caught his foot on the rope which extended obviously from John's bed to the interior of the tent. Though filled with fear and hardly rational, John recognized a connection between the "snake" causing him to dash away into the darkness and that lariat rope leading into Fred Stimson's sleeping quarters. He halted and confirmed the hunch. The prank became clear. The only reptile about was the human hand in that tent, the one which pulled on the rope to make the other end move like a snake.

John was angry. To beat up the culprit would have come easy at that moment. Seizing a guy rope, he pulled the tent to the ground, then yanked it away to expose the two men whose amusement was turning rapidly to alarm.

"Who did it?" John demanded, pulling blankets from both his boss and George Emerson. "Somebody's goin' t' get punched fo this. It's not funny."

His intentions were unmistakable. With visible fear, Fred Stimson took the gun from under his pillow and sprang to his feet. "What's the

matter with you, John. Nobody hurt you. What the hell's the idea —
pulling this tent down? Now, go back to bed before this gun goes off.''

"Noby hu't me, but somebody sca'ed me half to death an ah feels
lak sca'ing yo the same way. Ah thinks it was yo, Boss, who did it.
Now, didn yo?''

By this time, every cowboy in the camp was on his feet and edging
as close as caution would permit, to be a spectator if violence broke.
Even in the dark, they could see John's face without a smile and his
fists clenched defiantly. But Bill Moodie, knowing John would listen to
him, took his arm and said firmly, "Settle down, you. It was only a
joke. Now go back to bed and I'll help the boss to get his tent back
up.''

John obeyed and went back to his blankets, but he couldn't sleep.
Partly annoyed, partly ashamed of his own foolish feelings toward snakes,
he made up his mind he would leave Fred Stimson, get work elsewhere,
for a while anyway.

The roundup was completed; the cattle were back on the north side
of the Highwood River; and Tom Lynch, wasting no time, rode away
toward Idaho to get cattle for General Bland Strange and his recently
organized Military Colonization Ranch, a 70,000-acre lease on the north
side of the Bow River, east of Calgary. The retired general's first plan
was to raise horses and sheep, but on the advice of his foreman, Jim
Christie, he was turning to cattle. And, rather naturally, he'd try to secure
the one whose experience on the long drives was unsurpassed — Tom
Lynch. Lynch hinted that he'd like to have John go with him, but John
told both Lynch and Stimson he had agreed to work for the summer
with Smith and French at the Crossing.

"Well, what yo want me t' do?" John inquired after packing his
few belongings to the Trail and throwing them in John Quirk's house
where he was invited to sleep.

"We want you to help Dan to dig a ditch from the river to irrigate
our potatoes and oats," Oliver Hawkins Smith drawled.

"Who's Dan?" John inquired.

"Dan? Oh, Dan Riley, lad from Prince Edward Island. Just arrived
here. Looks like he could handle a shovel about as well as you. Come
with me and you can meet him.''

And so, two High River worthies met and went to work together,
shoveling earth and making a ditch to carry some of the first irrigation
water in the West. The digging was heavy, like all spade work, but the
two men were quick to become friends. Dan Riley related his experiences:
He had left "The Island" a year before, spent the winter at Winnipeg,
gone on as far as Swift Current by train and driven a cart from that

place to Calgary. He told John that the new railroad grade had been completed to a point twelve miles east of Maple Creek in the previous fall and that it would be built all the way to Calgary before the current summer was ended.

Moreover, Dan was glad to have work, even shovel work, because he had lost all his money the day his cart reached Calgary. It was all because he liked cleanliness and stopped to wash his shirt in the Bow River. Only after the shirt, left to soak in the stream, accidentally floated away with the strong current did Dan realize that the sum of thirty dollars — all the money he owned — was still in the shirt pocket.

John offered sympathy and a loan, and the two men talked about their chances of someday having some cattle of their own — somewhere in those foothills. In the evenings they visited the French and Smith store and listened to the stories about incoming settlers and ranchers. On one of those occasions, the stage driver who considered the communication of news to be one of his duties, told in a barroom voice that at least half a dozen big herds were presently on their way from the South. "There'll be critters everywhere, I'm telling you."

John Ware and the young fellow who later became Senator Dan Riley were in a good position to watch that rangeland parade of 1883. It was fascinating, like observing an infant learning to walk. Smith and French rounded up their cattle and drove them thirty miles west; and Stimson, worried because farm settlers with such accursed paraphernalia as plows and barbed wire were looking covetously at land near the Crossing, was getting ready to follow the Smith and French example — take herd and headquarters to Pekisko Creek, far back in the foothills. At the same time negotiations were under way to transfer the Bar U brand, which Stimson held in his own name, to the North West Cattle Company. The previous company brand, Double Circle, was not a good one, as time was demonstrating; it was too much enclosed, and there was a tendency for a hot iron to burn the hide to the center, leaving the mark blurred and indistinct.

Down Fort Macleod way there were several new enterprises, one of them the Winder Ranch started by Captain Winder, an "original" member of the Mounted Police and now retired. Having gone to Montreal to organize the Winder Ranch Company and raise funds, Winder received his first 1,200 cattle late in 1882. And then there was the Oxley.

John R. Craig tied his saddle horse in the Smith and French stable one night when John and Dan were there. Having ridden the forty miles from Calgary, he was glad to have shelter for the night and glad to have listeners for his story about the Oxley Ranch. It would be the biggest thing of its kind, Craig was sure. A year earlier, after resigning from the position of secretary of the Agricultural and Arts Association of Ontario, he had organized a company at Montreal. But when visiting England, where investments in Texas ranches were proving profitable, he was persuaded by A. Stavely Hill, Member of Parliament for Wolverhampton and resident at Oxley Manor, to abandon the original plan and reorganize with English capital. This, Craig agreed to do, and on March 25, 1882, Oxley Ranch Limited was formed with Lord Lathom as one of the bigger shareholders and Craig as manager.

Back in Canada, Craig secured two leases of 100,000 acres each, one near the mouth of the Little Bow and the other in the Porcupine Hills. The first cattle were bought in Montana late in the year, and Craig was a witness when Stavely Hill wrote a cheque for $115,000 in favor of a Montana rancher. During the winter, Craig bought more cattle, and the complete herd totaling 3,500 head was expected to arrive at the new headquarters near the Leavings of Willow Creek at the first of August. Craig was hurrying back to see that all was in readiness for the incoming cattle with the OX brand, little realizing the ranch and executive troubles that were to plague him in the next year or two.

Becoming well established at Pincher Creek was Captain John Stewart, not to be confused with the two-gun frontiersman, Rawhide Stewart, who liked to pretend he was shooting up the town of Pincher Creek now and then. And at Medicine Hat, James Hargrave and his brother-in-law, Daniel Sissons, were arriving during the season to trade and raise cattle. No longer were Fort Macleod and Highwood Crossing the only centers of ranching activity.

Cattle seemed to be moving in all directions, even southward, and at midsummer the two ditch diggers saw the Cochrane cattle, seriously reduced in numbers as a result of the disastrous winter, plodding south. After the heavy losses of two consecutive winter seasons, the Cochrane decision was to leave the range west of Calgary for sheep and horses and take the cattle to a "safer" range, between the Old Man and Waterton rivers. It seemed like a cattlemen's retreat, but it wasn't. Most people were still optimistic; and while the Cochrane cattle were being driven south, Fred Ings, who had worked alongside John Ware on the spring roundup, made a deal with Smith and French to buy all their cattle and the OH brand. Thus Ings, who expected his brother Walter to join him, started his Rio Alto Ranch.

He asked John Ware to come and work at the new place far back on the Highwood but John, happy in the thought that he was wanted by various people, explained a promise to return and work for Fred Stimson on Pekisko Creek as soon as the digging alongside Dan Riley was finished.

"Ah'm sho now," he said to Dan, "ah'm staying wight heah fo evah. Gollyme, fo anybody who twies t' behave lak a genelman, this looks lak the best place ah've seen. What you think?"

"Sure, John," Dan Riley replied. "We're saving twelve dollars a month right now. It's going to take a while before we can buy many cows of our own but we'll get them. It would help a lot if we could find gold along this river somewhere."

John smiled. "Yo think therah might be some?"

When Dan and John met at the Smith and French place on one of those late summer evenings to hear what news the stage drivers and travelers were bringing, they were informed about the railroad, now completed to Calgary. "We're just forty miles from rails and trains now," the sharp-eyed, sharp-tongued Smith observed. "Can you imagine that? Wouldn't surprise me a bit if they'll build a line right to this Crossing, someday. But, damn it, I don't know that I like the idea; it means civilization, and you can sure get too much of that."

"By the way," Dan Riley asked, "where's Laf French these days?"

"Hunting for the gold," Smith replied.

"Hunting for what gold?"

"Oh, the gold old Lemon found — bushels of it, if you can find the place."

John had searched for gold in Montana — unsuccessfully — and was only mildly interested in hearing the reason for French's absence. Dan, with a Maritimer's curiosity in hidden treasure, was plainly eager to know more.

"Where is the place?" he hastened to inquire.

"Oh, that's the point. Nobody except Lemon is sure and he's insane. There's supposed to be a curse on it, and everybody who's ever found it so far has either gone crazy or lost his life. Might be better to have Laf tell you the story — if he gets back safely."

"Sounds like something we should know more about, John," Dan said when the two were alone again. "We'd get into cattle in a hurry if we could pick up a few nuggets."

"An didn go cwazy," John answered, with a trace of worry. "Sounds so't a spooky t' me. But if yo decides t' go ahuntin fo it, ah guess ah should go too."

French returned, looking tired and tanned. He had followed Willow Creek to its source in the Livingstone Range and found no worthwhile traces of gold. But French was not giving up. He believed the mine existed and he believed he'd find it.

"Next time, I'll work our own river; stay with the north branch as far as I can go," he told Dan and others who listened wistfully.

"Next time?" Dan repeated. "You mean you're going again?"

"Sure, I'm going again, perhaps not until next year. But if the gold is lying there in one of those river bars, we might as well have it. Why do you ask? Do you want to come?"

Dan beamed. "Would you take John and me?"

"Sure, next summer."

CHAPTER 7

GOLD, GHOSTS AND A GLIMPSE OF CALGARY IN 1884

While Calgary people were gloating over the recent signs of progress — new railroad operating spasmodically, a weekly newspaper bearing the unabridged name of *Calgary Herald — Mining and Ranche Advocate and Advertiser,* and a committee seeking incorporation for the town — they were hearing about fabulous wealth at Silver City, near Banff.

"A mountain of silver," promoters J. J. Healy and "Clinker" Scott were telling, and there was the possibility these men were right. Moreover, every frontiersman was part prospector, and gold pans were about as common as Winchesters.

That old trader, Fred Kanouse, told of finding gold in the mountains in 1876, but he had an argument with local Indians — an argument accompanied by gunfire — and Fred didn't go back. A short time later, one of the cows slaughtered by the I. G. Baker Company to provide beef for an Indian contract was found to be harboring a handful of gold dust and nuggets in her stomach. "No doubt about it," men agreed as they rode stirrup to stirrup on the range. "She picked up the gold where she had been running, back there in the hills." The challenge was to find exactly where.

At the Crossing and farther west on the Bar U, John Ware's friends talked of gold as much as cattle, mainly about what they'd do if they found the Lemon mine, where nuggets were supposed to be the size of walnuts. Fred Stimson would make a trip around the world; John Quirk would build himself a castle in Ireland; and John Ware would ride to Montana or Idaho, buy himself a herd of cows, and turn them loose on Sheep Creek where nobody was using the grass.

"When you fellows ready to tramp back there and look for Lemon's gold?" French asked Dan Riley and John when he met them together one evening in May.

"Right after roundup, if that suits you," Dan responded. "Guess we shouldn't leave until those spring chores are finished.

It was Alberta's first general roundup, the cattle population having more than doubled in the previous year. Stimson's company had 4,500 head on its books; the Cochranes hoped to find 5,000 head; I. G. Baker and Company, 5,000; Oxley Ranch, 3,000; Stewart Ranch, 2,000; Winder Ranch, 1,500; Halifax Ranch, 1,200; and Lynch and Emerson thought they still owned 1,000. Cattle for the new Walrond Ranch, with lease on the Old Man and extending to the Porcupine Hills, were reported to be on their way from the Judith Basin in Montana, and did not figure in the roundup plans in that year of 1884. This new company, organized in the previous year by Dr. Duncan McEachern and financed by Sir John Walrond of England, bought its first 3,125 cattle for an even hundred thousand dollars. And coming with the Walrond herd was another able cattleman, Jim Patterson, the best available in Montana.

There were now six leases of 100,000 acres each and optimism was mounting.

Lighthearted men and frisky horses for the roundup converged upon Fort Macleod, still the acknowledged center of the infant cattle kingdom, just as it was the administrative center for law and order.

Although spectators were few, each ranch manager tried to field an outfit in which he could have pride. The Bar U, reflecting the showmanship of Fred Stimson, made the most imposing display — chuck wagon handled by the cook and expert driver, Cal Morton, bed wagon in the care of the night herder, about one hundred horses and at least twenty men, including Stimson, John Quirk, George Emerson, Fred Ings and John Ware.

At Fort Macleod the final plans were drawn for gathering the cattle in an area of 10,000 square miles or more. From there, half of the assembled crews, under the exalted leadership of range boss Frank Strong of Fort Macleod, went eastward to begin the gathering; and the other half, under Jim Dunlap of the Cochrane Ranch, went west to initiate the same operations.

John Ware and the other Bar U men followed Frank Strong, who was still attracting admiration for his part in getting the big Cochrane herd out of a snow trap in the previous winter. For the Cochranes it was the first winter in the south after two costly winter seasons west of Calgary. But, as though misfortune were following the big C brand, conditions completely reversed themselves; there was open grazing west of Calgary and heavy snows around Waterton Lakes. The Cochrane cattle were starving until the resourceful Strong offered, in return for a thousand dollars, to get the hungry herd out to a snow-free range nearer Fort Macleod. The offer being accepted, Strong and his cowboys rounded up 500 cayuses and drove them through the deep drifts to where the half-starved cattle were trapped by snow. Having opened a way of escape with the horses, Strong drove the cattle out to open range and the Cochrane herd was saved.

Fred Stimson didn't stay with the roundup very long that season. His purpose was to remain just long enough to meet and greet the new

Bar U foreman who was coming from Montana. The meeting was at Lethbridge; and the new man, George Lane by name, took his place like an old hand in the crew, to sleep on the prairie, be up before sunrise, eat his meals from a tin plate at the back end of the chuck wagon, rope a horse for the day's work and behave generally as one who enjoyed doing it.

But twenty-eight-year-old George Lane was not an ordinary cowboy. Born at Des Moines, Iowa, he had been digging gold at Virginia City when he was sixteen years of age and, after taking part in some Indian wars and riding the American range with all its vagaries, he was coming to Canada in fulfillment of an order placed by mail with the Montana Cattle Association for "the best cattleman available at $35 a month." Long and awkward, the new foreman didn't attract much attention at first, but time was to confirm him as one of the greatest stockmen of his generation.

Fred Ings recalled that it took a week to reach the point south of Lethbridge, near the International Boundary where the gathering began, and it took two months to work all the way back with the cattle. Riders brought the nearby animals together in the mornings and sorted, branded and moved on to new locations later in the day. Gradually, the herd became bigger — up to a point. As familiar ranges were reached, the appropriate herds were cut out and left behind, so that by the time the workers reached the place later marked by the town of Claresholm, the main body of cattle was becoming smaller instead of bigger; more and more cattle were being delivered as home ranges were overtaken.

The last days of the roundup were devoted to combining the Bar U range beside the Highwood and doing the last of the branding. That completed, John Ware collected his wages and rode to the Crossing to see Dan Riley and determine if Smith and French had more work for him. There were new faces down that way, and one of the signs of advancing progress was a ferry being built on the river, mainly for the benefit of stage coaches on the weekly service between Calgary and Fort Macleod.

Whatever may have been in John's mind at the time, Dan Riley had not forgotten about the proposed expedition and eagerly asked French when they might go.

"Leave tomorrow morning, if you like," the trader replied.

John, with thoughts of the alleged curse on Lemon's gold, would have been satisfied to forget about the trip, but he had no intention of deserting his friends — not even if the ghosts frequenting the scene of Black Jack's murder hunted in packs.

French's proposal to go in the morning was accepted. The men were traveling on foot. Saddle horses would be a nuisance when each bed of gravel had to be examined. But the water was low in the Highwood, just right for prospecting. And to make the adventure more inviting as the men started, the sky was blue and the water so clear that trout showed up as plainly as fish in an aquarium bowl.

Each man carried his own gun, shovel and blankets; and John, with shoulders like those of a draft horse, insisted upon carrying all the flour and dried meat for rations. Thus he packed a double load; but that was the way he wanted it and, at the end of the day, when French called for a night camp, John asked, "Why we stopping so soon?"

There beside the stream, the men built a fire, ate supper, and talked.

"Now," said Dan Riley, looking at Lafayette French, "You'll tell us the whole story about Lemon and what he found. We've heard bits of it ever since we arrived in these parts but let's hear the whole thing."

As darkness descended upon the valley and the campfire burned low, the old frontiersman lit his pipe with a burning twig and began to relate the fateful episode concerning gold and tragedy. Nobody except Lemon in his periods of sanity knew more about it.

In the light of the dwindling fire, John's face revealed conflict. Everybody who knew him recognized his unusual courage — the man didn't exist who could frighten him, but he had heard enough to know this to be a spooky story and John Ware didn't like spooks. But sitting against the blackness of night, he was determined that superstitions must not overcome curiosity about the gold or loyalty toward friends. As he licked his dry lips, he was reminding himself that it would be better to be captured by the cruelest hag in the spirit world than run out on Riley and French. Still, he wished that French would keep the story for telling in daylight.

"It was about ten years ago," French began. "Lemon and his partner, Black Jack, were mountain men, hated civilization like some people hate a snake. But they kind of liked the idea of finding enough gold to buy all the whisky they'd ever want. Couldn't blame 'em for that. Well, after a summer of panning in all these streams, they were making their way back south, going through these hills to winter in Montana.

"I don't know which stream they camped beside — might have been this one. Anyway, they got a good showing of gold in their pans; maybe right here — I don't know. Next thing, naturally, was to follow upstream to see where that yellow stuff was coming from, and, what d'you know, they walked onto a gravel bar with nuggets spread around like hail stones after a storm. My God, these two old tramps were standing in enough wealth to buy the whole damned Baker Company — or the biggest distillery in Uncle Sam's country for their private use."

Dan Riley tossed more wood on the fire and John Ware laughed to relax a feeling of tenseness. "Ah don want any pwivate distille'y," he muttered, "Ah'll just buy Fwed Stimson's wanch. But wheah do the ghosts come in this sto'y?"

Lafayette French continued. "It's funny how gold affects men. There was more'n enough for both men, but Lemon was greedy — wanted it all for himself. Well sir, that night, about an hour after both men should have been asleep, Lemon crawled out of his blankets and turned his gun on Black Jack — shot him dead while he slept. By golly, yes sir!

"Come morning and Lemon threw some dirt over his old partner's body, blazed a mark on a big tree and strode away with a feeling that he was the richest man in the world. And, dang it, I guess he was. But Lemon was a murderer as well as a rich man, and the killing began to haunt him. When he tried to sleep, he had dreams of bears tearing hunks of flesh from the bones of the dead man; and when he walked, the ghost of Black Jack seemed to be following. By God, by the time poor Lemon arrived back at his home base — a mission in Montana — he was a wreck — half-starved, half-naked and completely off his head."

French stood, stretched himself and asked: "You fellows want to hear the rest of it now or do you want to sleep?"

Quick to reply, Dan Riley said: "Go on, we're not sleepy."

And John, becoming more interested, inquired, "Did he tell about mu'de'in his fwiend?"

"Yes, he told them at the mission, and confessing brought the poor devil some relief. At first, I guess, the folks at the mission didn't believe the yarn, but, gradually, Lemon got better, and along toward spring they reckoned they could take time out from saving souls to help this man find his way back to his mine. Everybody wanted to go, and Lemon figured he could find the place. He was all right by this time and the people around were treating him like a hero instead of a murderer, at least, until they began to get close to where the mine was up in this country, and then Lemon got to acting queer again. Old Black Jack's ghost was hovering round there to torment the poor cuss. That's about the only way you can explain it. By God, in no time, Lemon was as crazy as ever, hopelessly crazy, and the gang he was leading was hopelessly lost. With Lemon gone nuts, there wasn't a chance of the men from the mission finding the gold, and they just turned around and headed back toward Montana. Lemon was no hero now, you can be sure. He was just a bloody murderer to that crowd."

"Did ol Lemon get bettah again?" John wanted to know, as he gazed at the bed of ashes.

"Yes, it seemed the curse or the ghost didn't range more'n a hundred miles from where the killing took place, and every time Lemon got far enough away, he got his sense back. The men down there tried to send another party with Lemon to bring back some of the gold, but exactly the same thing happened — Lemon went batty.''

"Looks as though the murderer was being forbidden to return to the fortune," Dan Riley observed and French nodded agreement.

Other expeditions known to French had followed, but all led to failure or tragedy. A Montana man, MacDougall by name, took up the search and was never again seen alive. A Fort Benton whisky trader followed MacDougall and did not return. A young Stoney Indian was supposed to have undertaken to direct one of French's friends to the place where the gold could be found, but on the eve of the scheduled meeting in the mountains, the Young Indian Judas died suddenly.

It was a terrifying record but, fearlessly or recklessly, Lafayette French pursued the search for years thereafter. Stoney Indians, he reasoned, knew something of Lemon's secret. Indian eyes may have witnessed the murder on that moonlit night, but the Stoney remained about as silent as the mountains. French believed the natives were bound by oath to Chief Moses Bear's Paw never to divulge what they knew concerning either the location of the gold or the murder. If the mine was rediscovered, white men would flock to that part of the foothills or mountain country and spoil the hunting of game upon which the Stoney Indians depended. That was the Chief's reasoning, and he was perfectly satisfied with the existence of the curse — that no white man could know the secret of the mine's location and live normally, and no Indian could disclose the secret and live.

Before French and his two companions retired to their bedrolls that night, John Ware recalled the stark events: Black Jack dead; MacDougall dead; a whisky trader lost; one Stoney Indian dead and Lemon crazy — all because of that gold. "And we'ah looking fo it." John was silent for a minute and then spoke: "Dan," he said, "do yo b'lieve in ghosts?"

Clouds hung low, but the night was still except for the soothing sound of water rushing over stones, when the men rolled into blankets spread on dry ground beside a grove of poplars. For Lafayette French, tough little squaw man with eagle-like eyes, sleeping in the open was as commonplace as washing his hands and he was quickly asleep and snoring. Dan Riley, though still new to this life, was taking to it with typical Maritime adaptability and he, too, was soon sleeping.

John couldn't sleep. He turned over and over, unable to get his mind away from the misadventures of Lemon and those demon spirits which remained to guard the site of gold. Of course it was silly to be worrying about the avenging spirit of a murdered man while Lafayette and Dan were enjoying detached rest, but he couldn't help it. If he could only meet an offending ghost on equal terms — get his powerful hands on one — he'd willingly take his chances in the tussle; but that was the trouble — nobody had ever caught one of the eerie critters.

Yes, he was being silly, he told himself. He'd think about other things — mother, father, brothers and sisters from whom he had heard nothing for the very good reason that none of them could write; he'd think about Old Murph and Mrs. Blandon who had been good to him, and about going back to see them some day. These were soothing thoughts, but just when he was beginning to feel relaxed, there was a rustling, swishing sound in the trees. Startled, John sat up. He could see nothing in the blackness of night, but at that instant there was a flash of lightning, momentarily illuminating the woods into which he was peering. If he had recognized the figure of a bear or a bull he'd have felt better; but, no it was, no living thing sould be seen. At once there was a crush of thunder and all John's inherent superstitions were back upon him. It might rain; that didn't matter. He could stand being wet, but he hated this eeriness. While he was still gazing anxiously into the night, something on wings swooped low over his head. This was too much for even his nerves of iron, and he reached for his revolver. As he did so, there was another rustling noise in the trees and, almost involuntarily, John fired his gun in the general direction of the suspicious sounds.

Lafayette and Dan, whose sleep had been unbroken by the thunder, bounded from their beds and seized their guns. Men knew they had to be ready for any emergency in this land.

"What is it John?" French was gasping. "Who's shooting at us?"

"That was ma gun," John explained. "Nobody else shot. Maybe ah'm mad lak Lemon but, gollyme, theah's somethin amovin wound heah. Ah thinks we'ah close to that gold — too close fo good sleepin, anyhow."

"Sure you're not dreaming, John?" Dan inquired. "Could be a Bar U cow you're shooting at, you know."

The lightning came again to make everything in the valley visible for an instant and again there was no sign of anything except trees in the direction of John's shooting. And apart from the sound of leaves swaying in the night breeze and water moving, all remained quiet.

"Sure, you were having bad dreams; I had 'em every night for weeks after the Piegan tried to take my scalp a few years back," French said. "You've been thinking too much about Black Jack's spook-devil. Now, forget all about the yarn I told you last night and get yourself some sleep. No more of that damned shooting in the dark."

John was apologetic. He'd try again to sleep. But from that point in the night, nobody could sleep; and before the sun was showing over the horizon, the three men were taking breakfast and making ready to continue upstream.

The second day was more or less like the first — gravel bars, majestic mountains becoming clearer as the men made their way westward, a few cattle coming down to the river to drink, wild life in abundance, and Stoney crossing the stream here and there. To questions about the gold, the Indians were as silent as the peaks on the horizon. They were taking no chances.

High on the river, where the water was swift and great banks overhung the stream, French found showings of gold in his pan. Interest quickened, and the gravel immediately above was searched meticulously. But nuggets were not found, and with an air of relief John turned his attention to fishing. His heart was not in the hunt for gold and, moreover, food supplies were almost exhausted.

With an appetite to match his strength, John had eaten most of the food and it was logically up to him to catch the fish. About his capacity for food, there was nothing new. Back on the Bar U, the cook had adopted the practice of serving his meat and potatoes on a special platter instead of an ordinary tin plate, and for tea and coffee, John's ration was administered in an old crockery jug holding something less than a quart and shaped like the glass mantle of a kerosene lamp.

After eating nothing but fish for a few days, the party began the downstream journey toward the Crossing. Actually, the return was the best part of the trip. Gold and ghosts forgotten; the three adventurers paused along the way to enjoy the August sky, ripening raspberries, whitening buffalo skulls, and the good grass still noticeably undergrazed by the new herds.

It was John Ware's only hunt for the Lemon gold, although French went again and again, sometimes backed by Dan Riley, who had unbroken confidence in the mine's existence, sometimes by Herb Miller. And, indeed, it was on one of those prospecting expeditions that French met his death. Returning from the mountains, he stopped for a night at a cabin belonging to George Emerson. During sleeping hours, the cabin caught fire and the little frontiersman was severely burned. Though taken to High River hospital and treated by Dr. G. D. Stanley, he died without regaining consciousness.

Gold was reported to have been found in the ashes at the cabin. But was it gold from Lemon's mine or was it from a cache connected with a theft in Butte, Montana? Did Lafayette French, on the last and fateful trip, really find the treasure and then pay with his life, like others who discovered the secret? Nobody knew, but the mystery of Lemon's gold deepened.

A day or two after returning from the upriver expedition, John Ware paid his first visit to Calgary, traveling over the rough trail by stage coach and stopping at James Reilly's prefabricated panel structure known as the Royal Hotel. The reason for coming to Calgary was to secure a homestead, one of those 160-acre farms a person could begin to acquire by payment of ten dollars. He wanted the quarter section immediately north of the Crossing of the Highwood. But in setting out to make entry for a homestead, he became aware that he was the object of a poorly disguised resentment such as he hadn't sensed since leaving the far South. It was surprising, shocking. Certainly this new Canadian community of fewer than 500 people, making plans for town incorporation, was the last place a stranger would have anticipated racial prejudice. Why was it different here than at the Crossing or at Fort Macleod, where he had been received like any other newcomer and made to feel at home? Here he felt alone, unwelcomed. There seemed to be nobody with whom he could talk or to whom he could direct a question.

Finally the answer came gratuitously from a tobacco-chewing charac-ter sitting on a fence in front of the I. G. Baker store. "Better behave yourself while you're in this town," the fellow said contemptuously. "They don't like your kind around here right now."

"What yo mean?" John asked. "What has ma kind eva done to yo people?"

"Don't you know about the killing? Just been one hanging here so far and that was Jesse Williams. Don't you know about that?"

John confessed total ignorance concerning the violence which had rocked the district earlier in the year. The stranger told the story. It was Sunday evening, and the news carried from house to house about the time residents were coming home from church service was that the popular young fellow, James Adams, had been found murdered in McKel-vie's store close to the west bank of the Elbow River, "throat cut from ear to ear." Everybody in the place turned out to help the police find the murderer; and the only Negro in the district, big Jesse Williams, was tracked to a shack at Shaganappi Point. "People were mad as hell and it looked as though there might be a lynching." Instead of mob action, however, there was a just trial, followed by conviction and Calgary's first hanging.

Unfortunately for the honest and gentlemanly John Ware, the memory of that tragic episode was still fresh, and he didn't remain long in Calgary.

Before leaving, however, John made official entry for the homestead quarter section he had been watching hopefully, signed as applicant with an "X" which was accepted from those who could not write. Now he was on his way back to the Crossing to build a log cabin and call it "home."

Dan Riley listened to John's tale of disappointment with Calgary, and assured him that any resentment toward colored people was nothing more than a passing emotion. "Next time you're there, chances are there won't be any trace of it," Dan said. "Don't let it worry you. Besides, as soon's any of those people get to know you, you'll have no more troubles of that kind."

It was comforting to hear Dan talk that way; John smiled again and said he was going to cut some cottonwood logs beside the river and drag them to the spot he had chosen for a cabin. The fact was that he felt happy to be back at the Crossing; he'd had enough of prospecting and enough of Calgary to satisfy him for a long while. He belonged with cattlemen and he knew it.

Moreover, the herds and flocks were still coming to stock this new grass. The stage driver confirmed that the Walrond cattle had arrived on their range between the Old Man River and the Porcupine Hills. Craig of the Oxley had bargained for an additional 2,600 cattle at a total price of $80,000 and these were being delivered to the Canadian range about the time John Ware and Dan Riley watched the first big band of range sheep splash its way across the Highwood, right beside the new ferry.

The "woolies" were creating about as much controversy as though they were ferocious. Nobody among the cattlemen liked sheep. "They graze too close to the ground," ranchers were saying; "ruin the grass for cattle." The antipathy between shepherds and cowboys was, of course, of long standing. When sheep came too close to cattle in Montana, cowboys were known to let herds stampede through the defenseless flocks, and shepherds loaded their rifles. The hatred was not forgotten, and the cattleman who was called a "sheep-herder" knew he was being maligned.

But the sheep in question — 8,000 of them — were on their way to the original Cochrane range, west of Calgary. They now called it the British American Horse Ranch, but it was still a Cochrane enterprise, with W. D. Kerfoot as manager and a newcomer from the East, A. E. Cross, acting as veterinarian and bookkeeper. As the sheep continued northward, men at the Crossing noted one consolation — the Bow River would separate the sheep range from the area to which the cattlemen felt they had exclusive right.

The celebrated and controversial sheep reached Calgary a few days later, and the Calgary *Herald* reported that most citizens turned out to see them being forced across the Elbow River. "The band," according to the paper account, "which is composed of Merinos and Shropshires and a cross of the two breeds, numbers about 8,000. They have averaged about six miles a day and came through with scarcely any loss and are as fat as butter. They will reach the Big Hill this week. We are persuaded that the interest which is just budding will in a few years be the largest and most important in this territory."

A few weeks later, 200 purebred rams arrived from England and the big experiment with sheep was under way, assured of the same curious attention as that directed at the Cochrane cattle brought to the same range three years before.

In short order, John had enough poplar logs cut and branched for a homestead house, and he faced the task of getting them from the river bank to the building site. The timbers were big and heavy; but cheerfully, as though they were of cordwood size, John began dragging them, one at a time, the quarter to half a mile, by means of a lariat rope looped round his middle. Each log would have been a load for an ox, but the man had demonstrated before that he could lift or haul as much as an ox. But one of his friends, seeing what he was doing, insisted that he get a horse for the job. Indifferently, John agreed; borrowed one from Smith and French and hauled the remaining logs to the building site that way.

But there was no reason for hurry in finishing the house because, ere long, John accepted Fred Stimson's invitation to return to the Bar U for the winter. Leaving the unfinished cabin, his intention was to come back to it in the spring. But before the next season came, John had other plans, and the house on the homestead was never completed. But a man can't do everything; and, certainly, John was never idle. Moreover, the year 1885 presented some new and terrifying problems.

CHAPTER 8

BEFORE AND AFTER THE DUCK LAKE TROUBLE

It was the year of the half-breed uprising at Duck Lake, an uneasy year in various ways. But for the people close to High River, 1885 began with four days of merrymaking, the most notable spell of gaiety seen in the foothills.

It was Buck Smith's party — Buck Smith, one-time buffalo hunter, now combining the post of ferryman with the operation of his stopping place beside the Crossing. Around Christmas, the one-eyed Smith had a run of luck at poker, and being ahead to the extent of seven cows, a saddle horse and a roll of paper money, decided to entertain his friends.

Everybody within sixty miles of the Crossing was invited, and ranch hands coming and going carried the message: "Bring your own squaw if you have one," was the sixty-five-year-old trader's instruction, "but come anyway."

It was an open winter, and mild. Cattle, with grass-fat from the previous summer still on their backs, grazed contentedly throughout. Trails, even back in the hills, were good; and over a hundred people, including John Ware and his friends at the Bar U, responded to the invitation.

Preparation for a party wasn't complicated by any thought of house-cleaning or fancy cooking. The main thing, as Buck Smith knew very well, was to have a fiddler and plenty of food and drink. The manufacture or sale of liquor in the Territories was prohibited by law and the Mounted Police were vigilant. But there were ways of getting whisky; a person could obtain a permit to import up to five gallons for "medicinal purposes" and nobody could be sure of escaping some prolonged illness calling for a lot of "medicine." Moreover, there was a place well back in the foothills, with a well-beaten path which wasn't made by range cattle. And, certainly, the molasses in barrels taken to that remote spot which acquired the name of Whiskey Coulee wasn't all used for spreading on chuck-wagon bread. Anyway, Buck Smith managed to have all the necessary refreshments and, as for food, it was a simple matter to slaughter one of the cows coming to his ownership at the poker table and to divide the carcass into roasts. Otherwise, the valiant Smith's idea of preparation for the festivities consisted of nothing more than inviting Dan Riley to be present with his fiddle to furnish music for dancing, and then getting himself ready by placing the black patch over the socket from which one eye was missing. Regardless of what other clothing which might hang on his shapeless figure, when the eye-shield kept for special occasions was in place, Buck Smith was "dressed up."

Guests were not all present at one time. It was a "come-and-go" affair, although a few people, with nearby places to sleep, remained for the four days and four nights, carving thick slices of roast beef when they were hungry, dancing on the dirt floor of the stopping place when there was music, and betting on horses when races were arranged.

A few Calgarians had taken to playing cricket; Fort Macleod men were going in for soccer; and at Pincher Creek, where E. W Wilmot had introduced English polo sticks a couple of years before, polo was gaining popularity. There at the Crossing, however, horse racing was still the unchallenged pastime, and no self-respecting cowboy or rancher wanted to leave home on anything except the fastest mount in his string because there was the constant chance he'd be challenged to a race.

Tom Lynch was always ready for a contest with a gray horse called Pete, and Fred Ings and Fred Stimson were never ones to refuse a challenge — even on the trail when spectators were absent. To make things specially interesting at Buck Smith's party, another Fred — Fred Kanouse, the old trader who had survived with his scalp on various occasions only because he rode a fast horse and drew a fast gun — came up from Fort Macleod with a long-legged nag on which he hoped to win some betting money.

The horse from the South won the best races on the first day and just about everything on the second day. Tom Lynch was worried; the honor of the local steeds was at stake; Kanouse's horse was just too fast for Tom's gray and the other good ones along the river.

"This is terrible," Tom Lynch was heard to say. "We've got to find something to beat the cayuse from Macleod."

Shorty McLaughlin had an idea. "Joe Trollinger's got a bronco down there at the ford on Mosquito Creek — built like a greyhound, and the blighter can run. Trouble is, he's a bloody outlaw and you'd have to break him before every race."

Lynch was interested. So was Stimson. "Let's get him here — fast," the latter proposed. "Suppose we send John Ware for him. He can take some of the bucking notions out of him on the way."

John was consulted and agreed to ride to Trollinger's place during the night and be on his way back with the dark outlaw before sunrise.

Of course it would be a big gamble. Nobody was sure the horse would be in Trollinger's corral; nobody except Trollinger and Shorty

McLaughlin had ever seen the brute run and then there was the doubt about an outlaw settling down to an honest race.

Half an hour before sundown John Ware made himself a roast beef sandwich — about as thick as a family Bible — and rode away on what a few spectators saw as a mysterious mission. It was seventeen miles to that place on the creek where the long, lean California squawman, Trollinger, was squatting and running cattle carrying the J brand. As darkness fell upon the trail, John jogged on, thinking of that day, many years before, when he rode and won at Fort Worth for Old Murph, sending that elderly Texan into spasms of delight. If only the good Hound Dog could have been brought back to live for a day the way he was at three or four years of age, the Kanouse horse would get a sound beating, John was sure.

Joe Trollinger and his Indian wife, Lucy, were at home and quite willing to let John rope the temperamental brown gelding they called Buck and take him along.

"He can run," Trollinger drawled. "But I'll be damned surprised if you can get him to do it at the right time. You know, he'll put up one hell of a battle before he goes with you. By the way, who's fixed to try riding him in the race?"

John didn't know who would be the jockey. All he had undertaken was to deliver the horse. "Ah'll start soon's enough light t' let me sna'e 'im in the mo'nin," John said, and then lay down to catch a few hours of sleep on a buffalo robe spread on Joe's dirt floor.

Lucy had an early breakfast of venison and home-grown potatoes for John. Trollinger's potatoes were already winning fame as far along the trail as Calgary. When a traveler had offered to buy a hundred pounds, Joe replied that to fill such a small order would be more trouble than it was worth; he'd have to cut a potato in two.

As John and Joe strolled through the dim light of early morning to rope the mysterious horse, the owner told in a measure of confidence of an inquiry he'd just received from a fellow representing the big Powder River Cattle Company of Wyoming. "He wants to buy me out. Likes this location, I guess. Damn it, I might sell."

Buck lived up to his reputation for meanness. When he was released with John in the saddle, there was a burst of furious contortions, such as would unseat any except the best riders. Laughing as he did always when a horse bucked, John waved farewell and shouted as distinctly as possible in the midst of such jolting, "ah'll bwing im back in a couple a days an pick ma own hoss up then — if ah don get maself killed about now."

Gradually the bucking became less violent; it was becoming more like "crow-hopping" as Trollinger watched horse and rider disappear behind a grove of native trees.

Fred Stimson and Tom Lynch were waiting, curiously and anxiously, when John arrived back at the Crossing. Buck, they agreed, looked like a runner; but he displayed the eye of a tyrant. Was there the slightest chance he'd co-operate long enough for a good race? Even John Ware wasn't sure about what they could expect. "He bucked fo the fust mile, an he lok lak he wanted t' eat me all the way; but ah thinks he could go 'bout as fast as a cowpoke's money ef he didn't stop t'buck."

"Do you suppose Mike Herman can ride him?" Lynch asked, turning to John. "You're too heavy for racing."

John showed his disappointment. He hadn't participated in a real race since Hound Dog died and secretly he wanted to try this rebel horse. "Mike He'man? Ah s'ppose he can, but Mike aint much smallah than me."

Actually, Herman had quite a substantial weight advantage and was called to try the horse before other people thereabout knew what was being planned. The agile Mike mounted, expecting that after a seventeen-mile ride the horse would be through protesting — for the present at least. But such was not the case. This horse was a fighter and had no intention of accepting any new rider without a rebel's retort, and again he bucked madly. Mike Herman, though a good rider, fell to the frozen ground. He picked himself up, bruised and sore, and any interest he might have had in riding this brute in a race vanished quickly. Half-breed Henry Meinsinger tried to handle the horse but his success was no better, and Fred Stimson turned away, satisfied to abandon the whole idea as a failure.

Tom Lynch was not as ready to give up. "What about it, John?" he asked. "I know you're about a hundred pounds too heavy but do you think you could give the Macleod pony a race?"

John beamed. "Ah'd sho lak t' twy. Tell yo, Mistah Tom, mak it a long wace 'cause this guy'd have t' do some buckin befo he weally sta'ted t' wun. In a long wace he might have time t' catch up. Mean hosses got lots a wind, an this ol scamp's mean 'nough t' wun aw day, ah figahs."

Fred Kanouse, trickling tobacco juice and radiating confidence, was ready for any challenge — even the long race Tom Lynch proposed. The contest would start two miles south on the trail and finish at Buck Smith's log house. But to Kanouse's disappointment there wasn't much interest in betting, not even at the four-to-one odds he offered. Nobody but the sporting Tom Lynch was willing to give any backing to this unproven nag weighted down with John Ware's 230 crushing pounds.

Only a few people saw the start, but Tom Lynch riding his own horse, witnessed everything. He couldn't hide his eagerness. The outcome could be humiliating; it could also be the triumph of the year for him.

Traveling southward to the starting point, the outlaw horse, supposing he was on his way back to the home corral at Mosquito Creek, jogged along amiably. But when the starter's revolver cracked to signal the beginning of the race, the temperamental brute balked at the prospect of running northward and went into one of his bucking tantrums. Tom Lynch breathed deeply to relieve the tensions. John, however, didn't lose the grin on his broad face. He was giving the gelding every chance to get the malice out of his system quickly. And Fred Kanouse, riding his own horse and concluding the race would be a farce, drew up about twenty lengths down the trail and turned to watch the show. That, as the man from Fort Macleod discovered too late, was a mistake, because while he gazed with some amusement, John's horse quit bucking and began running as though witches were after him.

Before Kanouse was able to turn his mount back into the course, John recovered half the distance separating them. John was right in his assessment; Buck could run like a pronghorn and now he was mad enough to give all he possessed.

Tom Lynch's heart was pounding violently as he watched John's horse become a threat at least. He shouted encouragement as the runner passed him and then tried to keep up with them to see the finish. At the one-mile mark, John was still eight or ten lengths behind but gaining perceptibly. Stamina was now being tested; and Buck, like most outlaws, had it. And not only was he put together like a greyhound, as Shorty McLaughlin had said, but he was running like one, with low-hanging head and unbelievably long strides.

Buck Smith's crowd had declined to risk money on the dark horse, but everybody was out to see the contestants come in. Almost too surprised to cheer, the spectators saw the outlaw pass Fred Kanouse's champion about where the trail entered the trees near the river. The scene was something to stir the heart of any cowboy. John's feet were out of the stirrups, his coattails floating like kites in the wind, and right arm high in the air to signal a feeling of mastery as he rode in, laughing boisterously. His mad gelding, with ears back and looking more like a man-eater than a domesticated horse, crossed the finish line with four lengths to spare. Tom Lynch, though not in the race, galloped in ahead of the horse from Macleod and leaped to the ground to shower his admiration upon John Ware and the brown rebel. It was a great day for Tom Lynch and John Ware, and the gelding never went back to Mosquito

Creek; Lynch bought the horse, renamed him Satan, and told John he'd have the job of educating him to become a reliable runner.

It was the last night for Buck Smith's party; it had to be that way because refreshments and beef were almost depleted. But with Indian and half-breed women present in larger numbers, the dance reached its highest pitch of hilarity and Smith's dirt floor had to be sprinkled with water to keep the dust down. Though disappointed that he had not had some bets on the winning horse everybody was talking about, Fred Stimson, with commanding personality and an enviable way with women, was trying to be the "life of the party." But this was not Fred Stimson's night; that distinction was going, unmistakably, to another — to John Ware, who sang southern songs with rich, bass voice, danced jigs tirelessly, laughed to make the sod-covered roof-poles shed periodic showers of soil, and entertained with feats of strength.

And then the party ended. Buck Smith removed the shield from his blind eye, indicating that he was back in working clothes. The cowboys could go home. John Ware made his return to the Bar U, riding with a new hand, Sam Howe, who had come to the North West in the previous summer with Tom Lynch and an immigrant herd of cattle for the Military Colonization Ranch. Sam was good company ånd told John about rumors that half-breeds living on the South Saskatchewan River, north of the new village of Saskatoon, were mad enough to start a war. They hated the idea of white men crowding in on them, and a fellow called Riel — Louis Riel — who had a bad reputation in Manitoba, was said to be with them.

"Did you ever think," Sam asked, "what'd happen if all these half-starved Indians decided to clean up on us? Gosh, wouldn't it be some slaughter?"

A few weeks passed, and on a clear evening at the beginning of April the stage driver, one day's drive out of Calgary, reported: "Hell's popping at Duck Lake." The telegraph messages received at Calgary told of a bloody clash between Mounted Police reinforced with volunteers and Gabriel Dumont's straight-shooting half-breeds — "a dozen men killed on the police side and a lot wounded."

That was only the beginning. A few days later, Big Bear's Cree attacked the settlement at Frog Lake, killing nine men and carrying away the women and children. The police were taking a serious view of the situation, as well they might, and settlers everywhere were feeling almost sick from worry. Naturally, the Indians were in sympathy with the half-breeds, and they might seize upon this as a signal to rise against the nigh defenseless whites living in isolated clusters across the West.

Inspector Herchmer and most of the Mounted Police stationed at

Fort Calgary were called to Prince Albert, leaving the town's people distressingly exposed to Blackfoot, Sarcee and Stoney Indians occupying nearby reservations.

The Canadian Government acknowledged a responsibility, and the Minister of Militia wired to Major General Thomas Bland Strange at his Military Colonization Ranch extending for twenty-five miles along the Bow River: "Can you get up corps? Would like to see you to the front again. Trust you as ever. Arms and ammunition will be sent upon telegram from you."

The old Imperial Army Officer, now a Territorial cattle rancher with four years' experience, wired to accept the assignment. Almost immediately there came General Middleton's message asking Strange to take command of the Alberta District.

Calls went out for volunteers and the response was instantaneous. Cowboys, including John Ware, offered themselves and their horses, but Strange advised against the removal of all able-bodied men from the ranching areas. A strong homeguard would be needed, and the General set an example by cutting gunslots in the walls of his ranch buildings.

Fortunately, nearly every district had someone who was able and willing to furnish leadership at such a time of emergency. The immediate need was organization for local defense, and keeping a cautious watch on the movements of Indians. Major James Walker, member of the original troop of Mounted Police and now retired after a fine record of service, was the appropriate person in the Calgary district and accepted the challenge readily. With the same forthrightness, Captain John Stewart, rancher at Pincher Creek, set about to organize the Rocky Mountain Rangers — predominantly cowboys — to patrol the south country as far east as Medicine Hat. One of Stewart's first successes was in persuading that Buffalo Bill personality, John George "Kootenai" Brown of Waterton Lakes, to serve the Rangers as guide and scout. Brown, former member of the Queen's Life Guards — until, as alleged, he became too friendly with ladies in the Royal household — was first won by the grandeur of his chosen section of the West when, in 1865, he looked down upon Waterton Lakes during a flight from pursuing Indians.

At the Crossing on the Highwood, a meeting of cowboys and others was called to assemble in the Smith and French store. There was discussion about building a fort for the particular benefit of the few local wives and children, but such a measure was concluded to be impractical because of insufficient time. Better, men agreed, to send the white women and children to Calgary where there was a Mounted Police fort. The Indian wives, like O. H. Smith's good Pokemee, weren't worried and would stay with their men. Newlywed George Lane, having married Elizabeth

Sexsmith earlier in the year, had already made plans to take his wife to Calgary.

There was good reason for fear, but the meeting did not pass without some loud expressions of bravado. Fred Ings, who was in attendance, recalled the bracing speech made by a little man who advocated boldness in meeting the Indians. But next day, when a few unarmed natives visited the Crossing for the purpose of buying or begging tobacco, the bold orator of the previous night was seen taking refuge in a shallow well.

The outcome of the meeting, however, was the organization of the Stimson Rangers, with two-fisted Fred Stimson in command. Every cowboy not accepted for active service now made himself available to Stimson and stood ready to do his part in patrolling the foothills region as far south as the Porcupine Hills. As far as possible, members of the Stimson Rangers would conduct their regular ranch duties; they'd carry rifles issued by the Government and travel in pairs, Stimson instructed.

Nor were communications being overlooked. Superintendent John Cotton of Fort Macleod was undertaking to organize a dependable system of dispatch riders between Fort Macleod and Calgary. Dan Riley was one of those assigned to this courier service, which the Fort Macleod *Gazette* described as "well nigh perfect. Two men are at the Leavings, two at Mosquito Creek, two at High River and two at Sheep Creek. Average time made, 12½ hours. Will probably be reduced to ten."

Eastern soldiers arrived at Calgary on April 12; and eight days later, General Strange, with the right wing of his conglomerate field force, left for the North, suppression of the Cree Indians and capture of Big Bear being his main objectives. But capturing the Chief and putting down his warriors was a bigger task than anticipated, and it wasn't until July 2, long after the half-breeds were beaten and Louis Riel was captured, that Big Bear himself gave up.

In the meantime, Indians of the South West were giving members of the Stimson Rangers and others concerned with home guard duties something to worry about. Chief Crowfoot of the Blackfoot tribe promised to refrain from joining the half-breeds, but in spite of the noble Chief's wise and good undertaking, the natives generally couldn't hide their restlessness and hate. Blackfoot, Blood, Piegan, Sarcee and Stoney snarled more arrogantly than usual. Boldly they shot cattle and stole horses. No white settler or cattleman could escape the consciousness of danger. The climate of fear favored rumors, and terrifying stories were being told.

The Stimson Rangers were carrying out their duties and watching all Indian movements. John Ware was paired with Fred Ings for much of the patrol time and left no doubt about how he would handle the troublemakers. Most ranchers and cowhands, thinking of self-preservation, admitted doubt about whether to be tolerant or tough with wayward Indians. John believed in firmness. Anything else would invite more trouble, he believed; and Fred Ings could tell of John's courage, even when outnumbered, forty to one, by the aggrieved natives.

Cattle killing by the Indians was not new — not at all. Nobody knew the destructiveness of which the red men were capable better than the Maunsells, George and Ed, who, after graduating from the ranks of the Mounted Police, bought 103 cattle from I. G. Baker Company in 1879 and released them between Fort Macleod and Pincher Creek. By late summer, the herd was down to fifty-nine head as a result of Indian depredations, and Commissioner Macleod of the Mounted Police was consulted with hope of protection. But the Commissioner was not encouraging. "If you can't identify the culprits, there isn't much that the police can do for you," he said; "and if you shoot and kill an Indian, you can expect to hang for it."

Discouraged, the Maunsells took the remainder of their herd to Montana and left it with a friend on the Marias River. By 1881, when the Canadian Government promised to do better in feeding the Indians the Maunsells went south with a double purpose, to meet a younger brother, Harry, coming from County Limerick in Ireland to join them, and to bring the cattle back.

For a time there was less cattle killing; and the three Maunsell brothers, using the IV brand, entertained fresh hope. Now, however, the Indian boldness generated a new outbreak of killing and men on patrol were seeing the viscera from freshly slaughtered animals from time to time.

When Fred Ings and John Ware were combining a range ride with patrol duty, they came upon a fresh carcass of beef and a couple of young Stoney nearby. The surly young bucks denied doing the slaughter, but John knew they were guilty and began uncoiling his rope as if preparing for a routine hanging back there in the hills. "If yo didn' kill this one, yo p'obably killed some othahs," he said as he looked around, pretending to be searching the landscape for a suitable tree. The young Indians were properly impressed, and after the hoax had been carried far enough they were allowed to go on their way.

Another day while Ings and John were on a similar ride they encountered a camp of Sarcee beside the Highwood, close to where cattle were grazing. With the air of a field marshal, John commanded the occupants to move. There was no response, but the man's face revealed his determination. Though the Indians were nursing hostility, John rode boldly to the center of the camp, roped the poles of the biggest teepee and pulled everything to the ground. When there was still no willingness to move, he seized a stout branch from a green poplar and proceeded to chase the Indians away. There were guns on both sides but, happily, they were not drawn.

The Sarcee couldn't understand John Ware. They were fascinated — almost hypnotized — by his courage and physical prowess, but he filled them with fear at times. The possibility of this distinctive fellow having some kinship with the spirit world was not overlooked. The wise men of the tribe rejected such a theory but were unable to offer an explanation for his color. To the tribesmen, any person who wasn't an Indian was a "white man." Understandably, John Ware became known to them as Matoxy Sex Apee Quin, meaning "bad black white man."

But in due course, the so-called North West Rebellion ended. The leaders among the insurgents either surrendered or fled the country. The danger of wholesale massacre was past and settlers and ranchers breathed more comfortably. General Strange returned to his ranch, knowing very well that his neglected range herd would be scattered and losses high. The circumstances added importance to the general roundup of that season.

For the most part, cattlemen saw their faith in the prairie and foothills grass being vindicated. Beef prices improved after the Riel trouble ended and now, for the first time, a few ranchers had Territory-bred steers to sell. Two hundred big three-year-olds and four-year-olds with imposing horns and fat on their backs were sold by the Stewart and Halifax ranches to Angus Sparrow for sixty-five dollars a head, delivered at the railroad in Calgary. It took twenty days to make the trail journey from Pincher Creek, but nobody complained when the price was around four cents a pound for good stock. Even the horsemen sensed prosperity when the Little Bow Ranch sold three carloads of horses to J. D. McGregor, of Brandon.

In approaching the roundup of that year, John Ware had a secret plan. Having saved his wages, he could now count a few hundred dollars with which to start in the cattle business for himself. The idea was to buy as many mavericks as he could pay for and place his own brand on them. Accordingly, as cowboys and chuck wagons converged upon Fort Macleod, the starting point for the roundup, on May 25, 1885, John Ware slipped away from his friends connected with the Bar U wagon and visited the office of C. E. D. Wood, recorder of brands, and announced that he wanted to register a mark for his own cattle.

"How many cattle do you have?" Wood inquired.

Chuckling, John replied, "None, but ah'm going t' have some jus as sho as a whale swallowed Jonah — an ah'm not goin t' steal 'em eithah."

"What brand do you want?" was Wood's next question. John answered, "Ah figahs 9 is ma good numbah. Ah've got enough money saved t' buy nine cows."

"All right," Wood replied, "I can give you the 9 brand. Want a single 9?"

"No, ah'd lak t' have quite a few. Would yo give me about fo' 9s?"

"You'll need big cattle to carry that many. But sure, there's no reason why you can't have them."

And so, Brand Recorder Wood, the man who was mainly responsible for starting the Macleod *Gazette* three years before, inscribed a new entry in his big book: "9999 on left rib registered to John Ware, May 25, 1885. Vent with tail of brand to tail of cow on left hip."

A hundred riders, fifteen wagons and 500 horses moved out of Fort Macleod, westward, for the spring roundup. Jim Dunlap, foreman of the Cochrane outfit, was chosen to be a captain; but after a few days half the party, led by Dunlap, proceeded toward Pincher Creek and the other half followed George Lane to cover Willow Creek area. It was a gigantic undertaking — something like 60,000 cattle gathered, demonstrating clearly the extent of expansion in cattle ranching where buffalo had still been plentiful an even decade before. Actually, it was too big for one organized gathering, and the men participating decided that for the next year they'd adopt a plan of district roundups, the representatives or "reps" attending from neighboring districts. Thus, it was the last of the general roundups.

Before those June operations were completed, John Ware bought nine young cow mavericks and paid about $300 from his savings to the roundup association which was trying desperately to establish its right to sell unbranded cattle to pay general expenses.

But regardless of the association's entitlement to the proceeds from unclaimed cattle, the colored cowboy now had cattle of his own buying, even though the number was small; and he had more friends than ever. More and more people were looking at this former slave with a special sort of admiration and respect. That fact was made very clear by an item appearing in the Macleod *Gazette* on June 23, 1885: "If there is a man on the round-up who keeps up the spirit of the boys more than another and who provides more amusement to break the monotony, this man is John Ware. John is not only one of the best natured and most obliging fellows in the country, but he is one of the shrewdest cow men . . . The horse is not running on the prairie which John cannot ride, sitting with his face either to the head or tail, and even if the animal chooses to stand on its head or lie on its back, John always appears on top when the horse gets up, and smiles as if he enjoyed it — and he probably does.''

The *Gazette* editor mentioned nothing about this local hero's race or religion or color. Quite rightly, it didn't matter. The abilities of a cattleman and the qualities of a gentleman were what mattered, and the outdoor people with whom John worked were big enough to acknowledge them.

Still rankling, however, was the memory of the rebuff he had received when visiting Calgary months before. And Calgary citizens, refusing to drop the bitterness engendered by the Adams murder, had recently demonstrated their resentment again by running a visiting Negro, Harrison by name, out of town. The man went to Lethbridge and had no trouble there.

Growing in John Ware's mind was a secret but compelling urge to conquer those Calgary prejudices, to convince the people living beside the mouth of the Elbow that there are gentlemen in every race — probably as many in one race or nationality as in another.

"Ah said ah'd neva go back t' that place," John confided to Sam Howe; "but ah've changed ma mind. Ah gotta go back — sometime."

CHAPTER 9

MORE OF CONFLICT

For John Ware and those around him there were other reasons for remembering the year 1885: local conflicts and disputes like the one at Oxley, an alarming increase in horse stealing, and an acknowledged need for ranchland organization. The Canadian range, still sparsely populated, was acquiring some of the evil as well as the good characteristics of a maturing community.

A man didn't need a university education in order to sense what was coming. The great open spaces were about to be invaded, to lose the tranquillity which John Ware had seen everywhere, except at Calgary, following his arrival a few years earlier.

"Ah likes people," John said, repeating what was obvious; "likes em any colah, as long's they behave; but gollyme, ef too many come, they'll spoil it fo cows. When they plants wheat o' cotton o' somethin lak that, they'll kill the best gwass the good Lo'd evah planted. Sutainly ah hopes they neva have big town lak Fo't Wo'th heah. Men'll live mo lak the Lo'd intended ef they wo'k that gwass an aint cwowded. They'll love thei neighbahs mo that way. When they' a lot a people, they'll be mo qua'els. Aint that wight, Mistah Dan?"

One of the cattleman's worries was the settler. From 1885 a homestead could be taken on land within the boundaries of a ranch lease. Some unpleasant and impossible situations were thus inescapable. To the rugged individualists with ranch herds, the thought of sodbusters crowding in on them was as repugnant as that of having sheep encroaching on their grass. Apart from the destruction of good native forage by the use of plows, there was the danger of squatters starting grass fires and helping themselves to furnish their own tables with beef. More than that, the cattlemen needed the waterholes, scarce enough at the best of times, which homesteaders thought nothing of enclosing with their hated barbed wire.

Dr. Duncan McEachern of the Walrond knew about the trouble and cost of getting rid of squatters, and of one in particular, ex-Mounty Dave Cochrane. Dave, regarded as a "slippery" fellow, moved onto the Walrond range and boldly made a home. People round about knew him as the man who stole the roof of a neighbor's cabin while the rightful owner was still in residence. It was natural, then, that until Dave agreed to move, for a consideration of $2,700, the Walrond men lived in constant uneasiness. How could it be otherwise when an unwanted squatter had the nerve to speculate about what would happen if the lighted match being held recklessly in his hand were allowed to drop in the dry grass on the Walrond?

It was the prospect of homesteaders that drove the Bar U policymakers to move more deeply into the foothills; and, now, with settlement advancing steadily, Emerson and Lynch dissolved partnership. Emerson, adopting the Rocking P brand, was following the Bar U example and relocating well to the west; while Lynch, taking the T over L brand, was accepting a location six miles west of the Crossing, on the south side of the river.

This was readjustment — not retrenchment. Expansion was continuing in most areas considered suitable for ranch operations. A. B. Macdonald was starting his Glengarry Ranch — 44 brand — west of Trollinger's place, and there was talk about new activity on Sheep Creek. Joe Fisher chose a Sheep Creek location, and now an English company known as the Quorn was making preparations for big operations.

And, as if to torment the cattlemen, more sheep were coming. Frank White, former manager of the big Cochrane Ranch, was on his way from Montana with 2,500 head for the purpose of stocking his Merino Ranch, west of Calgary. The move seemed to be foolhardy, especially in the face of troubles — fire as well as storms — which had plagued the 8,000 Cochrane sheep that had come the year before. The most devastating Cochrane loss was in a prairie fire early in the season. The sheep were trapped in flames which came upon them from three directions and 500 were said to have perished. Moreover, Manager Kerfoot believed the fires were started maliciously by cattlemen holding the traditional dislike for anything with wool on it. But in other districts, also, it was a year of devastating fires; and the month of November, according to the Macleod *Gazette,* found all the country between Cypress Hills and Lethbridge blackened, and fires still burning.

But the most obvious center of trouble in the expanding cattle kingdom during the latter part of 1885 was the Oxley Ranch. Everybody knew that Manager John R. Craig was having trouble with his aristocratic, cricket-playing directors in England, mainly in getting money with which to pay ranch accounts. In the month of May, 1885, some 3,000 of the company's cattle and 300 horses were seized on a sheriff's order and advertised for sale to meet a debt. Only at a late hour were sufficient funds to settle the account received from England. The bailiff's sale was canceled.

Craig, in whom the gentleman directors showed small confidence, was called to England for discussions, but mistrust continued. Cattle of his buying were said to be of inferior quality, and after Alexander Stavely Hill and Lord Lathom visited the ranch, Craig resigned in bitterness.

Australian-born Stanley Pinhorn was appointed manager of the Oxley, with James Patterson as foreman. But trouble didn't stop at that point. Craig, prior to his resignation, had sold some Oxley cattle to Angus Sparrow, and when the buyer came to take delivery, after the change in management, Pinhorn argued that the selling price was too low and refused to let the cattle go. The dispute continued for days, and ranchland sympathies were divided about as evenly as they were between Conservatives and Liberals when the first election was held in the South West. The Willow Creek and Mosquito Creek cattlemen stood with their neighbor, Pinhorn, and the High River men were with Sparrow. The possibility of open conflict with the sort of weapons men were in the habit of carrying could not be overlooked.

Sparrow, with a following of rugged men from the North, rode back to the Oxley and was met by Pinhorn holding a loaded gun and flanked by his friends.

"By God, Sparrow, you'll not take a hoof off this place while I can still hold a gun," Pinhorn shouted. And everybody knew he meant it. It was a tense moment, and only the good offices of the kindly George Emerson persuaded the cattlemen to return their guns to the holsters. Pinhorn kept the disputed cattle, and the Highwood men, including John Ware, rode toward their home ranges. The peace had been preserved, but for a time there were strained relationships between two groups of cattlemen.

Following that threat of a ranchers' war, the Oxley was reorganized as the New Oxley Ranch Company, with about 6,000 cattle carrying the OX brand.

By late summer it was the loss of horses that captured most of the conversation as men met at the Crossing. The rebellion-inspired rash of cattle killing on the part of Indians had subsided moderately, but horse stealing was more prevalent than ever.

The adoption of horses which had been brought to the Bow River Valley a mere century and a half before had completely changed the lives of native people; and now, having become skillful in the art of thieving, the Indians indulged freely. Inherently unsympathetic to the sanctity of private ownership of anything except wives, they stole horses as they'd play a game and found the pastime almost irresistible.

When Mounted Police vigilance finally suppressed their plundering of stock belonging to settlers and ranchers, the natives concluded that not even the white men's laws should prevent them from stealing from other tribes. Hundreds of stolen horses were being driven each way across the International Boundary.

In mid-1895 the editor of the Macleod *Gazette* estimated that 300 stolen horses were on the Blood Reserve alone, and by October the number was "very materially higher." Most of the animals were from reserves in Montana, and counter-raids for the purpose of recovering with usury were being made frequently. Snake Indians driving Piegan horses southward were known to meet Piegan driving Snake horses in the opposite direction. Such raids led, now and then, to pitched battles, one of the bloodiest being between the Canadian Blood and the Montana Gros-Ventre in the Sweet Grass Hills in 1886.

But the Indians were not alone in stealing horses, and many of the losses attributed to the natives were really the work of whites less deserving of forgiveness. The temptation of easy gain was strong and even certain members of the police yielded shamefully to it. Nobody on the frontier was likely to forget Mounties De Quoy and Carson who, three years before, had deserted from the barracks at Calgary and dashed eastward with a cut of horses belonging to the force. But the men were captured at Blackfoot Crossing and, tried before Stipendiary Magistrate James Macleod, were sentenced to six years in penitentiary.

The offenders may have thought it a severely heavy penalty, but they could be thankful that they had faced a Canadian magistrate rather than a vigilante "court" on the Montana side of the line. A few Canadian thieves who drove stolen horses southward into the United States territory never returned. The residents of Fort Macleod knew the two men, Counestie and McDonald, who were accused of stealing the North West Coal and Navigation Company mules from that place and running them into Montana. The Company advertised the brand in the *Gazette* and the mules were identified somewhere south of the border. According to the Macleod *Gazette:* "Jos. Kipp arrested the thieves and was on his way with them to Benton when he met a party of cowboys and was relieved of his charge. Very few preliminaries were bothered with. The thieves were taken to the nearest tree and very quickly paid the penalty for their roguery with their lives. Montana is an unhealthy retreat for such characters."

Montana ranchers were conducting what they admitted was a new type of "roundup" at that time — "a horse-thief roundup." The *Nor'-West Farmer* reported an organized sweep along the Missouri, from the Judith to the Poplar rivers, resulting in the hanging of about twenty men. "As soon as one was ushered into the presence of seventeen thoroughly aroused men, all armed with Winchester rifles," the report explained, "a few questions were asked, by which the prisoner was conclusively shown to be guilty whereupon the man acting as chairman of the assembly remarked, 'You hear what he says, what shall we do?'

" 'I move that we take the son of a — out and hang him.'

" 'I second the motion,' follows like lightning from another.

" 'You hear the motion, boys; those in favor say Aye.'

"One solid 'Aye' and it is unanimously carried. No trouble to get a jury, no fine points of law in prosecution or defence, no perplexity for the judge in making his charge, no long and harrowing suspense while the jury is trying to come to a decision, no pardon — nothing but five minutes for a trial and five minutes more for an execution."

In that early West, where a horse was essential to travel, a man on foot faced greatly increased dangers from starvation, storms, and treachery. Hence, the horse thief's villainy was regarded as being roughly equal to the crime of murder, and severe punishments were demanded. John Ware and Tom Lynch and Sam Howe had witnessed the work of Montana vigilantes — the cold eyes, blackened faces and protruding tongues of bodies dangling from tree branches. The only good feature was that the ordeal of trial and execution didn't last long. If the condemned man was on a horse, his hands were tied, the noose was placed upon his neck and the other end of the lariat was extended over a stout branch. Then, when all was in readiness, the gang leader would strike the condemned man's horse with a whip, and as the animal plunged forward, the unfortunate thief was left hanging. Without a horse, the thief was sometimes required to stand on a pile of stones while the noose was being adjusted, and then the stones were kicked from under him. Any way one looked at it, the operation was repulsive and disgusting.

To the credit of the Canadian ranchers, a better brand of law and justice was maintained; but the year did not pass without numerous proposals that a vigilante force be recruited to patrol the Canadian side. Such a step was suggested seriously at Medicine Hat and as far east as Whitewood. At the Crossing there were repeated discussions about "do-it-yourself" justice, but very few of the people there favored it.

If anything could have convinced the Highwood men to adopt the Montana method, the grand theft of 1885 would have done it — a hundred head of good horses whisked from the nearby range, and all at one time. Most of the lost animals belonged to Duncan Cameron, but some of them were the property of John Sullivan and some carried the brand of Fred Ings. Cameron, with the help of John Ware and Fred Ings, had branded his horses and turned them loose just the year before. Then, to use his time more profitably, he became a mail clerk on the Canadian Pacific Railway and was absent when the loss of horses was established. There were no clues, except that a big band of unidentified horses was known to have been driven across the Highwood, a few miles above the Crossing, and herded northward. Presumably, the horses were loaded on freight cars at a point east of Calgary and sent to Manitoba along with some horses bought in a legitimate manner for resale to farmers on the eastern prairies. The purchased horses confused the case for those who tried to investigate, and the thief was never brought to justice.

But one good thing came of the increase in horse stealing; it helped to convince ranchers of a need for organization. On September 7, 1885, a number of operators met at the Skrine Ranch, not far from the Crossing, and formed the North West Stock Association, with Alexander Stavely Hill as president and Fred Stimson as vice-president. Member ranches included the Bar U, Quirk, Oxley, Sheep Creek, Little Bow, Mount Head, Winder, Military Colonization, Skrine, Emerson, and Iken.

Just about the time of that ranchers' meeting, John Ware went again to visit the town of Calgary, as he had vowed he must do. The recently incorporated community could be a source of interest and entertainment, but John's chief object was to learn if the residents were ready to accept him as a fellow human, or if the prejudices of 1884 persisted.

In traveling to Calgary, John was helping to drive a herd of steers for George Emerson, but once in the town he sought work to keep him there for a period. The I. G. Baker Company wanted to hire a man for work in the store and John applied. The reaction on the part of the employer was frigid. "There must be a mistake," he told John. "We don't want a man for the store, but we might give you some work unloading freight from the bull wagons that'll be in from Macleod tomorrow."

John knew very well that the Baker man was bluffing. If he were honest, he'd say: "Jesse Williams was a murderer and a Negro; we don't want you working in the store, but we'll give you a job at the back."

Unhappily, John took the job. He tried to talk to people who were near. But the general feeling toward him was no better. His attempts to be friendly were met by coolness. When he went to the Methodist church on Sunday, the handshakes were perfunctory and limp. And then, to make him feel more depressed than ever, a Mounted Policeman working on the Cameron horse case came to question him.

"Do you own any horses?" the Mounty asked, curtly. "Do any of your friends own horses? Where were you during the third week of August?"

John answered truthfully, replied that he owned one horse, and tried to add that he owned a few cattle which he had bought with money saved from wages. But hateful was the thought of being under suspicion, unjustly. "Ah 'spose ef ah staid heah yo'd come t' me eve'y time theah was twouble in this town," he protested. "Well, Policeman, ah won't be stayin. Ah' be going back t' the grass wheah Geo'ge Eme'son says, 'A good man o' a good hoss is neva a bad colah.' "

Fred Ings drove to Calgary, but arrived too late to prevent this pointless interrogation. With obvious discouragement John confessed he had had enough of town life. "They don't want colah'd boys heah," he said, "an ah won't stay. Ah'm going back t' the hills."

"I'm returning tomorrow," Ings announced. "I'll take you back."

John paused for a moment as he leaned against a wheel of the Baker freight wagon, and then spoke: "Say, Mistah Fred, yo ben a twavellin man. Is theah any count'y that is all cow count'y — no fences, no fahmahs, no towns — just cow count'y?"

"We'll talk about that when we're driving back," Ings replied. "But where do you figure on going?"

"Might stop at the Stoney Cwossin' an see Ba'tah. Yo know Ba'tah who's got the good hosses on Sheep C'eek. He tol me ah could wo'k fo him any time ah wanted t' come. What'd they call his new outfit with the Z bwand? Yes, that's it, the Quo'n. Ah'll stop theah."

CHAPTER 10

THE QUORN AND A PRINCE ALBERT COAT

Irish John J. Barter, tall, lean, and dignified by a gray goatee, looked more like a professor of Latin than the manager of a new ranching company having uncertain boundaries and ill-defined purposes. As a former servant of the Hudson's Bay Company, he was familiar with the Indian and buffalo country; and as a close friend of Fred Stimson, he had welcomed the opportunity of accepting this position in the foothills. It was while Barter was supervising the building of a fence near the big rock, west of Stoney Crossing, that Fred Ings reined his sweating ponies to a halt and smiling John Ware leaped from the democrat to inquire about work.

"Give you a job? I said I would and to be sure I will." Barter's Irish accent was clear as the meadowlark's morning call. "But mind now, I'll be counting on ye staying a while. None o' this here-today-and-gone-tomorrow like a Belfast beggar. We'll not be having many beasts until spring, but there are buildings and some fences to put up this fall and winter. God man, you're bigger'n what I thought when I see you on yon roundup a few months back. You're strong like a stall-fed bull. I know all about you; you'll be handy when we have to move this big rock at our corner."

"What yo mean?" John was visibly worried. "Yo mean this chunk a mountain that stwayed ova heah?"

Realizing that Barter was not serious in his reference to the barn-sized stone, later recognized as the biggest erratic or glacier-transported rock known anywhere, John grinned and asked, "Wheah yo want me t' put it?"

"You can look after the saddle ponies and saddles this winter, John; and when you've got time to spare, you can peel poles for the fences. We'll be running coyotes the odd time too."

Behind the Quorn enterprise was a syndicate of fox-hunting English capitalists, and the ranch name was adopted from the Quorn Hunt Club in Leicestershire. Under such circumstances, nobody could expect ranch plans to be strictly commonplace. Cattle were to have a part in ranch operations, but company directors, with romantic dreams about horses, planned to specialize in remounts — one or two crosses of Thoroughbred on native mares — for the British cavalry.

There was no shortage of capital, it seemed, and ranch buildings then under construction on the south side of Sheep Creek and eight miles west of Stoney Crossing — later Okotoks — were well constructed and elaborate for that time and place.

Barns? There would be five of them; and practical ranchers located to the south snickered benevolently at the extravagant ideas. As for the ranch lease, it extended southward from the Sheep and westward from the big rock to distant points never accurately identified. But the exact limits of a ranch lease meant little because grazing critters wouldn't stop at them anyway.

John was directed to the Quorn bunkhouse, where he unpacked the grain bag used to carry his personal belongings and started to work at forty-five dollars a month. As the ranch herd had not yet arrived from the South, nobody was very busy and the winter passed quietly and pleasantly enough. Sam Howe, working for John Quirk, came that way quite often and stopped to spin some stories. George Emerson and Fred Stimson stopped to visit Barter a few times; and Joe Fisher, who had settled farther west on Sheep Creek, called when going to Calgary or the Stoney Crossing for supplies. And toward spring, Barter instructed Tom Lynch — still the acknowledged King of the Long Trail — to bring breeding stock from Montana.

Before the snow was fully melted in early 1886, Lynch was on his way back from the South with 500 better-than-average broncos — mostly mares. Upon their delivery at the Quorn headquarters, John Ware assumed full responsibility for them; and Tom Lynch assured Barter he'd get the cattle on the next trip but, first, wanted to stay around to handle the Bar U wagon for the spring roundup in the Highwood-Mosquito Creek area. There'd still be plenty of time to drive in the thousand head of ranch cattle already ordered for the Quorn.

For John Ware, spring brought delight in unsuspected ways. Being more than an ordinary ranch hand, he had the full responsibility for the horses, and was determined to merit the trust. Many of the Montana mares were foaling, and John watched every new-born with a paternal interest.

In time for spring breeding, the first of the imported English Thoroughbred stallions arrived and their magnificence was something to inspire any true lover of horse-flesh. Here were twelve equine aristocrats, and each was allotted a spacious box stall in the new stallion barn. Instead of displaying a timidity becoming to new arrivals, the studs acted like noisy proprietors, especially while the breeding season lasted. Often they were unruly. But John Ware loved them all, particularly the big bay, Eagle Plume, which rancher and horseman E. D. Adams pronounced, "the best Thoroughbred I ever saw." In the corral he would stand like a massive statue, with head held high and tail carried gaily. "Ol Ploom,"

John called him. Then there was Acrostic, notable winner on English tracks, and Grand Coups and Yorkist — bluebloods all.

In the preceding months, the Cochrane Ranch Company and the Halifax Ranch had brought purebred Percheron stallions to their respective ranges, but these Quorn horses were the first Thoroughbreds possessing such quality and breeding. Fred Stimson and a dozen of his friends on the Highwood rode across on a Sunday to inspect and admire them.

Often after all others had retired for the night, John was still in the stable, grooming his stallions by lantern light and either singing or talking to them in tones they seemed to understand. One stallion with an Old Country reputation as a man-killer behaved like a big kitten when John was in his stall.

Barter knew his horses were in good hands, and after the cattle arrived he left almost every decision concerning the horses to John Ware's judgment.

Accompanying the shipment of imported stallions were several hound dogs with long legs and expressions of perpetual hunger. They were for chasing coyotes and entertaining English visitors. Like the horses, they were placed in John's care.

Old Country visitors may have thought of coyotes as wild things created essentially for man's entertainment, but to the residents of the cow country they were pests and killers deserving nothing less than destruction. Timber wolves were the big and crafty destroyers, but coyotes were more numerous and accounted for the deaths of some calves and foals in most spring seasons. Regularly their shrill barks broke the night stillness and sent shivers up the spines of newcomers unaware of the cowardly nature of these animals.

About the first of May, the ranch democrat was sent to Calgary to meet incoming "guests," sons and nephews of Quorn Company directors. They might not know which end of a steer eats grass; but in the course of a two- or three-weeks' stay they expected to learn all about "rawnching," mostly from well-cushioned chairs in the ranch house. The titles may have been borrowed for the occasion, but there was "Lord Harold," who came intent upon shooting buffalo and sulked when he found the race had completely disappeared from the prairie; there was "Earl Alfred," with wing collar, huge bow tie, and mouth like a half-open door; and then there was Mister Ernest, with a constant longing for a drink. For the first few days the guests kept their own company completely, ignoring the workers, white as well as black. When they chose to go for a canter, their request for horses, saddled and readied, was made through Barter to John Ware.

And John, with good nature and patience, selected horses unlikely to humble the visitors by dumping them far from home. He made sure the cinches were tight and the saddles clean. And when the riders returned, he was on hand to take the horses, always with the best of humor. Gradually the guests found themselves admiring this constantly pleasant personality. But still there was a smug reluctance about inviting his company or conversation.

Then came the Sunday when the imported hounds were to be put to a test. The English visitors chose to accompany them. Fred Stimson came from the Bar U to join the hunting party; and at mid-afternoon a dozen mounted men — three on flat saddles — rode away from the river bottom with five dogs which were strange to the countryside and totally unaccustomed to coyotes.

The sky was blue and warm, the mountain outlines were sharp and clear, and the mosquitoes came in murderous waves. The young Englishmen complained bitterly as welts arose on all exposed parts of their tender bodies. And John, with the best of intentions, observed that the pests would be much worse near sundown. Why, on the night before, according to his telling, when he had built a smudge for the protection of his mares and foals, he had had to shoot a hole through the clouds of "Skitters" before any smoke could get away!

But all talk about mosquitoes ended when Fred Stimson sighted a coyote. "Halt!" he called. "Now, how do we want to handle this situation? We'd better cut that gent off from the river, because if he heads for cover there, we'll lose him for sure. Suppose we cut west and make him run to the open country southward."

Nobody wanted to argue with Stimson — about coyotes or anything else; and the party turned toward the mountains, the dogs still unaware of the coyote.

"You fellows keep close to me," Stimson instructed in a loud whisper, as his Mexican spurs touched his horse's flanks and he cantered away. "Hold back, you!" he called to Lord Harold, who obviously resented taking orders from anybody. "Stay behind until I tell you to run."

Defiantly the young Englishman pressed his horse into a fast gallop, making it necessary for Stimson and the others to follow or abandon the chase for that particular coyote. The man from the Bar U cursed as only he could do, knowing that the alleged aristocrat was incapable of giving leadership under these or any circumstances.

John Ware, feeling some responsibility for horses and men, held his own mount at the rear of the group. He knew exactly what evil thoughts were going through Stimson's mind: "It would serve that arrogant English ass well if his horse dumped him."

Horses and dogs were now running hard and bearing down upon the coyote when, as though Fred Stimson's curse had gathered power, Lord Harold's horse stumbled and the rider hit the prairie sod, sprawling awkwardly. Stimson pretended he didn't see the accident and rode on. To stop now would be to lose the coyote, and nobody wanted to miss the concluding act when the dogs would close in for the kill.

But John Ware couldn't close his eyes to the accident, even though this highborn fool was getting exactly what he deserved. He knew he couldn't decently leave the humiliated and perhaps injured fellow on the ground. The man was lying motionless; he might even be dead. But nobody was more eager than John to witness the hunting climax and he hated to stop. As other riders galloped on, however, he drew his horse to a stop beside the prostrate form, bounded to the ground, placed a powerful right arm around the Englishman's middle and, in an instant, was back in the saddle, holding a semi-conscious horseman the way a bartender might hold a towel, and galloping away to overtake the other hunters.

The embarrassed Lord Harold had suffered nothing more serious than loss of wind; and being suspended on the stout Ware arm while the horse raced forward served to revive him. By the time the two biggest and fastest dogs seized the coyote from their respective sides and pulled him down, Lord Harold's curiosity was fully recovered and he and John Ware were there to see everything.

Fred Stimson's anger waned; and the foolish young man, who had been winded, shaken and humbled, needed no further rebuke. Other cowboys caught his horse and quietly he rode back to the Quorn headquarters.

"Damn it," he said to John, "I ignored you for days. Really though, I'm a bloody fool at times; you'd better take care of me from now on, and if I'm making an ass of myself, you tell me!"

"Look afta yo? Sho, I'll do it," John replied, showing his good white teeth with a grin which closed his eyes to mere slits. "Fust yo gotta lea'n to wide a man's saddle instead of that leatha sweat-pad yo call a English saddle. Then, while yo out heah in this cow count'y, yo betta foget those fancy names lak Lo'd and Ea'l. Sho, ah'll look afta yo."

The young man received the advice with silent surprise, listened the way a pupil would to a wise elder. Then the slightly inebriated member of the trio changed the subject. "I say, Mister Ware, we are invited to attend a concert at High River tomorrow evening. Will you ride with us — cowmen's saddles all around?"

John beamed his pleasure, but this was not an invitation he could accept without the consent of the ranch manager. Lord Harold understood and added, "Mister Barter will agree; I shall see to that."

The boss agreed and John, with clean shirt, red handkerchief around his neck and trousers with stains from the last branding, set out with his English friends on the sixteen-mile ride to the Highwood Crossing. As they rode he pointed out places of interest — home sites of incoming settlers, the spot at which the Indians conducted a Sun Dance, and camping places offering good spring water. He told them, too, how a man should sit in a stock saddle, and about the long trail journeys from Montana to the Highwood. Now, instead of shunning this colored man, whose grammar and clothing were unrefined, the Englishmen were pressing close to him to get every word. Instead of being ignored, he was the center of attraction as he talked on with intermittent bursts of his own laughter.

But the men from the Quorn never did get to the concert at the Presbyterian Mission. Unexpectedly, there was a counter-attraction at the Economy Livery Stable, where most cattlemen quartered their horses and loitered when they had time. As John Ware led his horse into the stable, his eyes fell upon a young transient Negro sitting and dozing. Leaning against the wall beside the fellow was a banjo. Boyish surprise showed plainly on John's face as he gazed momentarily at this sleeping member of his own race. Before throwing a feed of hay to his horse, John awakened the stranger with a slap on his shoulders such as might have loosened a man's teeth.

"Ma names' John — John Wa'e," he said. "What's yos?"

"Sam," came the drowsy reply, "from Dixie."

"Man, yo sho a long way f'om hom. An what yo think yo doin with that banjo thing?"

Sam continued to sit on the livery stable watering bucket, but before many minutes he was strumming and John was singing and clapping his huge hands. As the words and music of "My Old Kentucky Home" filled the stable, men from the street stopped to listen. One song led to another and people forgot about the concert at the church.

With a lull in the singing, there was a certain searching for other forms of entertainment. It would have been easy at that moment to promote a wrestling match there on the plank floor; but instead, there was a demand from Sam Howe for John to demonstrate his strength, already recognized wherever Canadian buckaroos met to gossip and tell tales.

John had no desire to stage livery stable vaudeville and shook his head. The request being repeated, John moved cat-like to seize Sam Howe by the loose of his coat and, with one hand, raise him above his head, keeping him there until repentance was unmistakable.

Of course the growing number of spectators wanted more. "Jake says you can't lift a barrel of water," one of them called challengingly.

"There's a barrel — nearly full. I'll buy your supper if you lift it clear off the ground."

"Ah can always use the suppah," John mumbled, striding to the barrel kept for watering patrons' horses. "Ef it had ho'ns o' somethin' fo handles, ah migh be able t' do it." Placing his long arms around the barrel, he paused to take a deep breath and then made a pretense of lifting, but nothing happened. He could play at showmanship as well as anybody, but his smile revealed that he was holding back his best effort.

"Try again," somebody called, and John braced his feet and heaved. This time the barrel and its great weight of water were lifted well off the floor and set down on a stoneboat kept nearby for hauling manure.

It was now past the hour set for the concert, but the livery stable crowd showed no inclination to leave. Instead of wandering to the mission, fascinated spectators called for more entertainment. "There!" shouted one of them after looking about for something still more challenging than a barrel of water and pointing to a wagon box on wheels. "A cigar you can't take it off the wheels and set it down, all alone."

It was a standard box, capable of holding seventy-five bushels of wheat, and like all such boxes, it was long and heavy and awkward. Transferring such an object from one wagon gear to another was difficult enough for two men.

John didn't want a cigar any more than he wanted flat feet or a monocle, but the English boys from the Quorn were enjoying it all and John was ready to do anything for their pleasure. Throwing a horse blanket on his shoulders to protect human muscles, he placed himself at a midpoint under the box, hefted a few times to test his estimate of the center, and then raised it a foot above the bolsters.

"Wheah you wan me t' take it?" he gasped at the man who had challenged him. The admiring English boys clapped and cheered, and when there was no further instruction about the box's disposition, John let it settle back on the wagon gear. Walking away, he said, "ah'm thwough now!"

The colored boy from Dixie took to singing and playing his banjo again, and one by one the spectators walked away. Mister Ernest found a friend with a bottle of wine and helped to empty it. Lord Harold engaged in conversation with a High River remittance man, and John Ware accompanied Sam Howe to visit with Tom Lynch and Dan Riley.

Lynch, as always, knew exactly what was taking place across the vast prairie spaces. Howell Harris, who was among the earliest traders in the country — he had built a post on the Highwood River in 1872 — was now returning from Montana with 3,000 I. G. Baker cattle to be grazed on a range north of Lethbridge. Lynch had much to tell. A.

E. Cross, who had been bookkeeper for the B. A. Horse Ranch, was starting his own operations on Mosquito Creek. The Bar U was believed to have 10,000 cattle on its books; and the Powder River Ranching Company — better known by its "76" brand — had brought the Trollinger place on Mosquito Creek and was driving 6,000 cattle from Wyoming. "Deaf" Murphy would be the "76" manager; and over East the Medicine Hat Ranching Company, first big outfit in its area, was being started by owners Ezra Pearson, Thomas Tweed, W. F. Finlay and John Ewart.

"How many cattle do you figure you've got for yourself now?" Dan Riley inquired, turning to John Ware.

"Me? Ah figahs bout seventy-five, countin' eve'ything. Cou'se, they's all out on wange; don' know xactly wheah they ah, but if the cows keep on having calves an ah can bwand 'em befo' anybody else does, ah'll soon have a pwetty good he'd."

"Better get yourself some land pretty soon," Dan hinted. "At the rate these nesters are coming in and homesteading on the leases, it won't be long before there's no range. Cowmen hate barbed wire; they hated the wire the Cochran's nailed up to keep their cows with their own bulls, and cut the stuff to pieces every time it got in their way. But cattlemen will have to come to using it themselves. You'll see every rancher carrying a hammer and a pocketful of staples before long."

"I tell you," Tom Lynch added, "things are changing. The day of trailing cattle from down South is just about over too. I know the "76" is herding in a big bunch, but they'll be having a merry time. Nesters! Hang it, they're all along the trails now, stretching fence wire and ready to shoot the cow herds and the cowmen too. I wouldn't mind going down for more horses — and I think I will — but, if we want more cattle, we gotta raise 'em. I suppose we might rail some in from the East, the way the Quorn is going to do this year. Maybe that'll work — but, damn it, it might not. I'll wager those Ontario or even Manitoba calves they're talking about bringing are not the tough and hardy critters like the ones from Montana and farther south. You can tell us next spring, after you've spent a winter with these eastern dogies, John."

About sundown, John and his English friends saddled for the ride back to the ranch. The Mission concert had been a failure, but the few hours in High River were pleasant and the friendship between John Ware and the visitors was now cemented more firmly than ever. The Englishmen would be leaving in a few days, and they asked John's permission to ride with him on his range duties as long as they could be together. John agreed, and on the last evening of their stay at the ranch the young men insisted that he be their guest for dinner at their special table in the ranch house. The Englishmen dressed in their formal clothes and

John came in the only clothes he owned, the ones he wore every day, but he wasn't in the least embarrassed. But he admired the dress suits and pressed his rough fingers on the cloth to judge its fine texture. With unhidden admiration for the splendid tailoring, and some pardonable covetousness, he tried to put on Lord Harold's Prince Albert coat.

The garment was too small for him. His disappointment was plain. He wanted to see himself in that beautiful coat. But Lord Harold, sensing the cowboy's thoughts, said, "Mister John, you've been good to us — better than we deserved — and we owe you something. When we get back to London, I shall see that a dinner suit is sent to you — a big size. I don't know when you'll find a chance to wear it, but that will be for you to worry about. You can wear it when you're chasing coyotes if you want. Anyway, you'll get one of these coats, I promise!"

The very day the young Englishmen left the ranch, a dozen carloads of yearling stocker steers and heifers from Ontario and Manitoba — 300 head — arrived at Calgary. Barter and a few of the cowhands went to town to drive the young cattle to the ranch. John, still the man in charge of horses, remained behind. It was better that he should not go to that town because he'd worry about the cool reception he might get again.

The young cattle were predominantly red in color, and mostly of Shorthorn breeding. The one good thing about them was that they were a better type than ranchers could expect from the hundreds of scrub bulls at large on the range. They were well grown for their age, but when released on the grass west of Okotoks, they bawled incessantly and walked aimlessly. They were looking, it seemed, for familiar barns on hundred-acre eastern farms and the friendly faces of men carrying pitchforks and bent from thinning turnips.

"Ah don' think they lak owah company ve'y well," was John's observation as cowboys tried to hold them together, "o' maybe they just got no sense. Don' know 'nough to be sca'ed of a man on a hoss. What those little critters gon' t' do when cold weathah hits 'em?"

"If the fool things don't quit traveling," Barter replied cynically, "they'll be back in Ontario by Christmas. We've got to try keeping them near home until they settle down; may be hard on horses, but it'll have to be done."

More English travelers visited the ranch in time for the fall shooting — again, well-tailored young men with the finest of guns. Unlike those who had come before, however, these guests lost no time in cultivating John Ware's acquaintance. Moreover, there were no "Lords" and "Earls" among them. From Lord Harold they had received a briefing, and had learned about the Quorn's strong man and superior horseman, with the unusual capacity for friendliness. And for delivery by one of the guests was a package for John Ware: "With appreciation and best wishes, from Harold"

Lord Harold had not forgotten, and John Ware was now the proud possessor of the most luxurious English Prince Albert in the Northwest Territories — tails and all. His smile was broad like a Hereford's loin as he tried the coat for a fit. "Ah neva thought ah'd have anthing lak it," he muttered, recalling that, except for the work clothes on his back, every other garment he owned was crumpled in the grain bag which served at times for a pillow.

"Gollyme! Ah didn't think it would weally happen. Ah wish ah could w'ite a lettah. Ah'd tell Misah Ha'old ah sho thanks him. Wondah when ah can weah ma good clothes?"

Late in the autumn there was a Thanksgiving social at High River, and the Quorn men resolved to attend, largely to give John a chance to wear the best clothes seen in the foothills at any time. Unfortunately, there was neither artist nor cameraman present to capture the spectacle of John preparing for and riding to the party. Wearing his work boots — the only ones he owned, heavy woolen socks, big-brimmed hat, scuffed red shirt, and the finest Prince Albert coat ever turned out by a London haberdasher, John Ware settled into his saddle for the two-hour ride to the Crossing. The coat was fully as incongruous as a silk hat on a stonemason's assistant, but nobody objected. By the time of arrival at the social, the elegant clothing was fouled with dust and the marks of horse saliva; but it was still lovely, and John Ware was the best-dressed man in and about High River.

"I never thought it would happen," John Barter said with good humor as the cowboys rode home through the darkness, "one of my cowboys turning out to be a fashion plate. All you need now, John, is a stovepipe hat; and if I can find where they sell those things, you're going to have one. But by the way," Barter continued, with sudden seriousness in his voice, "there's a change of weather. Wind's shifted to northwest and it's getting cold. Could be we'll see some winter weather tomorrow. By gee, there's snow in the air right now."

Barter was silent for a moment and spoke again. "Hope we get a mild winter. A hell of a lot of cattle in this country now and not much hay put up. One of these times we'll get caught like a cowboy without a horse. A bad winter would ruin most of these cowmen, and I hate to think what can happen before they learn their lesson."

Barter's next remark, as the horses plodded on, facing wind and snow, revealed the substance of his fears: "Father Lacombe is predicting another mild winter. Hope he's right. But Chief Bullhead at the Sarcee Reserve says it'll be a rough one."

Serious thinking is always easier when the snow is falling, and Barter's men agreed with him. "Ah think yo' wight, Boss," John Ware replied. "Not nough hay piles fo' all these cwitters in a bad wintah. Too bad cowmen gotta get hu't befo' they lea'n."

CHAPTER 11

THE WINTER OF HUNGRY CATTLE

The next day was October 26, 1886, and snow blanketed the cow country from Calgary to Oldman River. With shocking suddenness, like a fall through river ice, the range was plunged from Indian summer into winter. Still, most people were undisturbed; October storms were not uncommon, and a chinook would soon clear the range just as it had done many times.

The Calgary *Tribune* (of October 22, 1886) had just published its comment about this area's "unsurpassed climate . . . very similar to that of Southern Europe." And Sam Livingstone — trader, Indian fighter and first farmer close to Fort Calgary, made news by setting out 350 fruit trees on his land close to the Elbow River.

Optimism was fashionable. Pessimism was akin to treason. The cattle bonanza born on Canadian soil when Sergt. Whitney of the Mounted Police had turned a few cattle loose on the public domain at Fort Macleod exactly ten years before, had experienced only a few reverses in that period of time. Men on the frontier were not inclined to dwell on dangers like long periods of snow. The cattleman's kingdom appeared about as secure as Caesar's.

The only visible uncertainty seemed to lie in the outcome of a war between the ranchers demanding open range and the "nester" fellows who threatened to wreck the old order, "turn the grass upside down," and enclose the land of their choosing — and sometimes good watering places as well — with their contemptible barbed wire.

Cattle numbers had increased rapidly; 100,000 head were feeding on the Canadian ranges south of the Bow River. Unfortunately, however, the summer having been hotter and drier than usual, some ranges showed signs of overstocking and overgrazing. Equally serious was the fact that only a few cattlemen had hay in stacks; many of them didn't even own mowers, hayracks and pitchforks.

"Ah don' lak t' be sad," John Ware told the boss in mid-November, "but ah've a mise'able feelin' in ma bones that ol man Winta's got it in fo us this yeah. We've justa nough hay fo the studs an a bit mo in case theah's some sick cwitters. Gollyme, boss, do yo think yo could buy us a lil mo hay in case we have twoubles?"

Barter listened with silence betraying an anxiety he had recently come to share. "Damn it, John," he said finally, "we might have made more hay, but it's too late now and you can't buy the stuff today — unless you're willing to pay a fancy price like twenty dollars a load. No, I reckon we'll just take our chances like every other cowman between here and the boundary. But I wish we'd get a spell of warm days. Those young things from Manitoba are getting thin and it's too early for that."

"Ah'm worried bout ma own lil bunch a cattle scatte'ed all the way to Montana. If ah evah have a place of ma own, ah'll sho wide he'd on my own cwitters so ah'll know wheah they ah. An, Boss, ah'm wo'ied about yo bawlin little cow cwitters f'om Manitoba," John added. "Wheah is that place, Manitoba? Betta get these cwazy lil cattle gathe'ed up, ah'd say, cause theah's gona be anotha stom in about five days."

"Storm? In five days? What are you talking about?"

John's face was serious as he leaned momentarily on a six-tined fork behind the stallions. "Didn yo see that wing wound the old moon last night, Boss? An just five stahs inside that wing? Five days they'll be a stom."

Barter chuckled. He knew all the weather signs observed by Ireland's superstitious people — but did not believe in them. "Maybe those stars mean five weeks or five months till the next storm," he said jokingly.

But strangely enough, snow was falling heavily four days later, and then a wind arose to wrap the foothills and plains in blizzard. Hardy western cattle shook their long-horned heads and looked for shelter along the river, while the soft and infantile specimens from Manitoba and Ontario seemed ready to drift like tumbleweeds in a wind. Having neither fear nor cow sense, they refused to be turned or guided by men on horses. Now, with snow on their backs, icicles dangling from their nostrils, and expressions of hopelessness in their eyes, they scattered aimlessly in a southerly direction.

Cowboys tried to turn them and drive them to shelter along the river, but when one of the dogie cattle was being turned, a hundred others were going their separate and aimless ways with the snow-laden wind.

"We weren't doing a thing except wearing out our horses," a new hand explained that night. "Might as well have been trying to round up coyotes. We might as well sit here till the storm quits and then we'll have a chance to get those fool cattle back. But, by the way, where's that big slave tonight?"

Barter replied: "John Ware, you mean? Why do you say 'slave'? Sure he was a slave but that's no reflection on him. And sure, he's colored but what's wrong with being born that way? By God, don't you or anybody else in my employ speak disrespectful of John. Show me a white man who's half as good and I'll hire him too. But if you fellows who gave up and came home in the storm today want to know where he is, I'll tell you; he rode to the Highwood Crossing. The big stallion's been having colic off and on all day and John insisted he'd get some linseed oil and turpentine for him. I told him I'm paying some men who'd let a stud die before they'd ride in that storm. You might just consider that before you cast any reflections on John. But I hope he won't try to come back till the wind goes down."

It was sixteen miles by trail from Quorn Ranch to the Crossing on the Highwood but on this day, even with the wind blowing from the rear, it seemed more like twenty-six. John's choice of a mount for the trip was a mare known as Molly — big, white and awkward. Stamina would count for much on a journey like this, and Molly was thought to possess it.

With no beaten path to follow and no opportunity to travel faster than a walk, the mare took four and a half hours to cover the ground to the Crossing.

"What in tarnation brings you here on a day like this?" Buck Smith exclaimed after John had tied his weary horse in Smith's stable to feed on a big ration of oats, and then presented himself inside the stopping place in the hope of securing some food for himself.

"Gotta sick stallion at home," John replied while rubbing his cold hands. "Need some tu'pentine and oil fo him. But will yo give me a little bit a bwead and tea an then ah'll get ma oil and start home."

"Start back? Tonight? Man, you're locoed! You'd be stiffer'n a frozen carrot by morning. You'd never get there in a night like this. Hell, no, John; I'm not letting you leave here tonight. There's a spare buffalo robe — biggest one in the house — I shot that bull through the eye when he was charging me. You can make a bed on the floor and start north in daylight. As a matter of fact, you were damned lucky to get down here alive. Now get your oil and turps fixed up tonight, and you can make an early start in the morning — if the storm lets up by then. Now mind what I'm telling you and no arguing."

The warmth from Buck Smith's potbellied stove was as acceptable as nuts to a hungry squirrel, and John remained close to the heat while he munched a meal of tea, bread and cold beef. He mumbled something about Eagle Plume, the sick stud, but knew very well that Smith's advice was right. It would be folly to start back before the light of morning and perhaps never succeed in delivering the turps and oil.

"Ah s'ppose yo' wight, Mistah Buck," he said, stirring his tea with his jackknife. "Ah'd lak to be goin but ah'll stay till mo'nin. Ah must leave ea'ly though. Ah'll just go now and give ma Molly hoss some hay and get ma jugs filled an then ah'll woll up in that buffalo skin and do some of the dangdest sno'in yo evah hea'd.

Before the first rays of morning light, John was up and lighting a lantern in order to feed Molly. The weather had changed without improving. The previous day's wind, which John said was "the laziest ah evah saw—wouldn't go wound a fellow; just wanted to blow wight th'ough," had subsided and visibility was more favorable but the snow was deeper and the frost more intense. The sixteen-mile ride would, at best, be a hardship. John knew he'd have no trouble finding his way; but with so much snow, the journey would be slower and more tedious than ever. Moreover, there were the jugs of oil and turpentine, one to be tied on each side of the saddle; and they'd add to awkwardness and difficulty in travel.

Hurriedly John devoured the bread and prunes and tea Buck Smith set for his breakfast, and minutes later turned his saddled mare's head northward and waved farewell.

Bareheaded and shivering, Buck Smith watched as John's horse labored through the drifts, one heavy step at a time. "By gee, I'm not sure he'll get through to the Quorn," he whispered to himself. "I'm not sure a horse can carry that load and fight sixteen miles of snow and drifts too. But John knows he can come back here if he can't get through."

It was just as tough as Buck Smith surmised.

Molly wanted to go home; but she was still tired from the hardships of the previous day, and three miles away from the river the mare stopped, needing a rest. John dismounted, rubbed the icicles from her face and said, "Molly, yo old scamp; yo got a long way to go. Yo shouldn' get ti'ed yet."

Another two miles and Molly was again showing signs of fatigue and begging for a rest.

John was puzzled. Was this horse sick too? Or was the hardship of plunging through soft snow, with a heavy man on her back, just too much for a saddle horse? In any case, progress would be slow. At this rate of travel and the necessity of periodic delays for rest. John knew he'd be fortunate to be back at the Quorn by nightfall.

It was close to midday when man and mare stopped for the third time. John's fingers were now numb from cold, and Molly was coming ever closer to exhaustion. The mare's head, with frosted whiskers, seemed at times to be dragging in the snow, and her ears flopped irresponsibly. Moreover, there was no shelter along the trail and no food for man or beast. Molly might have performed some equine pawing to reach snow-covered grass, but she was totally uninterested in anything calling for physical effort.

For the first time on the trip, John was worried. He was still six or seven miles from home and his mare was playing out. Of course, he could abandon the horse and all the animal was carrying, and walk on to save himself from freezing, but that wouldn't be good; he wanted to complete a task, to deliver mare and saddle and crocks of colic cure. New urgency spawned in his thought. Violently he swung his arms against his body and ran in a small circle to improve circulation of the blood to his cold extremities. Then, cutting the rest period to a few minutes, John shouted, "Come on, ol Molly, yo gotta try it again."

Back in the saddle, John concluded that his mare was refreshed. But any revival of strength which might have been noticeable was brief. Before going half a mile, Molly's steps were again becoming short and the poor brute was stumbling. The situation was now perfectly clear; with a heavy man and some crocks on her back—300 pounds at least—and bad footing, the mare would not make it to Sheep Creek. And even without a man on her back, the outcome was doubtful.

At that moment John spotted the forms of two animals, with coats filled with snow, in a nearby clump of trees. He wanted to know more about them. Leaving Molly to stand and rest, he walked toward the objects and at once recognized them as red yearling heifers. Just as he had suspected, they were two of the stupid young cattle brought from the East and wearing the Quorn's Z brand. Objects of pity, the heifers were half-perished and half-starved. Momentarily John forgot about the seriousness of his own plight. He wanted to drive the heifers back to the ranch headquarters, but that would be impossible. Recognizing the futility of trying to save the yearlings, he considered using the revolver he carried on his belt and ending their suffering—but he reminded himself that the boss should be consulted before such drastic steps were taken.

When John returned to his horse, the unhappy creature was lying in the snow, satisfied to remain there and freeze. "Wall bless ma soul, Molly. Yo sick o' jus done out? Guess ah'm going to have to leave yo heah and tak myself home without yo. Gollyme, ah hate to do this, Molly, but ah can't see anything else to do."

John loosened and removed the saddle, placed it to one side in the snow, picked up the crocks—one in each hand—and strode away, taking as long strides as deep snow would permit. He'd make better time this way and be sure of getting to the ranch before dusk. But after going a few hundred yards he looked back, saw Molly's head raised inquiringly, and thought he could detect a pleading in the animal's eyes.

"Gollyme—ah can't do this," John said to himself while turning in his tracks. "Ah can't leave that ol hoss theah to fweeze. Maybe she can walk in ma twacks and we'll both get home."

Backtracking, John urged Molly to get up; and then, taking the reins as lead lines, he tugged gently, saying, "Come on, ol scamp, yo can make it if yo got nobody t' cawy on yo back."

Molly did follow, not very briskly, about like a man carrying a sack of potatoes through a pool of mud. But it was all right; and weighted down with oil and turpentine, John wasn't anxious to make fast time through the unbroken and unmarked sea of snow.

There was another halt for rest, and another. But even without a rider on her back, the mare's strength was not returning. Her gait was becoming steadily slower, and more and more she was drawing back—almost leaning against John's hold on the lead straps. And even John, with his well-nigh superhuman strength, was getting tired.

A few minutes before sundown the Quorn workers saw the figure of a big man, jugs in his hands, more or less pulling the exhausted horse through the snow.

Barter rushed out to take the heavy containers from John's near frozen hands. "Thought you'd know enough to stay at the Crossing till weather was better," Barter scolded. "Don't know whether you're a hero or a fool, John—blamed if I do. But if you weren't even stronger than a horse, by God you never would have made it. And you'd carry those bloody crocks! Carry them!"

"Sho did, Mistah Boss. That's tu'ps an oil fo ol Eagle Ploom. That's what ah went fo an ah wasn comin home without what ah went fo. How's ma ailin stud hoss?"

The stallion, Barter reported, was still experiencing spells of colic. "But see here, John, you go right to the house and get thawed out and get some food into you. The boys'll take care of the horse."

"Oh no boss—ah'll see ol Molly gets some feed afo ah do. An ah wants to give that stud some stuff f'om those cwocks. Then ah'll eat."

"Damnest fellow I ever saw," Barter remarked, half in admiration and half in annoyance at this man who should be at the point of collapse. "Pull a horse through the snow, carry a load of colic cure from the Crossing, go all day without eating, and still in no hurry to take care of himself! Beats all!"

John smiled much as usual and went about the tasks of drenching the ailing Thoroughbred and making sure Molly had plenty of hay and bedding. When there was nothing of consequence left to do, John Ware sauntered to the ranch house to wash and eat and fall asleep on a chair beside the long ranch table.

After being left to sleep, balancing on his chair for an hour, he was awakened by Barter and told to go to bed. In the meantime, as John was quick to observe, somebody had removed his heavy boots and placed on his feet a pair of soft slippers. It was a considerate and kindly thing to do. But who had done it? It was the new ranch hand known as Slim—the one who on the day before had inquired in a tone of disrespect, "Where's that big slave tonight?" The "big slave" had made another conquest.

Sure it was a tough winter and it was just starting. For weeks after the November storm, there was no chinook to ease the cow-country hardship. The snow persisted; and cattle, rustling only a fraction of the feed they needed, grew steadily thinner. Many of the Manitoba dogie cattle were known to be dead already, having drifted and piled up in remote coulees. Some had traveled south to the Bar U and OH ranges, and Fred Ings sent word to the Quorn for somebody to come down and take care of them.

John Ware told Barter he was willing to go if there was a reliable man to tend the horses. The arrangement was made, temporarily, and from the OH headquarters John and Ings rode together and found plenty of the Quorn dogies—many in drifts and too weak to get up. None had enough strength to carry them back to the home quarters. What could be done? Barter had authorized any action John considered proper and John Ware was a man of action. He hated to see an animal in needless pain; and where there seemed to be no hope of saving a steer or heifer, he resorted to his six-shooter and speedily put the animal out of misery.

Christmas and the 1887 New Year came, and still there was no relief such as a good chinook would bring. What little hay was available soared to thirty dollars a ton. Ranchers generally were in trouble, but those near the Highwood and around Medicine Hat and the Cypress Hills were suffering the biggest losses. Near Calgary, where the snow was light, the losses were correspondingly less; and Walter Huckvale, wintering his "fiddleback" cattle on the Blood Reserve, experienced relatively good fortune. But A. E. Cross, having made a beginning on Mosquito Creek, knew that his losses would be around 50 per cent. And Ezra Pearson, at Medicine Hat, lost not only half his cattle but almost lost his own life while traveling in a storm from the "Hat" to his ranch.

At one time, according to Mounted Police estimate, there were 40,000 near-starving cattle within twenty-five miles of Fort Macleod. And the STV outfit south of the Cypress Hills lost nearly all the cattle driven in from Texas just a couple of years before. By February the Quorn men knew that all or nearly all of the Manitoba and Eastern dogie cattle brought to the range in the previous summer were dead. As for John Ware's friends, John and Mrs. Quirk, they, with Sam Howe's help, kept their herd from disaster by cutting and gathering willow twigs for feed.

Even the wild animals like deer and antelope and rabbits died by the hundreds. Only the Indians and coyotes, eating sumptuously from the thousands of beef carcasses strewing the ranges, fared better than usual. Ranchers found it difficult enough to keep themselves alive at times, and anything resembling optimism had the appearance of being forced and artificial.

Even when winter departed in March there was new trouble for the cattlemen—floods on all the foothills streams, and a drop in cattle prices. All of this, coupled with the foul strench of rotting carcasses rising from the range when weather became warm, intensified the gloom.

The statistics from the spring roundups confirmed the crippling losses. Nobody with cattle on the open range escaped. John Ware's little herd was reduced to half the number branded 9999 in the previous season.

"Is this the end of cattle ranching?" people were asking. Many observers believed it was. "The present blow will hasten the obliteration of the large cattle companies," an editor wrote, and according to another: "The present paralysis of the industry heralds its end."

With the great pessimism pervading the cattle kingdom came a new interest in horses. With an inherent ability to paw their way to grass beneath the snow, horses would be less of a risk than cattle on the Canadian ranges. Stockmen as far away as the foothills nodded understandingly when they heard the story about a Medicine Hat settler who brought his oxen and horses through the winter by tying an ox to each horse and turning all loose. The horses pawed the snow and both oxen and horses got enough grass for survival.

Moreover, there was a promise of a good demand for horses. Farm settlers needed more horses than the farming districts would ever produce; Mounted Police needed them; the British War Department would be looking this way for cavalry horses; and, altogether, it was easy to see the hardy horse stock as offering more than cattle on ranges where winter climate held the seeds of disaster. Horse ranching was bound to profit from the failing popularity of cattle ranching, and the demand for breeding mares improved immediately.

"Guess ah'll get me some hosses," John Ware told Mike Herman. "But ah'm not agoin' t' quit cows. Ah've gotta get me a place wheah ah can cut hay fo bad wintas; an ah've gotta show that an ol slave boy can be a good wancha an a good Canadian. Sho, ah should get me some hosses."

"You've got one you can call your own right now, you know," Barter said. "I'm giving you that Molly mare you carried home through the snow."

John giggled. "Ah didn cawy the white maah home; ah just dwagged her. But thanks, boss, ah'd sho lack t' have a foal f'om Molly an Ol Ploom."

CHAPTER 12

COWMEN BECOME HORSEMEN

Cowboys loved good saddle stock at any time; and now, in 1887, bunkhouse conversation showed how completely the ranchland hopes had shifted from cattle to horses. Why would anybody be surprised at this with well over half of the previous year's crop of calves now dead?

From as far as Moose Jaw, reports were the same—countless winter deaths among cattle and small losses in horses. Again and again, John Barter and John Ware heard a Cypress Hills story concerning the disastrous loss of cattle experienced by the STV outfit; while, almost on the same range, Michael Oxarart, best-known horseman in Western Assiniboia, had wintered 700 horses with practically no write off. The lesson was perfectly clear.

Everybody between Calgary and Fort Macleod remembered Oxarart as the reckless Frenchman who had driven horses from Montana three years before and found himself in a series of troubles with the police. First he was accused of smuggling horses into Canada. When that charge was dropped, there was another—of undervaluation for purposes of the import duty. Then, after his horse herd was seized for the second time, at Calgary, some of the animals disappeared, and the fabulous Frenchman was arrested on a charge of "stealing" his own horses from the police. John Ware and his friends chuckled every time Oxarart's name was mentioned.

Moreover, there was a matter of markets. This year, for the first time, Mounted Police officials were buying all their horse requirements in the Territories, paying up to $125 for good ones instead of going to eastern Canada for them. At last the hardiness of western horses was being recognized and appreciated, as a statement from the Assistant Commissioner showed: "I have no hesitation in saying that the bronco horses are the most suitable in every way for the services, both teaming and saddle."

Horses in use by the Mounted Police at that time numbered 921, and annual replacements would assure a market for close to 200 head. The police wanted horses standing fifteen hands, short in backs, and with hard-wearing feet and legs. Buyers for the force believed the best ones were to be obtained from Frank Strong, of Fort Macleod, and the North West Cattle Company. The Quorn horses possessed undisputed quality, but there was fear of their being too rangy. They were considered better, perhaps, for the needs of the British Army than for the fatiguing labors of police patrol day after day.

And certainly, a bad winter hadn't halted the influx of "nesters," those annoying fellows with wagons, plows, manure forks, and unpardonable nerve in squatting—with or without homesteaders' claims—on the choicest ranchland sites. They needed horses—a thousand times as many as the police. The typical landseeker came with a pair of horses, and at once needed more to make up a four-horse team. Nearly every day in June, John Ware saw newcomers visiting the Quorn, anxious to buy any horses gentle enough to be harnessed.

Regardless of type of horse the importance of quality was obvious. To become more salable, ranch horses everywhere would need to be improved through better breeding; and stallions of widely different sizes and breeds being brought to the foothills ranges reflected the new outlook.

Horse lovers about Calgary were receiving inspiration from stock brought in by the Halifax Ranch—Percheron stallions imported and delivered at the home quarters on the Elbow River a year before, the first of their kind in Alberta. Pride of the shipment was Marcus, a beautiful dappled gray four-year-old, standing 17 hands and weighing 1,980 pounds. How this noble horse and another Halifax Ranch Percheron called Caesar were regarded may be judged by the service fee of $40, more than the market value of an ordinary bronco.

Arriving about the same time as the Halifax Ranch Percherons and the Quorn Thoroughbreds was the shipment of stallions for Frank Strong, including Clydesdales, Thoroughbreds, Standardbreds and Hackneys, altogether the sensation of the south country.

Some people held interest in horses for business reasons, some for pleasure; but, in any case, every rangeland citizen was a horseman, and names like Eagle Plume and Marcus were about as well known as those of Frank Oliver and Frederick Haultain, who were making platform pleas for self-government in the new North West.

And while Quorn mares were delivering the first foals from the imported Thoroughbred sires, and John Ware had words of admiration for every "baby," regardless of how crooked its legs might be, Barter was expecting a big band of imported mares, mostly from Ireland, for his breeding program. They arrived late in the spring, a hundred of them, including a few English Thoroughbreds. And itinerant cowboys who considered the transmission of foothills gossip as their responsibility reported new horse ranches springing up, both north and south. Along the Bow were the Critchleys—Harry and Oswald—making a studied beginning, and the Rawlinsons, with ambitions to raise world-champion Hackneys. And from the south came word of the McPherson and Ross Ranch, started beside the Highwood one year earlier, now changing from cattle to horses.

McPherson and Ross were well-to-do Britishers anxious to start sons on the road to fame and fortune in one of the Colonies. Rather often at that period, English fathers saw a ranch in the Canadian North West as a solution in rehabilitating wayward progeny, even though their erring ones might not be sure of the difference between a Longhorn and a Leghorn.

Having acquired the buildings and ranch location at which the North West Cattle Company operated when the first cattle were brought to Canadian grass, the new owners needed livestock. Ontario Shorthorns were shipped out in 1886, but none survived the winter. Ross withdrew from the partnership and another would-be empire-builder, Major Haldane Eckford, took his place. Then, in the spring of 1887, young Duncan McPherson arrived from England to "manage" operations. Some time later, he was joined by Herbert Eckford.

For families with Imperial Army and Old School traditions, it was easy to decide in favor of horses, and the place became known as the High River Horse Ranch. The first foreman was George Baker, and before the end of summer the ranch was assuming the same sort of equine distinctiveness as had characterized the Quorn. Clydesdale mares and stallions with the finest of Scottish pedigrees were brought from Ontario. Two Thoroughbred stallions and two Norfolk trotting stallions came from England, and with trail-wise Tom Lynch directing the overland journey, 392 ranch horses were driven from Oregon.

For John Ware's friend, Tom Lynch, it was the last of many northward drives with cattle and horses. With settlers crowding in along the routes, the days of trailing were passing, and Tom Lynch had to accept the change.

On a Sunday morning in September, Barter, on a Thoroughbred stallion whose grandfather had won the Derby, and John Ware, on his white mare, rode south to see the new horses Lynch had turned over to the High River Horse Ranch and the 100 mares which he had brought in at the same time for himself. Unsurpassed as a trail driver, Lynch had other talents, one being as a judge of horses, and the mares selected to stock his own ranch were the best Barter and Ware had seen—well-muscled mares with good shoulders, flat bones, long pasterns and nicely shaped feet. But for the day's visitors there were two horses of special interest: Grey Eagle, a gelding with which Lynch hoped to win some races and reform the nearby betting men; and Dynamite, a bucking horse with the reputation of having humbled about every rider trying to stay on him.

Quite by coincidence other local buckaroos arrived to inspect new horses and to visit. Present were George Lane, Fred Stimson, Herb Miller and brother Charlie from the Bar U, and that great rider, Frank Ricks, who had ridden into the country with horses from Oregon in 1883. There on the pleasant riverside ground where Howell Harris had swapped beads and whisky for Indian furs many years earlier, and the North West Cattle Company, W. E. Cochrane, and Walter Skrine had made ranch headquarters successively, the stage was set for races and bucking contests. Any horseman would sense the possibilities.

The Bar U men, with some home-grown conceit about the speed of their nags, and John Barter with his pedigreed English Thoroughbred, would be hard to convince that Tom's new gray gelding might be the best horse on a short track. But in the gray's first test on the Canadian side, he removed all doubt about his ability to get away faster and finish sooner than any of the assembled Highwood River rivals.

For McPherson's best imported Norfolk Trotter no competition was available that day, but the tall dark stallion, said to have been driven sixteen miles in a hour, performed convincingly for the Sunday guests. Then, before the neighboring stockmen considered saddling for homeward rides, the vociferous Fred Stimson was promoting a bucking contest, waving a five-dollar bill and challenging that Frank Ricks, thirty-three years old and big and broad-shouldered, could stay on Lynch's outlaw longer than John Ware could.

Barter had heard of the Ricks skill, but Ware was his man and loyally compelled support. The two men, strangers to each other until this day, but similar in size and shape, agreed to ride; so Tom Lynch went for Dynamite, the big bay horse with switching tail and hate in his eyes.

Stimson tossed a ten-cent piece. "If it's heads you ride first, Frank," he called. "It's tails. You're first up, John. If you should stick, don't take all the buck out of him. Leave some for Frank."

John removed a revolver from his belt, handed it to Barter, hitched up his corduroy pants, pulled his shapeless hat down to make it stay on his head, and said, "Ef that fella kills me, yo can bury this ol' slave wight beside that Indian twee wif its stems hitched t'gethah."

As the bad horse switched and eyed the cowboys defiantly, John leaped into the saddle and shouted, "Le' me have 'im."

Dynamite felt spurs raking his ribs and sprang skyward; he groaned in anger and twisted unbelievably in midair. Stimson stared in amazement. The horse was better than his reputation. He was a bucking sensation, and onlookers were sure that neither John nor anyone else could stay on such a brute.

Dynamite's fury was undiminished. Men cheered and laughed as they overheard John's mumbling to the horse: "Yo mad at me, yo ol cow hoss? Well, why don yo buck me off? Come on, buck lak yo weah some good, yo ol plow hoss."

"Come off him now, John," Stimson shouted. "Leave some kick for Ricks."

John bounded to the ground and walked away as though he had done nothing more unusual than to stir a pot of porridge.

Now it was up to Frank Ricks, but that great rider changed his mind.

"No sir," he said to Stimson, "you can award that ride to John. I couldn't beat that and I wouldn't try. Nobody could beat that and you all know it."

Before the visitors saddled to go back to home ranches, McPherson served tea, and conversation turned to many topics, including a report about a dread horse disease called glanders, detected at the Brown Ranch on the St. Mary River; the continued arrival of settlers; and the ruinous state of the cattle market.

The very name of glanders made older horsemen cringe. Speculation was that the infection had been carried by Blackfoot Indians returning from a foray onto the Montana range.

And as for cattle markets, raw-boned George Lane said, "Terrible!" Bovine survivors from the first crop of calves dropped by Bar U cows after coming to Canadian grass were now four-year-olds, and the steers were ready for sale. But buyers were indifferent, and Lane vowed he wouldn't take the thirty-five dollars per head being offered for those big cattle. He and Stimson had resolved to conduct an experiment—ship to the English market and accept the consequences.

Barter had nothing to sell except a few dry cows, but he was interested and sought Lane's promise to let him know the result of the experimental shipment.

"As a matter of fact," Lane said, "we'll round up next week and be cutting out the big steers. Could do with some good help to trail the fat critters to Calgary. Could you spare John Ware for a week or ten days? I'd feel better if he was going along."

Barter hesitated a moment and replied, "Dash it, John's got lots to keep him busy, but if he'll trust our breeding horses to somebody else for a spell, I guess it'll be all right."

John had no desire to visit Calgary, where he had encountered less than decent respect on every previous visit, but he wanted to help George Lane. So the necessary arrangements were made for work in the Quorn horse department.

A few days later John, in high spirits, rode south and west to the familiar range beside Pekisko Creek. The late-September weather was warm and altogether delightful as cattle were gathered and steers segregated for the drive. The four-year-olds were fat, making it difficult to believe them to be the same cattle which had lingered at death's door at the previous winter's end. The foothills ranges were odd. They had their own way of making men forget troubles. But what George Lane couldn't forget was that he'd have had at least 40 per cent more steers to ship if it had not been for the utter destructiveness of that killing winter.

"All right, John, you're in charge of the drive," George Lane said when all the ranch hands were present to hear his orders. "Don't rush 'em—ten or twelve miles the first day, but you know all about that. There'll be plenty of blankets and beans and beef in the wagon, and I'll join you before you get to Calgary."

As trail trips rated, this was not a long one—not like the one of five years earlier when John had helped drive the mothers of these steers from Idaho. On that occasion he had started by occupying the dirtiest and lowliest position at the drag end. Now he was in charge, and commanding the respect of every cattleman and horseman who knew him. But how would he be received in Calgary? He worried about that.

CHAPTER 13

CALGARY ALMOST FORGIVEN

As planned, George Lane overtook the herd north of Fish Creek and rode ahead to see if the CPR cars were ready for loading. Requests for freight cars were sometimes filled slowly, and as Lane discovered, the railway company had assembled only half enough stock cars for the 700 cattle in this drive. The rancher was annoyed. But no benefit would come from complaining, and his decision was to load the available cars, bill them to Montreal, and hold the remaining cattle on the outskirts of town until more cars were brought in.

Only a few residents of Calgary were present to see the big steers driven across the Elbow and westward on Atlantic Avenue to the holding pens beside the railway track. But when it was time to start prodding the 1,500-pound steers up the chutes and into the cars, spectators lined the top rail of the stockyard pen like sparrows on a garden fence.

Neither George Lane nor John Ware had ever loaded stock in cars before; but both men possessed a cattleman's resourcefulness, and before long both were commanding ringside admiration for their skill.

By nightfall, half of the herd was loaded and ready for shipment, the remaining half being temporarily secure in the railroad pens. Bar U cowboys could now relax and see the town and celebrate. Since John had seen the place about one year before, the community had changed greatly. On November 7, 1886, fire had raced savagely through fourteen tinder-dry log and frame buildings on Atlantic Avenue, and that tragedy had led to an interest in more enduring buildings such as could be constructed from the sandstone to be quarried nearby. There for John Ware and his friends to see, was the recently completed Knox Presbyterian Church, the first sandstone structure of importance. But a sandstone courthouse was being started; also three buildings of consequence at the intersection of Stephen Avenue and Scarth Street — the Alexander Block, the Bank of Montreal and the Alberta Hotel. Quite clearly, the business center was shifting from Atlantic Avenue to Stephen (from 9th Avenue to 8th in present-day terms).

The evening wore on and the Bar U cowboys, taking John Ware with them, visited each of Calgary's hotels, drinking too freely and becoming too noisy. The town's police officers, Chief John Ingram and Constables Bob Barber and Bob Barton, bored with weeks in which there had been little for law officers to do, welcomed an opportunity to demonstrate their worth to the community. Swooping down upon a cluster of cowboys intoxicated to one degree or another, the police had no difficulty in making arrests — until they came to John Ware, who was not drunk and could see no reason why he should be taken to jail.

The arrested men were escorted to the town lock-up, and the two constables returned to concentrate on John Ware. "All right colored boy, you're coming with us this time," one of them announced.

With a policeman seizing each wrist, John looked puzzled and then angry. Easily he could have drawn upon his great strength and knocked these officers to the ground, but he restrained the impulse. And, unfortunately, his friends had been taken away; he seemed to be alone.

"What yo mean? Why should ah come wuf yo? Ah'm not misbehavin. Wheah is Mistah Holmes o' Mistah Lane? Ah'll go t' jail ef they say ah should. Ah'm goin t' find em."

Two Calgary constables soon discovered their error in supposing their combined strength would be sufficient to overpower this man. Though hoping to impress street-corner spectators, they found themselves dealing with superstrength and being placed in a ridiculous light. Instead of hustling a prisoner to jail, the humiliated policemen, held by their coat collars, one in each of John Ware's powerful hands, were being marched down Stephen Avenue in the opposite direction from the jail.

As the helpless constables protested and vowed terrible punishment for John, the cowboy continued to mumble: "Mistah Lane o' Mistah Holmes can tell me if ah should go t' jail t' night."

Billy Holmes, who had driven from Moose Jaw to Calgary by team and wagon in 1882, and had ridden in from the south with John that very day, commanded the Negro cowboy's respect; and as fortune would have it, John knew where he was likely to find his friend.

"They'ah twyin t' put me in jail, Mistah Holmes," John complained; "an ah ain't dwunk an ah ben mindin ma business jus fine. Ah don mind sleepin in a jail an ah'll go ef yo say ah should. But ah won't go ef you say ah shouldn."

Billy Holmes was amused. But knowing the error of defying the law, he muffled an irrepressible chuckle at this scene: two Calgary policemen in the custody of a visiting cowboy. "Better go along, John," he advised. "I don't think you're drunk, but you better go with the police and I'll be there to talk to the magistrate about it in the morning."

That was all John needed. He yielded and peacefully let the two constables, whose backs he could have broken, take him away and push him into a cell with a Bar U man. Now John was tired, and after repeating his dislike for this town of Calgary he stretched out on the cell floor and went to sleep.

In the morning men from the lock-up, one by one, faced the magistrate. When John's turn came, the man on the bench eyed him resentfully and said, "Well, what excuse have you got, Stranger? And who invited you to this town, anyway?"

"Ah wasn dwunk, Mistah," John exclaimed nervously. "Ah was jus a twyin t' take ca'e a ma fwiends an yo policemen figu'd cause ah'm colo'd ah should be put in jail. Ah wasn dwunk. Yo can ask Mistah Holmes. He neva told a lie."

"Mr. Holmes?" the magistrate inquired. "Is he here?"

Billy Holmes was there and stood to speak. "As far as I know, John Ware was never drunk in his life. When I saw him with the police last night, he certainly wasn't drunk. I believe he was along with the cowboys from the South — to look after them; and the police jumped to the wrong conclusion."

"Cowboy? A Negro cowboy? Are you a cowboy?" the magistrate asked John, obviously surprised and satisfied to change the subject. "Can you break horses?"

Holmes spoke up again: "Probably the best horse breaker in this country."

"Charge of drunkenness dismissed," the magistrate ruled. Then without hesitation or change of voice he asked, "Any chance you'd have time before you leave town to come around and saddle a bronco I just got in from the Cochrane Ranch? A nice brown gelding, shanks like a deer and he looks like he's got breeding. But the beggar's never had a saddle on his back. Would you have time to ride him around once?"

John regained his usual ease. "Sho thing. Ah got time. It wouldn take as long as spendin a week in jail. If yo lil policeman fellas can't wide a hoss fo yo, ah'll do it. Ah'll do it wight now ef yo don want me heah."

Court was adjourned; and the magistrate, a voiceless policeman, Billy Holmes, a dozen courtroom spectators walked a couple of blocks to a corral at the back of the magistrate's home.

"There's my horse," the proud owner said with a flourish. "Beautiful, isn't he. When he's broken, I'll have one of the best between here and Macleod. But I don't feel that I want to undertake the breaking myself. I grew up with horses in the East, but I don't profess to be any expert with these broncos. You're looking for the saddle? I'll get it. It's in the house."

The horse was attractive, no doubt about it, and a bit spooky like every range-raised horse. As John's lariat fell over the gelding's head, the animal fought viciously, but was soon snubbed to a post, then saddled and bridled.

"Now, yo lil fella," John whispered to torment the policeman who had gone along to watch, "do yo wan t' wide im fust? Ef yo do ah'll help yo into the leatha. Ef yo don't just stand back out a ma way in case yo gets yoself hu't."

The constable tried to ignore the indignity and John drew himself into the saddle. Reaching down he loosened the tie rope and released the bronco.

"Open the gate an let's out," John shouted. As the gate swung, the horse dashed for the open country on the south, mixing his spurts of running with moments of rare bucking. Magistrate and other townsmen gazed with fascination as man and horse disappeared into the Elbow River Valley. Thoughts of trouble in the stream entered the onlookers' minds; but just as quickly, horse and rider reappeared on the opposite bank, the struggle in no way slackening.

"That man can really ride," the judge said to one of the Bar U boys who had spent the night behind the jail bars.

"Ride? Nobody's yet seen that man beaten by a horse. Nobody's ever seen him dumped. Every man in the hills wishes he could ride like John."

After a few minutes John was seen returning, guiding the subdued gelding with a steady hand. In front of the magistrate he halted, dismounted, patted the horse's face, mounted again, rode in a small circle and stopped, saying: "Yo got a good hoss heah, Boss. He won't give yo' any twouble." Smiling broadly he added: "Be ca'fu that no lil police fellas steals him on yo."

The horse was returned to the corral; and as a cluster of small boys gathered to gaze admiringly at John, the magistrate stepped forward and said, "Thank you very much. Now, it's just about noon. I want you to come to my house for dinner."

John didn't know what to say. But before he realized it, he was following the magistrate and being introduced to the man's wife. He couldn't understand it, but for some reason he felt very much at ease. While they sat at dinner, John answered his host's friendly questions, telling about his boyhood years in slavery, and the unsettled times after the Civil War. He recalled how he had never had shoes on his feet until he was about twenty years of age; and finally, he expressed a growing hope to be a rancher in this country and a good neighbor.

"Hope we'll see you in town often," the magistrate's wife said as John was leaving. "Any time you're here, you might drop in and see us. We'd like to know you better."

John knew she meant it and he was speechless. Apart from Mrs. John Quirk, who welcomed him to her house beside the Highwood, there had been no opportunity in his life to talk to white women. This lady's friendliness made him happy and he beamed broadly.

As John and his friends rode south from Calgary, they encountered another herd of fat cattle about to be shipped to England — 600 head of Oxley steers being driven cautiously to preserve their precious fat. Lane's men offered some advice about driving into Calgary and loading the cattle, and John Ware added something about "stayin outa jail."

But John was happy, and before leaving his Bar U friends at Sheep Creek Crossing he told how glad he was to have made the trip. "Calga'y isn as bad as ah thought it was," he confessed. "Ah wasn su'p'ised they wanted t' put me in jail, but ah neva expected a magist'ate would wan a know me betta. Sho, ah'll go back t' Calga'y, any time. Might get t' lak the place. Might even get t' lak those lil police fellas ef ah knew em betta."

CHAPTER 14

JOHN SET A POND ON FIRE

Cattle fortunes rose and fell like a chorus girl's legs. A good winter with uninterrupted grazing followed the wicked one, and George Lane's net return of forty-five dollars per head for cattle shipped to England made the experiment a joyful success. Many stockmen who were ready to quit cattle in favor of horses now revised their plans and added to their beef herds.

Dr. Duncan McEachern of the Walrond, constantly in dispute or litigation with the hated settlers, sounded the keynote of 1888 by advising ranchers to stay with cattle but to reduce risk of loss by stacking hay and keeping some horses. In pursuing his own advice, McEachern was expanding the Walrond cattle operations and bringing 150 pedigreed Clydesdale mares and four of Scotland's best stallions to the range. But this did not mean that the bonny Clydes, supported ardently by all good men with Scottish accents, were to escape breed competition; and before the year was out, George Lane brought in thirty purebred Percheron mares, driving them all the way from Montana.

John Ware's white mare gave him a bay foal from Eagle Plume, and his joy was akin to that of a human father gazing upon his first offspring. The wobbly-legged thing brought the confidence born of creativeness. To Joe H. Brown, who drove horses from British Columbia to Fort Macleod in 1884 and worked for the Bar U Ranch before ranching for himself with the 7U brand, John declared a determination to be riding herd on his own cattle by the time the foal was old enough to carry a saddle.

The Quirks, who made headquarters beside the Highwood Crossing for six years, were bent on getting a new location deeper in the hills, "where the nester fellows won't be acrowding in." So, later in the season they drove their 800 head of Q brand cattle to a place on Sheep Creek. It was half a day's ride above the Quorn, close to what was later the Kew post office. That the Quorn people coveted the Quirk brand was no secret, but the Quirks had it properly registered and the Quorn men had to be satisfied with the Z.

"If you're going to be ranching for yourself by time that colt's big enough to carry you," Sam Howe said to John Ware, "you better get some more cattle and a claim on a place to run 'em pretty soon. Maybe you and I better take a ride back there where Quirk's going and look it over."

John was well aware of his need for more cattle, his little bunch having almost disappeared in the bad winter. There were still two ways of acquiring more. One was with a fast horse and a hot iron on a range with a lot of mavericks. Some men were getting their start that way and nearly everybody knew it. But, years ago, John had promised Old Murph: "Ef ah evah owns ma own cows, ah'll get em honest; ma ol pappy an mammy wouldn steal an John Wa'e isn goin t' staht."

Acquiring cattle by purchase was slow for a man on a cowboy's wage — exasperatingly slow, but every spare dollar from John's pay was going to that purpose. True enough, he was gaining ownership of some maverick cattle and marking them with the 9999 brand on their ribs, but he was getting them in the most legitimate and honorable way. Up to that time, the stockmen's association claimed all unbranded cattle gathered in the roundup nets and either butchered them to supply beef for the working gangs or sold them to pay association expenses.

On March 21, 1888, A. E. Cross, as secretary-treasurer of the High River Stockmen's Association, wrote J. J. Barter, stating: "John Ware's account with the High River Association stands thus:

Mavericks sold	$89.50
Mavericks sold	6.50
	———
Total	$96.00
Amount received	7.00
	———
Balance due	$89.00

"Would be obliged to you and John Ware if the above amount was placed to my credit in the Bank of Montreal, to me as secretary-treasurer, and notify of such as I pay out the disbursements in the form of checks. Yours truly."

The amount covered nine young cattle. After the bad experience of the earlier winter, John was taking no chance of losing these animals and left them with a settler near the Highwood to be wintered. They came through well, and John's total cattle count was almost back to what it had been two years before.

But some of the big ranch companies were not recovering from the disastrous winter as readily. The Bar U was all right, also Walrond, Cochrane, and Quorn; but the STV, south of Maple Creek, and the Powder River Cattle Company on Mosquito Creek were reported to be in serious financial straits, perhaps facing liquidation.

"Well," said Sam Howe, "when do we look for some good places west of here?"

"Ah'm weady ef Mistah Ba'tah says ah can go fo a few days. But maybe we shouldn go till afta we wound up the steeahs. That'd be what month? Octobah?"

By autumn the range industry was throbbing with new interest. No longer were the huge herds being driven from the south, but shipments of purebred animals from Ontario and the Old Country reflected the new concern for improvement.

The spring roundup for purposes of sorting, counting and branding was still the biggest organized effort in the cowman's year; but the fall roundup, started in a small way the year before, gave assurance of becoming an institution. Now that most ranch outfits had steers old enough and big enough to sell, the fall gathering would be needed in order to cut out the stock to be marketed.

Fewer riders were needed for the fall operations, but Barter asked John if he would go as Quorn representative. Of course he'd go, provided a competent person would watch Molly and the bay foal to see that they had enough feed and water and salt and other comforts which they as favored members of the horse world might expect.

As usual, the men who congregated in the course of roundup operations were a distinguished lot — two-fisted fellows, self-reliant, aristocrats of the early Cattle Kingdom. There was soldierly John Herron, who had come with the Mounted Police in 1874 and later entered into partnership with Captain Jack Stewart in the Stewart Ranch near Pincher Creek. Walter Huckvale, an Englishman who saw the first railroad train arrive at Calgary and then went south to buy O.S. "Hod" Main's ranch at Fort Kipp, was on the job, watching for cattle with the fiddleback brand. John Sullivan, with corncob pipe and the map of Ireland on his face — he for whom Sullivan Creek west of High River was named — was one of the riders. Howell Harris, who had crossed onto Canadian soil as a Montana freighter twenty years before, was there as manager of the Conrad Ranch, better known as the Circle and situated between the Belly and Bow rivers. Archie McLean, with provincial politics in his teacup, and who had started the CY Ranch east of Lethbridge a year or two before, was one of the personalities nobody could escape seeing. Lem Sexsmith was riding for his brother-in-law, George Lane. A. H. Lynch-Staunton was present from Pincher Creek. And Manager Murphy, from the fading Powder River Company, seemed to have more to worry about than most riders.

John's main assignment on the roundup was to supervise the gathering of any Quorn steers big enough for shipping. But, as always, he was there to help anybody who needed him and his versatility was never in doubt. Billy Holmes was a spectator when a Quorn cow was found to have an unbranded two-year-old steer following her and still interested in milk. Branding irons were hot; and John Ware, after roping the big maverick, jumped from his horse and with his herculean strength held the steer against the corral fence while cowboys seared the Z brand on the animal's hide.

In the case of the Powder River cattle, riders were looking for more than fat steers; they were cutting out everything — cows, calves, steers, everything carrying the 76 brand. And appearing periodically was a bumptious little Englishman, talking incessantly and riding precariously on a "pancake" saddle. Sir John, they called him. He was Sir John Lister Kaye, purchaser of the big herd which had until recently been the property of Powder River Cattle Company. His new ranch manager, D. H. Andrews, with less ostentation, was diligently counting cattle.

According to book count, there were to be 7,300 cattle in the deal; and except for such steers as were ready for shipment to the English market, all animals found with the 76 brand would be driven to one or another of Sir John's ten new agricultural holdings along the CPR between Balgonie on the east and Calgary on the west.

The little man with big ideas struck the West like an August tornado. A 7,000-acre farm at Balgonie was too small to contain his energies, and in 1887 he organized the Canadian Agricultural Coal and Colonization Company with English capital, then secured ten additional blocks of land, each about 10,000 acres in size. He'd grow wheat, cattle, sheep, and scores of things. He'd milk the hostile range cows and make cheese for sale in England. He'd irrigate his expansive wheat fields with water hauled in horse-drawn tanks if the rains failed. And then he'd bring families from the Old Country and settle them on his land.

Just prior to the fall roundup in 1888, he reported his plans to the Edmonton *Bulletin* (Oct. 6, 1888): two million feet of lumber on order for farm and ranch buildings, 500 Clydesdale mares coming from Ontario, pigs and 50,000 sheep to come later, and now the Powder River cattle. The idea was to divide the 7,000 or more cattle among the ten new properties.

To beat the threat of drought on his dry wheatfields in the next season, Sir John was ordering forty-four pine tanks from wagon-makers Ryan and McArthur of Winnipeg, each tank to hold 575 gallons of water. And to insure improvement in cattle, he could report ninety-nine Aberdeen-Angus and Galloway bulls on their way from Scotland to the Northwest Territories. If determination and big ideas could compensate for lack of rain, poor markets, and inexperience, success would be assured.

When the roundup ended, close to 5,000 steers belonging to various ranchers were separated and on their way to railroad points and shipment to England. Each big animal was thought to be worth forty-five dollars and cattlemen were cheerful. Enough of the 76 brand steers were cut for fifteen carloads to be shipped out of Calgary, while cows and young cattle with the same brand were being herded northward and eastward toward Sir John's properties forming the long chain. The remainder of his recently bought cows would be recovered in the more complete spring roundup.

"All right, John," Sam Howe said again when the roundup work ended, "Barter says for us to make that trip back into the hills, to see how it would do for you and me."

With blankets tied to saddles, Sam and John rode away from the Quorn to inspect the grass higher on Sheep Creek and its tributaries. Nobody knew exactly where to find the western boundary of the Quorn Ranch lease, but it didn't seem to matter very much. The big ranges toward the mountains appeared to be ample for those who wanted them, and they were not likely to attract the wheat-conscious settlers. Joe Davis was pleased with his decision to locate there, and the Quirks were moving with full confidence in the taller grass and greater growth of trees.

"Maybe mo snow back heah," John speculated. "A cowman would jus have t' put up hay — but, gollyme, it's pwetty. Ah don think even ol Ca'oline was as nice t' look at as this. Ah want t' build me a little house beside this cweek, someday."

"And settle down with a wife, I suppose," Sam added.

"How evah would an ol slave boy get a wife up heah? Spose ef ah staid in Texas o' some place in the South, ah would have me a wife an a hahd of young ones now; but they's nobody of ma kind t' mawwy up heah. Ah'll waise cows and hosses ah guess an foget about mawwyin."

It was when the men were making their way homeward, traveling half a mile apart because one of them wanted to examine the grass and water in a nearby valley, that John had his biggest fright of the season. It was close to Sheep Creek in the broad valley later known as Turner. At a pool of water John halted to allow his saddle horse to drink. The animal lowered its head, then reeled quickly, repulsed by the odor of the water. Puzzled, John dismounted, noticed a scum on the surface, and cupped some of the water in his hand to taste it. The horse's assessment of the water was right — the flavor was no better than the odor.

For a reason which not even he could explain, John lit a match and threw it on the surface of the pool. Immediately, the whole body of liquid seemed to burst into flame. In shocked surprise John jumped back-ward. Not knowing what this flaming meant, he bounded into his saddle and struck off across the range at full gallop to overtake Sam, nervously glancing back to make sure the fire was not following him.

"Gollyme, ah don know what ah did. Ah jus th'ew a match on the watah an it blazed at me. What yo make of it, Sam?"

The fire ended almost as suddenly as it had started, and Sam and John returned to the mysterious body of water. The former scum was no longer to be seen. Sam scratched his head as he speculated. "Think we better take some of that crazy water with us and maybe ask somebody what's in it."

From a nearby pool a sample of similar water and scum was taken in a bottle used for Sam's tea. After reporting the spectacle of the flaming pond to Barter, the sample was submitted to Dr. G. H. Mackid for such examination as he might be able to perform. In due course a report came back: "Probably seepage from a nearby vein of coal."

"Seepage?" John repeated when Barter read the report aloud. "What is seepage? Ah figu'ed it might be oil an we'd bu'n it in the lamps. Maybe they will find oil in that valley someday."

"I suppose it could be oil seepage," Barter added. "Sure, somebody who knows how to do it will come along someday and strike the oil that seepage is coming from — and make a million dollars. They'll never know that it was you who discovered it either, John Ware."

CHAPTER 15

A MATTER OF PEDIGREE

While conflict between ranchers and homesteaders increased in bitterness, lines were being drawn for another battle, the "Battle of the Breeds." John Ware, still at the Quorn, was in the best possible position to witness it.

In the earliest years of ranching, rather little thought was given to controlled breeding. At best, the unrestricted range gave practically no opportunity for controls, and an owner turning superior sires on the public domain was not likely to derive much if any direct benefit. Herd bulls, recognizing neither ethics nor loyalties, ignored the brand characters on cows to which they gave attention. Moreover, those men who bought cattle to fill Indian beef contracts paid as much for a glassy-eyed brindle longhorn as for an animal with refined type and plutocratic pedigree.

Now, however, things were changing. Barbed wire fences were appearing, and interest in the English market for Canadian beef cattle was growing. Five thousand western steers were exported in the year 1888 and the practical importance of quality could be overlooked no longer.

A few progressive cattlemen had imported pedigreed bulls on earlier occasions, but in this year of 1889, both bulls and cows of pure breeding were being unloaded from freight cars at Calgary and herded to new homes where their progeny were expected to raise the standards of beef excellence and give every steer a higher dollar value.

As the red, roan and spotted cattle on the range would indicate, the old Durham — later the Shorthorn — was the first imported breed to exert an influence for good upon the thinly fleshed native stock brought from the South. Without loss of more than moderate length of horn, the Powder River cattle purchased by Sir John Lister Kaye showed the benefit of one or more crosses of the English-Scottish breed.

But other breeds were coming to challenge the revered Durham. The. progressive Cochrane Ranch was the first to introduce Hereford and Aberdeen Angus bulls to the range, and the Walrond followed the example, adding five Hereford cows, three Aberdeen Angus cows and a Galloway heifer in 1888.

Now the year of 1889 was proving to be by far the biggest for purebreds. The same two ranches, Cochrane and Walrond, received shipments of Herefords and Aberdeen Angus, the Cochrane outfit gaining special publicity from its selection of red color in that breed which was normally black. "Senator Cochrane's red Angus," an editor wrote, "are full of promise and should become as famous as the Stony Mountain buffaloes."

Other breeds? There were lots of them, both in cattle and horses. Black Brothers of Fort Macleod brought in a Devon bull; John McKay, Qu'Appelle, imported twenty West Highlands, and C. D. Geddes of Pincher Creek became the owner of the first pedigreed Holstein cattle in the area, seven females and a bull.

Things were stirring in Thoroughbred horse circles, too, with the most dramatic events still taking place at the Quorn. With a horse count now totaling a thousand, Quorn Manager Barter was expecting four more Thoroughbred stallions from the Old Country, and John Ware was sure the current crop of foals was the best yet.

One of the encouraging sales of the season involved a team of Quorn-raised horses sold to the town of Calgary for the purpose of hauling the new fire engine. Calgary's Boynton Hall burned down early in the year and citizens were showing ready willingness to spend money for fire protection. A good fire engine needed good horses to pull it.

And just at dusk on an evening when John Ware figured he was at the end of the foaling season, Tom Lynch, mounted on one horse and herding four others of striking quality, crossed the creek at the Quorn headquarters and asked if he could corral his tired animals for the night. The weather-beaten and aging "King" of the old cattle trails, who accounted for so much of ranchland history, was unconsciously making some more — more than he or anybody near him would have suspected.

Of course he could corral his tired horses. Nobody was ever refused overnight accommodation. John was glad to see the old friend with whom he had made his initial entry on to Canadian grass. Before the two men went to the Quorn kitchen for supper, Tom, having left Calgary before daylight, remarked about the long day.

But why would Tom leave the town before daylight? There was something mysterious about it all, and for a few minutes John's questions were being evaded. Then Tom eased himself against a corral rail and related all he knew about the circumstances, the aftermath to some recent horse races at Calgary.

John listened attentively. An American by the name of Reynolds, it seemed, had breezed into Calgary, bringing four Thoroughbreds for the races. They were good horses — superior horses anywhere; but at Calgary there had been some misfortunes of a kind not unknown to horsemen. The man had borrowed quite a substantial amount of Canadian money, naming his race horses as security. Then, unable to make repayment and facing the prospect of seizure by the Calgary sheriff, he had inquired in a whisper if there was anybody who might undertake to whisk his good horses away and out of reach of sheriff and Canadian law.

"Tom Lynch is your man," he was told. "Nobody can move cattle or horses like Tom."

Lynch was contacted. He listened carefully and thought he recognized justice on Reynolds' side. Yes, he'd move the horses by little-used trails in the hills to Montana. But there'd have to be some reward for his time and effort. He offered to take the Thoroughbreds to Montana with the understanding that one of them, the one of his own choosing, would be his. In other words, he'd take the four noble race horses to Montana and bring the one he most fancied back to High River.

While the sheriff and all other citizens of the town of Calgary were still asleep, the skillful Tom Lynch turned the four high-lifed Thoroughbreds loose and kept their heads to the south. There was a brief stop for rest at Fish Creek, then upstream and southward toward the ranch buildings on the Quorn.

"Tomorrow," Tom told John, "we'll bear farther west and then south through valleys back there. But by the way, which one do you like best? I figure to bring one back and I'd be a damn fool if I didn't pick the best one."

John studied the graceful creatures. All looked good to him, but his gaze returned repeatedly to a clean-limbed bay mare with an expressive personality. "That one Mistah Tom. Yo might as well have a maah and she's gotta face lak an angel. F'om that one an Ol Ploom yo might get a wo'ld beatah."

Tom nodded agreement. "Sangaroo, they've been calling her. She looks like the one I'll be bringing back with me."

At daylight next morning Tom Lynch was on his way again, and John Ware waved farewell, momentarily wishing he were free to ride out on another long journey with Lynch, just as he done after meeting the man for the first time in the state of Idaho.

After a couple of weeks Tom was back at his TL ranch on the Highwood — with Sangaroo, and proud of her. But under the circumstances the mare needed a change of name, and she became Froila. Lynch raced her successfully. After a time she was bought by Duncan Cameron, and in line with John Ware's hope, she produced a filly foal from Eagle Plume. And what a Thoroughbred that foal turned out to be!

Tom Lynch didn't live to see it happen, but John Ware watched Froila's filly, May W, with special interest and pride as her fame extended ever farther. She was trained at Calgary and, proving worthy of her story-book mother, became one of the greatest runners of her generation. According to James Speers, "She was the best mare ever bred in Canada."

Finally, this daughter of Tom Lynch's Sangaroo and John Ware's Eagle Plume was sent to England, where she won distinction even among the best Thoroughbreds in the world.

But beyond question the biggest breed news of the year, bigger even than Tom Lynch's recovery of Sangaroo, was made at the Quorn when nearly a hundred purebred Aberdeen Angus cattle arrived from the Old Country.

After being unloaded from freight cars at Calgary late in August, this herd, which was to provide the best single foundation for the breed in Western Canada, was driven south as far as Fish Creek in one day; then to Stoney Crossing, where travelers could choose between Kenny Cameron's stopping place and McMillan's stopping place, the second day; and then over the Barter Trail to the Quorn headquarters the third day.

Springing from the best blood lines in their native land, these good cattle were registered in the name of Hon. Walter F. C. Gordon-Cumming, noted big-game hunter and Quorn Ranch shareholder. They were smooth, black, beefy animals — polled, and saucy in appearance. Conspicuous among six bulls in the shipment was Donald Dhu of Mulben, with surly expression, broad back, and a proud walk such as would do credit to a general superintendent.

John Ware was fascinated and in high glee proclaimed: "That's ma breed a cows. Ah lak they'ah colah! Things a getting bettah an blackah all the time at the ol Quo'n."

Soon after the cattle were delivered, J. D. McGregor of Brandon brought a shipment of eastern dogie cattle to the Quorn and tried to buy all the imported purebreds. At that point he succeeded only in acquiring an interest in the cattle he so much fancied; but later he did buy outright most of the Gordon-Cumming cattle, and with them founded his Glencarnock herd which was to win international fame.

With the ninety-seven "dodded" cattle came four Thoroughbred stallions and seven long-legged Scottish deerhounds to be used to pester the foothills coyotes and wolves: And in charge of all while in transit was one of Scotland's stalwart young sons, George Scott, nineteen years of age and eager to learn the ways of the Canadian frontier.

Well-known to Alberta cattlemen in later years as a brand inspector, Scott set about his first job — to ride herd on the pedigreed cattle, to keep them from wandering far, and to keep strange bulls away — all at forty dollars a month. Everything was understandably new and strange to him, including the ways of the people. Most conspicuous among the twenty workers on the ranch was John Ware, and Scott found the first flush of curiosity in this fellow changing quickly to respect and admiration.

"We were pretty green," Scott said, referring to himself and Joe Whitbread, who had come from the Old Country with him, "but John was friendly and we needed a friend. He must have laughed at us, but he was never too busy to show us how to swing a lariat or handle a western horse. He told us stories about his boyhood days in slavery and his first experience on a horse, when the slave-owner cracked a long whip to frighten the horse and amuse himself and his friends. Powerful John Ware, always good-natured, never tired, soon became our hero."

The boys learned quickly that when they were in trouble resourceful John Ware was the man to see. Stray bulls, some of them old and truculent, were worrying George Scott as he tried to protect the black heifers. "I just can't keep them back," he told John, "and some are pretty mean."

"Ah'll wide out with yo t'mo'ow," John said, thoughtfully. "We gotta keep em away f'om those good heifahs. Ef we can't do anything else, we'll paunch em."

Just as Scott had said, bulls of strange kinds and colors were coming in; and one refused to be turned. "We jus gotta be tough on that kind," John said and proceeded to demonstrate his paunching technique guaranteed to make a bull yield to reason. Skillfully he rode alongside of the running animal, aimed straight down and pulled the trigger to send a revolver bullet through the left flank and paunch and into the ground.

"That'll make him awful sick," John commented.

"Might he die?" Scott asked.

"Not a no-good ol bull lak that," was John's reply. "He won die — but he'll fo'get about those black cows fo a few days."

John's reliability and usefulness became better and better known. George Lane invited him to return to work at the Bar U; and Sir John Lister Kaye, who hadn't bothered to speak to him when they met at the fall roundup in the previous year, was now anxious to have him and directed an offer of work with either horses, cattle or sheep on one of the "76" places. Sir John's sheep had just arrived, 18,000 of them, having been driven overland from United States ranges to Maple Creek.

But John didn't fancy the idea of working with sheep; and he didn't want to leave the foothills and the Quorn with its splendid Thoroughbreds, friendly colts, and fine barns with each stallion's name spelled out with big letters made from coyote feet over the box stalls.

Moreover, Barter was an understanding and offhand fellow and John liked working for him. When Lord Stanley, Governor General of Canada, came that way to see some ranches in October, 1889, and remained for the night before driving the 28 miles to Calgary, John donned his Prince Albert coat and made certain that the barns were spotlessly clean. Then the royal visitor was invited to inspect Donald Dhu of Mulben and the

Thoroughbred stallions. Each one was shining like a polished plate, and John Ware led the horse closest to his heart, Eagle Plume. With head held high and joints flexing in a gay prance, the horse displayed a pride equaled only by that of the man at the halter. The Governor General gazed severely, and the guard of Mounted Police stood at a painfully rigid sort of attention. All was tenseness until John halted his "Ol Ploom" squarely in front of the guest and released one of his great smiles directly at the sober-faced man of noble pedigree. Barter, standing beside Lord Stanley, forgot his hurriedly rehearsed protocol, and in his fine Irish way said, "John, let me present the Governor."

"Good day, Mistah Lo'd," John replied with perfect foothills composure. "How'd yo lak ma Ol Ploom? He's got so much pedig'ee, it's a wondah he even lets you o' me touch him."

In London or Ottawa the performance might have appeared shocking; but on the Canadian range, where pedigrees were important only in stallions and bulls, nobody objected.

Tempting as was George Lane's offer to return to work at the Bar U, still more tempting was one from Duncan McPherson to go as foreman to the High River Horse Ranch with its familiar surroundings — at fifty-five dollars a month. John would consider that proposition; but accepting it or not, his determination to start ranching for himself as soon as he had enough cattle was a firm one. He longed to give full time to his own animals, use the 9 brand more extensively, inoculate his own calves with garlic or whatever else the men in the livery stable at the Crossing said was good to prevent blackleg — more prevalent this year — and live in a house of his own making beside a foothills creek.

In any case, the wonder of it all was growing steadily. Notwithstanding the handicaps — an ex-slave's scars visible like an old brand on his back, total lack of formal education, and still a job as a lowly hired hand on a remote ranch — to George Scott and Joe Whitbread, privileged to work closely with him, "John soon became our hero."

CHAPTER 16

MEET MISS MILDRED

John Ware decided to move. Early in the spring of 1890 he went again to see the country higher on Sheep Creek and fix upon a homestead location. On returning, he announced his intention to work a while as foreman at High River Horse Ranch, where horse numbers stood at 913 — not quite as many as on the Quorn. There at the Horse Ranch he would follow George Baker, Mr. McPherson's first foreman.

The range country was showing signs of maturity. Indians, long sources of worry to the ranchers because of wandering habits and readiness to kill cattle, seemed rather more settled than formerly. A few more ranchers were adopting barbed wire; but the big operators, like the Bar U with 9,661 cattle and 761 horses on its books, were still resisting it. Railroads were about to be built from Calgary north to Edmonton, south to Fort Macleod. Most farmers and ranchers were bachelors, but the CPR was offering excursion rates to eastern Canada as an inducement to young settlers to go there for wives.

Nothing would change ranch life as much as wives and homemakers, but nobody could overlook the risk that many young women would not adapt themselves to frontier hardships. Advice about selection of help-mates was offered freely, very much as settlers were told how to choose the most useful specimens in work horses and herd bulls.

Writing to an agricultural magazine, one "authority" with a practical turn of mind had this to say: "In the first place, the prime qualification to be secured in all cases, at whatever sacrifice, is toughness. Our climate is a hard one and it will not pay to import those classes [of women] which cannot be reasonably expected to stand our winters without expensive quarters. A competent authority should make a thorough examination to see that they are sound in wind and limb and have good teeth. Bad teeth are a frequent cause of indigestion because in the winter our frozen foods are hard to masticate . . . Large and rangy females with good bones should be selected as this aids materially in handling an ax or pitch fork."

"You better be thinking about getting a wife, too," one of John's friends said again; but with wistful expression, John replied, "No, don' think so. Nobody heah fo me t' ma'y. Ah know some a ma friends lak Laf Fwench an Ol Kamoose a'e squaw men. But unless the Lo'd sends me a nice colo'ed gal, ah think ah'll stay wuf hosses and cows. Besides, ah undahstands how t' handle 'em."

Leaving the Quorn wasn't easy. John was lonely for "Ol Ploom," and for George Scott and the other boys; but the new place had good horses. And there were the inducements of an additional five dollars a month in wages and more coyote hunting with dogs.

John loved dogs almost as much as he loved horses; and when he was leaving the Quorn, Barter gave him a gangling and friendly hound pup. Where John went the young dog followed, even to bed at night. Duncan McPherson's hounds were confined to pens most of the time, but not John's dog. Moses was the dog's name, and Moses was a privileged character about the ranch.

But just weeks after John went to the High River Horse Ranch, Moses disappeared. John called loudly, whistled and searched east and west along the river. Moses was nowhere in the vicinity. That the dog would stray away seemed most unlikely. If the animal had been shot, the body would have been found. As John fretted and pondered, the thought struck him that Indians might have taken his pet. A band was in camp in the generous cottonwood trees beside the Crossing, a few miles downstream, and stragglers from the tribe had been seen shuffling along the river in recent days.

The very idea of theft angered John Ware. His cabbage-sized fists were clenched as he gazed in the direction of the Crossing. "Ah gotta find out, good an soon," he told McPherson. Saddling Molly, he galloped away.

When John rode into the circle of tents, where the George Lane Park is located today, dogs barked and scores of Indians emerged from teepees to see what this intruder wanted. John jumped to the ground and, ignoring hostile glances, led Molly as he peered into one tent at a time. Indian resentment mounted, and squaws as well as bucks stood in John's path to express their defiance. But John was bent on completing the search; and just as he was about to admit failure, his eyes fell upon Moses, tied to a tent-peg in an out-of-the-way location.

Joy mingled with anger as John rushed to embrace his dog and release the brute. That accomplished, John stood and faced the Indians defiantly. It was one man against a tribe, but the Indians seemed to sense the folly of taunting this man. Squaws and bucks remained stationary while John shook his fists and assured his astonished listeners of what would happen if natives ever again stole a pup dog from him. The subdued tribesmen were still standing as though frozen in their places as John and Molly and Moses triumphantly took the trail leading back to the Horse Ranch.

Dogs were almost as conspicuous as horses on the McPherson and Eckford Ranch. Coyotes and wolves were constant menaces and their pursuit was partly for sport and partly for purpose of control. After the destruction of the buffalo herds, members of the wolf family began to concentrate their attack on calves and colts. In the spring of this year, A. E. Cross reported the loss of twenty foals, and ranchers were angry.

Several of the big cattle companies kept hounds. Cochrane dogs killed 110 coyotes in one month during the autumn of 1889; while the hounds owned by the Quorn, North West Cattle Company, and High River Horse Ranch accounted, collectively, for "200 coyotes and two wolves" earlier in the year.

Ranchers vied with each other to own the best pack of hounds, just as each aspired to have the fastest horses. Among the dogs imported by Barter of the Quorn was a famous English greyhound called Joe, very successful in hunting coyotes but too light for the powerful wolves. The High River Horse Ranch followed by getting one of the best dogs available in Montana, a 150-pound boarhound named Prince Bismark, powerful but not fast enough for the Alberta coyotes and wolves.

It was a great occasion when the leading packs came together for a day of hunting and John Ware was always present, riding Molly, with or without saddle, and enjoying the excitement. No red coats or hunting togs were worn, but the outing was readily admitted to offer the best entertainment of that time. Even urban people were attracted, as evidence a disorderly hunt at Lethbridge, reported by the Macleod *Gazette* (Oct. 5, 1889): "Lethbridge has gone wild over fox hunting. The first experience of this invigorating sport which the citizens of Lethbridge have enjoyed was on a recent Sunday. A number [of foxes] had been captured and on this particular Sunday the town turned out almost en masse to give chase. As many as could get anything in the shape of an animal with four legs were mounted. Having arrived at the spot the foxes were let out one by one and the pack of hounds, from fox terriers up to Newfoundlands, let loose. Then the fun began. Another fox turned toward town and arrived, followed by a wildly enthusiastic crowd, both mounted and driving, just as the children were going to Sunday School. The fever seized the latter. The fox darted across the railway track and the children joined pell mell in pursuit. Religiously inclined people felt much shocked and we hear that the matter was reported to the police."

The numerous coyotes in the country invited chase but the most serious annoyance was the wolf, big, crafty killer. Added was the fear that human life was not always safe with these brutes about. George Lane could tell about being attacked when riding near the Highwood. Being handy with a revolver he shot one, but another leaped at him as he sat in the saddle. It was an unhappy moment; but afterward, from

Lane's description, Western artist Charlie Russell made a picture of the scene.

Coyotes were fairly easy to catch and kill with good dogs. Wolves presented quite different problems. Light hounds were helpless. Even with fast dogs, it took two to stop a mature wolf — usually one on each side to seize the wolf by the neck. Even at that a shot from the rider's gun was often required to finish the wild animal.

When John Ware went to High River Horse Ranch, all settlers west of the Crossing were talking about the "King" wolf, a particularly big and particularly bad one. For two years this stealthy predator eluded men with guns and dogs, and ranchers were sure it had destroyed more than a thousand dollars worth of calves and foals. Nearby stockmen offered a reward of fifty dollars to the person who would kill the killer. English visitors who had hunted lions in Africa and tigers in India set out to end the depradations of this bad wolf, and men of the High River Horse Ranch were constantly on the alert, ready to give chase. But the big, gray "King" wolf was too smart and continued to pull down young domestic animals as they retreated from him.

While the big wolf was still a common topic of conversation along the river, John Ware's curiosity was directed in quite a different direction. He could scarcely believe it when John Barter, having returned from Calgary, sent the message. Among settlers from the East was Negro Dan V. Lewis with a family including an attractive daughter of marriageable age. The Lewis family, from Toronto, had taken a homestead two miles south of Shepard; and Barter could tell of meeting the father, mother, and four Lewis children on Stephen Avenue in Calgary. "They come to town with eggs every Thursday and I'll be there on that day next week," the message explained.

John tried to hide his interest but he couldn't, and his friends teased him. Duncan McPherson's humor was poorly disguised: "Think you should go to Calgary for a load of groceries — about next Thursday."

John made no immediate reply but on Wednesday he hitched a team of half-broken cayuses to the ranch democrat and started northward. It was early May and the grass was turning green. The horizons were clear except for some unusual tufts of smoke eastward by Gladys Ridge and beyond. It had been an extremely bad spring for prairie fires, and John expected to see the smoke spread in the unmerciful manner of grass fires. Instead, the smoke curls remained slender and the truth dawned upon him — they were Indian smoke signals. But what did they mean?

In Calgary, the significance of the spectacle became clear; the curls of smoke were indeed signals; Crowfoot, the great Blackfoot chief was dead. John remembered seeing him during one of the roundups — a fine, lean physical specimen, a quiet but thoughtful man, and perhaps the greatest Indian leader of his generation. "The Chief of Chiefs is gone," men meeting on Stephen Avenue said with sorrow in their voices.

There was other news, also. The Cochrane Ranch Company had bought the STV cattle which ranged by the Cypress Hills — 6,000 head, to give the Cochrane outfit a total of nearly 15,000. The price of twenty-seven dollars a head for everything was considered a big one, and the former owners, J. H. Conrad and C. S. Hunter of Montana, were glad to liquidate because of new customs and quarantine regulations being imposed upon cattle coming into Canada. And with the prospect of more Indian beef contracts coming up for tenders, the Cochranes believed they could profit from the bigger herd.

John Ware was only mildly interested in the news of cattle sales. His mind was on other things. And, good as his word, J. J. Barter was at the recently opened Alberta Hotel — architectural pride of the town. "I'll meet you early in the afternoon," he instructed John Ware. "We'll take a walk to the Baker store and you can get your groceries."

Barter knew exactly how long it would take Dan Lewis to drive from his homestead at Shepard, and at two o'clock he and John Ware "dropped in" at the sandstone store on the corner of Stephen Avenue and McTavish. John scanned the store's interior, saw tins of tea, bags of sugar, bolts of gingham, and rolls of barbed wire filling the shelves; and sides of bacon, watering pails, and kerosene lanterns dangling from hooks attached to the ceiling. But no colored people were to be seen.

"They'll be here," Barter said assuringly, while John made a pretense of being busy by searching for boots to fit his massive feet. Ever since he had begun wearing boots, he had had trouble getting them big enough; and too often, the biggest available pinched. Then, to confirm the accuracy of Barter's estimate, Dan Lewis, carrying a crate of eggs and followed by wife and three children, entered the store. John's glance flitted from one Lewis to another, but he saw no daughter fitting the description of "marriageable."

Barter advanced to greet the homesteader, saying, "I brought along a friend of mine you should know. Here. you, John Ware, come and meet Dan Lewis and his family."

Bashfully, but plainly thrilled, John said a collective "Hello." Quickly he forgot about the boots. There was an exchange of questions about places of origin and Mrs. Lewis volunteered, "We have another daughter; oh, here she comes now."

Entering the store was the nineteen-year-old daughter, and Mrs. Lewis made the introduction: "Mr. Ware, this is Miss Mildred."

The girl was medium in height with round face, smooth skin, bright eyes and soft voice. John beamed radiantly but could think of nothing to say. Surely here was the most beautiful picture he had ever seen, and his eyes were keeping no secrets.

Mrs. Lewis spoke again. "Will you come and visit us some Sunday? It's not far to Shepard. Come Sunday after next and I'll fry some chickens."

John didn't know how it could be arranged but he said he'd be there. What could possibly be more important than getting to know these good people better — and seeing Miss Mildred wearing an apron and serving fried chicken?

As he drove back to High River, John revived the experiences of that moment and counted the days until "Sunday after next."

At the Horse Ranch he was quizzed and teased, but he enjoyed it all and McPherson said he could take the team and democrat again for the drive to Shepard.

John brushed the Prince Albert coat, polished his boots with soot from the kitchen stove and drove away on the Saturday afternoon. By trail it would be twenty-five miles and there was the Bow River to ford. But no obstacle seemed great, and the horses jogged on until nearly dark when preparation was made to unhitch and spend the night beside the trail. In the morning, with benefit of daylight, John found the river crossing without difficulty and was at the Lewis homestead by mid-forenoon.

Dan and Mrs. Lewis greeted John like an old friend, and Miss Mildred appeared like an angel out of a cloud, wearing a freshly ironed cotton dress and a white ribbon in her hair. But what does a man whose life is cast with cows and horses talk about when in the presence of women? On the drive from High River John had worried about the answer to that question and tried to rehearse some conversation. Now he could think of nothing to say except to agree with the Lewis elders that the morning was bright and the horses were tired. But a beaming smile confirmed his joy, and Miss Mildred's was equally revealing. Neither was so bold as to stare, but shyly and often they glanced at each other.

Mildred appeared unbelievably lovely; and John though slightly stooped and ungroomed was athletic and manly and big. Nervously he twisted some stems of buffalo grass, but the mutual admiration was not well-hidden.

Other guests, Jim and Mrs. Hanson, joined the party. The men got around to conversation about range cattle, and the women addressed themselves to the task of dinner. Mildred flitted between kitchen and where the men were sitting; and when dinner was called, fried chicken never tasted better. And so, the day wore on, all too quickly.

After the meal, somebody proposed a leisurely drive to let the Hansons see the crops. John's team, now rested and more docile than when leaving the ranch, was hitched to the Lewis democrat with double seating facilities. The Hansons took the back seat! And Miss Mildred, erect and smiling, took the place beside John in front. As they drove away Dan Lewis shouted, "Don't go far. It might rain."

There were heavy clouds in the west, but the four happy people out for an hour or two of sight-seeing were completely carefree. Threat of rain was scarcely noticed. But three or four miles north of the homestead the storm clouds became suddenly blacker and there was a peel of thunder, close enough to be under the vehicle. John realized he had driven too far and no shelter was in sight. He turned the team, but one flash of lightning followed another and the thunder became deafening. Rain fell lightly and John tried to shelter Mildred with the coattails of his Prince Albert.

With each flash of lightning, the horses started and crowded against each other in their fear. Mildred and the Hansons were frightened; and just as John urged the horses to a faster gait, the sky seemed to crack open with a bolt of lightning that struck right beside them. The women shrieked and the horses went down as though they'd been shot through their heads; then all was still again. It was an awful moment as John sensed exactly what had happened. The four rain-soaked occupants of the democrat were uninjured but the horses — still in harness — were dead.

"Pwaise the Lo'd," John breathed as he looked around to verify that his friends were safe. "Yo all alive! Now, what we goin to' do?"

In an instant John was out of the democrat, loosening harness to give the horses a chance to get up if any life remained. But the horses were dead — positively dead — and John accepted the fact. Without more delay he removed harness, collars and neckyoke, threw them in the back of the democrat, pushed the vehicle back to completely separate gear from the dead horses and glanced at his friends to make certain they were still alright. Then, while the three rain-soaked passengers held firmly to their seats, John, with the strength of a Samson carrying away the Gates of Gaza, picked up the democrat tongue and began pulling the vehicle in the direction of Mildred's home.

It was late when the party arrived back at the homestead. John remained for the night; and next morning, with a borrowed team, he set out for High River, wórried about Duncan McPherson's reaction to the loss of his two horses.

McPherson, with more than 900 other horses, listened sympatheti-
cally as John related the trying adventure and said, "Guess we can spare
those two nags easier than we could spare you. Forget it, John."

There at the Horse Ranch John found that the "King" wolf had
returned to dinner-table conversation. The killer had struck again. Foals
were long known to be its favorite meat, and one of McPherson's riders
pointed to the partially devoured carcass of a Horse Ranch colt. John's
anger burned as it hadn't done since Indians had stolen Moses. Something
had to be done. No wolf would continue to kill helpless foals if he could
prevent it. He announced that he was taking a day or two off.

The wolf would return to the tender foal meat, and John made up
his mind to be nearby. Taking blankets, lariat, bread and cheese, and
making certain his revolver was loaded, he rode away to patrol the area
where the foal was killed. The wolf, he reasoned, would not go far while
the meat lasted. It would return at intervals to feed gluttonously and
spend much of the daytime in sleep. John's hope was to encounter the
brute at an early morning hour when it was gorged and sluggish from
excessive eating.

During the afternoon and evening John saw coyotes and foxes visiting
the carcass, but no wolf. To spend a few night hours in sleep, the cowboy
chose a wooded knoll a safe distance from the carcass; and just as daylight
was returning, he heard growls which sounded like those of a wolf protect-
ing his store of meaty food from coyotes. He rolled his blankets and
rode toward the sounds as soon as he could see clearly. By keeping
bluffs of trees between himself and the carcass, he could ride quite close
before being seen by any animal feeding there.

Precisely as calculated, the big wolf was there, lying on his belly,
distended with meat and still munching. Instead of galloping forward,
John maintained a walking pace and the wolf paid little attention — until
man and horse were quite close. John prepared to send a bullet into
the animal, but the bloated brute turned to run. Nobody had ever shot
a running wolf with a revolver, and John realized he would be wise to
adopt some other technique. Impulsively, he put spurs to his horse and
gave chase.

Normally a wolf would have been too fast for the horse; but this
one, its belly protruding from load of foal meat, was running with difficulty.

For a few minutes, the distance between wolf and horse was maintained without change. Then John and his mount seemed to draw nearer.
But the wolf was running toward Sheep Creek, and once it reached the
scrub and trees it could easily evade its pursuer. John pressed his spurs
hard against the bronco's flanks, and at the proper moment, swung his
lariat and threw it. The full length of the rope was required but the loop

fell over the wolf's head with all the precision that would characterize an expert marksman.

John pulled with a jerk. The wild thing, feeling the rope tighten about its neck, leaped savagely into the air, snarled at its pursuer and fell back on its rump. Again it unleashed all its latent fury, seized the rope in its teeth, plunged forward, and fell still more heavily from a frantic leap. Turning his horse, John now rode off in the opposite direction to drag the protesting wolf with him. Before long, the old "King" wolf was exhausted and John reined his horse to a stop.

John considered momentarily. He might have dragged the hated wolf, with some of its life remaining, to the ranch headquarters; but why cause needless pain, even to a killer wolf? Drawing the revolver he was able to use with skill, he finished the great wolf with a bullet in its forehead.

Triumphantly, John returned to the ranch with the trophy draped across his saddle, the biggest wolf anybody thereabout had seen or measured — seven feet, six inches from tip to tip.

Duncan McPherson reminded John that the destruction of the foal-killer would save him far more than the dollar value of two horses killed by lightning and, "There's the fifty dollar reward, you know, for the person who managed to kill the big one. What are you going to do with fifty dollars?"

"What am ah goin t' do with fifty dollahs? Ah figu'es that would just be enough t' build me a house back theah on the Sheep — buy the windows and doahs an things. Ah figue'es t' dwag logs outa the bush this wintah an John Qui'k'll help me put 'em up. Ah might need a littah biggah house than ah tended t' build — maybe one big 'nough fo a woman t' live in. Yo jus nevah know what a fellah might need."

CHAPTER 17

"A HOME — AH MA OWN"

After the spring roundup in 1891, John drove all the 9 brand cattle to the higher ranges, away west of the Quorn, and took up bachelor residence in an unfinished log house beside Sheep Creek. Surveying the rough log structure set on stones and still unchinked, he proclaimed from his heart: "Ain't it beautiful! Ah nevah thought ah'd see a house as pu'ty as that'n. An its ah ma own."

"If you make many more trips to see the Lewis girl, the chances are that house won't be all your own," John Quirk said cynically. "But s'ppose you might as well git into the family business, jist like the rist of us nincompoops."

Now, less than ten years after riding into this country, the former slave boy was a rancher in his own right, counting 200 branded cattle. The thought of being his own boss and riding over his own range and coming home to fry bacon on his own cook stove brought secret pride, and as soon as he was properly settled, he instructed Mrs. Quirk to write a letter to his mother and father in Carolina, urging them to come to Canada to live with him for the rest of their lives. But communication by letter was uncertain, especially when no members of the Ware family could read or write. Perhaps the letter was never delivered, perhaps the parents were dead; in any case, there was no reply, and John was never to learn more about the members of his family.

John Quirk, who had helped with the log house, now needed assistance in making an irrigation ditch to take water from Sheep Creek to his hay flat. It wouldn't be the first irrigation project in the Canadian West, but close to the first. John Glenn, who shared with Sam Livingstone the distinction of conducting the first farming operations in the Calgary district, took water from Fish Creek to irrigate twenty acres of bottomland beside the present village of Midnapore in 1879. Quirk knew very well that irrigation was still an experiment in this country but was showing an Irishman's determination to try it.

The idea was still so new it seemed ridiculous to most people, but John Ware was happy to be doing something for a loyal friend and patiently he guided a walking plow and then horse-drawn scraper, following contour lines laid out by means of a carpenter's spirit level in Quirk's hands.

As John soon discovered, his new home was in an isolated section of the cow country. News from across the far-flung range was slow to reach the upper branches of the Sheep. But ultimately, reports of events in the Cattle Kingdom came to John Quirk or Joe Fisher or Sam Howe or some other rider from the Quorn and were dutifully passed on. The month of May brought word of prairie fires being unusually serious in the south — one fire having swept from the Oxley Ranch clear to Lethbridge. Then there was a report about the old and reliable and versatile trading firm of I. G. Baker and Company selling out to the Hudson's Bay Company. Cowmen agreed the country would be strangely different without the Baker Company, whose bull teams had hauled most of the pioneer freight, and whose trading stores at Calgary and Fort Macleod and elsewhere rendered every conceivable service from selling United States stamps to guaranteeing transportation and care for incoming brides.

From the Oxley there was sad news — Stanley Pinhorn, manager, had taken his own life. Why should he have done it? John Ware had met him on the roundups on various occasions, and had seen him as the young Australian with an evident love for range life and meeting with success in his work. It was all so strange and cast a shadow across the hills.

There was also cheerful news. Notwithstanding a drop in cattle prices — from forty-five dollars for a four-year-old steer to thirty-five dollars — more men were being attracted to the industry. George Lane resigned from the North West Cattle Company to ranch for himself, having bought the Flying E Ranch in the Porcupines. And while cattlemen were painfully conscious of falling prices, sheepmen found their trade to be increasingly brisk. The market for both mutton and wool was good, and Sir John Lister Kaye, who loved nothing better than entertaining editors with stories of big farming and ranching operations, reported the sale of sixty tons of wool, the season's clip from his company's ranches. The "76" ranches, incidentally, could account for more than half the sheep population of the Northwest Territories. The current crop of wool, Sir John added, was being shipped directly to France.

The year 1891 did not bring any improvement in relations between ranchers and settlers, especially where the Walrond Ranch was concerned. Some grazing leases had been canceled for the express benefit of homesteaders, and cattlemen wondered if this encroachment would mean the end of their industry. "Farmers and ranchers can't live together any more than cattlemen and sheepman can graze the same range," stockmen repeated.

Dr. Duncan McEachern, who continued to divide his time between the post of Dominion Veterinarian and that of manager of the Walrond, was constantly ready for battle with settlers who came too close. He'd have welcomed the sight of homesteaders' hides hanging over corral fences to cure. Walrond cowboys pulled down a homesteader's house erected in such a position as to cut off a good watering place; and, days later, the Walrond people lost 300 tons of new-stacked hay — by fire.

Spectators, thinking of the range wars in Wyoming and Montana, wondered where this conflict might end. Discouraging to the ranchers was the fact that the greater political strength would be on the side of the hated sodbusters and government policy was being fashioned accordingly. Had not Sir John A. Macdonald admitted as much? "The bull," said he, "must give way to settlers."

But the worst blow of 1891 came in September, when the British Government placed an embargo on Canadian cattle because of alleged or suspected contagious pleuropneumonia. It appeared very ridiculous; western cattlemen had never heard of the disease. Canadian authorities insisted the diagnosis was incorrect, nothing more serious than "corn-stalk disease," according to Dr. McCauchaiu.

English interests, perpetually objecting to the competition created by imported cattle, were suspected of fabricating the disease scare. John Quirk, with an Irishman's distrust of the English, was sure the embargo was a plot and pronounced the western range cattle as the "hilthiest" in the world. Actually, the two or three cattle responsible for the overseas scare of pleuropneumonia were from Ontario farms, but that didn't make the debacle any less costly for western stockmen with beef to sell.

Canadian authorities protested vigorously about the injustice, but the embargo remained long enough to further demoralize the Canadian cattle trade. Steers which earlier in the year had dropped ten dollars per head now dropped another five dollars.

John Quirk took 150 tons of hay from his irrigated field but didn't need that much because the winter was mild. But to the colored cowboy living alone for the first time in his life, the month of November seemed like a long winter. Now and then he spent an evening with the Quirks or Fishers or rode back to see how things were with the 5,000 cattle and 1,200 horses at the Quorn. And early in December he drove to Calgary and on to Shepard to visit members of the Lewis family — Miss Mildred in particular.

"You'll come back for Christmas, John," Mrs. Lewis said in a tone that was almost a command. Without waiting for a reply, she added, "Might as well stay a few days when you come. We can sleep the boys on the floor and you can have the straw bed."

"A few days? Gollyme! Ah'd lak that. Ah'll ask John Qui'k t' keep Moses an' th'ow some hay t' ma thin calves an see the ice is bwoke in the cweek. Sho, ah'll come Misa Lewis. Ah neva ate a real Ch'istmas dinnah cooked by a woman. Ah'd sho like t' do it."

"Mildred will help me," the Lewis lady added as if to make a point clear. "That gal can bake bread and cook a chicken better'n I can."

The day before Christmas, two unemployed roosters lost their heads at the Lewis chopping block, and at about the same time, John Ware saddled for the long ride from Sheep Creek to Shepard. With snow in the hills and bare trails in the vicinity of Fish Creek, neither sleigh runners nor wheels would have been satisfactory. But such a distance by saddle held no fears for the man who had traveled the long trails from Texas to the Highwood River that way. Anything he had to take along could be carried in a grain sack tied like a blanket across the back of the saddle. Actually, the sack held nothing more than a feed of oats for the horse and a few little packages containing Christmas gifts — one in particular, a silver brooch which Sam Howe had been commissioned to select when in Calgary. The brooch was for Mildred, and John hoped it would tell her something of his interest in her, something he felt he'd never have the courage to express in words.

Darkness was falling when John rode into the Lewis farmyard. His horse was tired but its every step in the crisp snow sounded clear like a Blackfoot drumbeat. A kerosene lamp threw light from the kitchen window, and as John drew near, all members of the Lewis family came outside to extend a Christmas Eve welcome.

It was a happy meeting and the humble Lewis home glowed with Christmas warmth. Mrs. Lewis expected the guest to be late and had thoughtfully kept supper for him. As though it had been rehearsed, Miss Mildred, in a freshly ironed white apron, took charge, serving homemade sausages dripping with goodness, preserved raspberries with the wild tang of scrubland beside the Bow, and thickly buttered pieces of johnny cake — almost too good to be true. Every morsel was a treat, and Mildred seemed unbelievably attractive as she flitted between kitchen cupboard and family table. John wanted to gaze at her the way one might study the colors in a lovely sunset or beautiful painting. He wondered if all this could be real.

After supper Mrs. Lewis offered the guest a pair of her husband's slippers and invited him to relax. Such pleasure and comfort! Here was kindness such as he had never known. "Wouldn it be wonde'ful to have somebody to take ca'e of a man's home lak this," John was thinking as he stared in silence. "Wouldn it be g'eat to have child'en!"

Christmas morning was cold, as Christmas mornings are expected to be, but a wood fire in the Lewis kitchen range banished all chill from the house's interior in short order. Dan Lewis' shout, "Merry Christmas everybody," was the signal for all to get up and acknowledge the day.

Younger members of the family had to examine the contents of stockings hung on a chair in front of the stove. There were exchanges of gifts — the silver brooch from John to Mildred and a pair of hand-knitted socks from Mildred to John. Breakfast followed and then singing — Christmas carols and Negro spirituals. Farmhouse rafters vibrated when seven strong Negro voices joined in singing "Silent Night" and "All God's Children":

"I've got a song, You've got a song, All God's children got a song, When I get to Heaven goin' to sing a new song, Goin' to sing all over God's Heaven."

John enjoyed singing, and today, more than ever, he wanted to sing with all the volume he could command.

Christmas dinner was another experience — two roasted roosters bulging with rich dressing, suet pudding, and everything spread on a white tablecloth to make John think again of all the home life he had missed. And Miss Mildred, having overcome all trace of bashfulness, talked and teased and laughed. She seemed too good to be real. John tried to hide his admiration and wondered again if he might ever bring himself to the point of telling her what was in his heart.

He was almost sure he could never say the proper thing to a young lady; but his fears to the contrary, opportunity came with practically no trouble at all. Considerately, all other members of the Lewis family went to bed early, leaving Mildred and John sitting beside the kitchen stove. The wood fire crackled mildly and the reflection of flames danced on the wall. The girl inquired tenderly about John's recollections of boyhood in the South and about the size of the new house on Sheep Creek.

"It's an awfu' nice house," John replied, sort of carried away; "nicest house ah evah saw — an' ef yo evah think yo'd like t' be an ol' cowman's missus an' have that house, ah'd sho like t' know."

"What do you mean by that?" she asked.

At once he realized what he had done — unconsciously introduced that subject he thought he could never present. Now he had to say more and say it in terms a romantic girl would naturally expect.

Clumsily he managed to say it in words which left no doubt about his intention, and in an embrace in which he surprised himself, he heard her breathe, "Yes, John."

Until kerosene burned low in the lamp, the two lovers talked in whispers, talked about the home they would make and about children. They'd meet at the Baptist minister's home in Calgary about the end of February and be married.

"This was the most joyful time in ma life," John told Mr. and Mrs. Lewis next morning as he prepared to ride back to the house in the hills, the house which would become Mildred's home. And as Molly walked and jogged on, John unconscious of frost and distance, lived again every event of that Christmas day and repeated a prayer of thanksgiving for the prospect of making a home with that girl the good Lord had sent into his life.

On the second last day of February, when snow lay deep in the hills, John borrowed Joe Fisher's jumper for the trip to Calgary. "Ah'll get back late tomo'ow night," he said, "an' with the p'ettiest lil wife anybody evah saw." Dressed in a new shirt, new boots, new trousers and the Prince Albert coat of Bond Street styling, he drove away.

Next day — Leap Year Day — the Rev. George Cross, B.A., Minister in charge of Calgary's new Baptist Church, performed the ceremony and signed the certificate, recording the fact that "Mr. John Ware of Sheep Creek and Miss Mildred J. Lewis of Calgary, were by me united in Holy Matrimony, according to the ordinances of God and the Laws of the Dominion of Canada, at Calgary on the 29th day of February, 1892."

The newlyweds bought some groceries, dishes, sheets and towels at the big stone store and drove away over winter roads and into a new world of romance, with more happiness in their hearts than either had ever known.

It was a long trip over snow-covered trails and should have been both chilling and tiring. At the Quorn Ranch the honeymooners stopped for supper. J. J. Barter extended a welcome, thinking of the day on which he had planned the meeting of John and Mildred. With unrestrained pride the groom introduced his bride to the others at the ranch house.

After more hours of travel through that moonlit winter night, they were at their own log house, warm because John Quirk had been there to make a fire.

The very next evening, the Negro Wares had company — the Irish Quirks, the American Sam Howe, the Mexican Ferdinos, and the half-breed Fidlers arrived over the snow to extend a foothills welcome to the newlyweds. The women in the party brought buckets of sandwiches, expressing the genuineness of rangeland neighborliness.

Nobody on that frontier talked about Brotherhood, but everybody practiced it and graced such practice with the dignity of sincerity. Mildred thanked her new friends — Irish, American, Mexican and Indian, and urged them to come again, saying, "I'm going to love it here."

CHAPTER 18

THE STEER WRESTLER

According to some writers, Canadians saw steer bulldogging for the first time when an itinerant Negro performer, Will Pickett, staged his show in front of the exhibition grandstand at Calgary in 1905. The rooting-tooting Guy Weadick, seeing the City of the Foothills for the first time, was Pickett's manager and traveling companion, and presented his star in the black silk stockings and gold-trimmed pants of a Mexican bullfighter.

The performing cowboy rode a fast horse, leaped and seized the steer's horns and twisted the head in such a way as to upset the animal. Then, gripping the steer's upper lip in his own teeth and hanging on bulldog fashion, he'd throw both hands in the air. All the while, the inimitable Guy Weadick, talking in the manner of a circus salesman through a megaphone, made this performance sound like the greatest show on earth.

"First time anything like it was staged outside of Texas," it was asserted. But something was being overlooked. The Canadian range country had witnessed steer wrestling — privately and publicly — for years, and credit for the first performances must go to John Ware.

As those who worked with him knew, Ware combined athletic skill with unusual strength. Notwithstanding great bulk of body, he could sprint like a hound and jump like a white-tail; and nobody in the roundup gangs had ever bettered him in a wrestling match. Who else could have held a two-year-old steer by the horns and crowded it against a corral fence while another cowhand branded? Who else could catch a bronco with the loop of lariat around its middle and, while standing in a catching pen, bring the unwilling animal to a stop?

Anyway, the first time Canadian cattlemen saw steer wrestling, the act was unpremeditated and uninvited. It was the spring of 1892, and a longhorn cow in a Walrond corral beside the North Fork of Oldman River decided the time had come to annihilate the human race. Suddenly she was a wild-eyed demon, charging viciously at anybody within reach. Cowboys scrambled madly for safety on the pole fence — all except John Ware, who seemed to be so preoccupied that he did not sense the danger until the brute was lunging at him.

Springing like a startled cat, he seized the widespread horns and drew himself to a position behind the left one. The cow dragged him for a distance, tried to gore him, and tried to shake him off, but he stuck like a weasel at the throat of a rabbit.

"Gosh a'mighty, he's in trouble now! How's he going to get free?" Worried thoughts occupied the comparatively helpless spectators. Sure, he was riding in a place of relative security, where the cow could not reach him with her horns; but how could he now let go and escape being injured by this man-killer in a cowhide? Anxious friends, watching him being swept from one side of the corral to the other, wondered if they should try to effect a rescue. One of John's riding companions, surveying the situation from a top rail, was ready with his revolver to send a bullet into the infuriated cow.

But shooting wasn't necessary. At a proper moment, John freed his left hand, reached for the animal's muzzle, and with firm grip upon the nostrils, wrestled to twist the cow's head and throw her off balance. In an instant she rolled awkwardly on her right side; and John, keeping her head pointing skyward, was in complete control.

Surprised and relieved, the onlookers cheered. And when John walked away from the completely pacified cow, they wanted to know if he could do it again. He wasn't sure, but tried to reconstruct the technique. One thing was certain — having done it once of necessity, he would be called upon to repeat for the entertainment of admiring cowpokes.

John Ware was no show-off, however. He had no ambition to be a Wild West performer. He wanted to be a rancher and a good one. Through the summer of 1892 he was on his own place, making fences, helping John Quirk to extend the irrigation ditches, and fixing the house to make it more comfortable for Mildred.

The season was saddened by the sudden death of John's old friend, Tom Lynch; and the murder down at Pot Hole of the well-known Dave Akers, who was once the keeper of the notorious Fort Whoop-up. On the other hand, a new man, E. D. Adams, squatting on Quorn lease at the south side of Sheep Creek, close to Malcolm Millar, seemed to promise another friendship.

"Ol' Tom is dead," John told Mildred, sorrowfully. "Nobody could move cows lak Ol' Tom. An' ef it wasn' fo' Tom, ah wouldn be heah."

Everybody in the Cattle Kingdom knew Tom Lynch. In the words of William Henry, "Everybody was his friend," even to a heavily armed gunman wanted for murder, who had once ridden up to the Lynch cabin seeking shelter for the night. "Sure," was Tom's reply. "Anybody can stay here as long as he likes."

The gunman had remained for two nights, then disappeared as quietly as he had arrived. But a few weeks later there was a report of another shooting in Montana. This time it was Lynch's ungrateful guest who had been shot and killed in a barroom brawl.

John's new downstream neighbor, E. D. Adams, a mild-mannered twenty-four-year-old, born in India where his father was serving in the Imperial Army and educated in England, had recently been employed as a clerk in the service of the Hudson's Bay Company at Lower Fort Garry and Rat Portage. Now the young man was bent on ranching, and the spot presently marked by Millarville was his choice of all the country he had seen on world travels.

The young man wasn't sure whether he should go into cattle or horses or both. Ranchers were still angry about the British restrictions requiring immediate slaughter of Canadian cattle at point of arrival in the Old Country. And an intensive search by veterinarians failed positively to reveal any trace of the contagious pleuropneumonia in Western Canada. "These western cattle are still a lot healthier than anything they've got in England," the Walrond's Dr. McEachern repeated.

But the depressed state of the cattle trade led Hon. Walter Gordon-Cumming of the Quorn to send a trial shipment of ranch horses to England — about 100 head — and John Ware's friend George Scott went back with it. At the same time G. E. Goddard of Bow River Ranch sent two carloads of horses, selling at London and Liverpool. Some of the Alberta horses were sold for general farm use, some to be hunters, some to become cavalry mounts, and some to pull the recently introduced horse-cars on London streets. Altogether, the venture was not profitable; and the Quorn people and others like them decided to concentrate again' upon cattle.

But John Ware was not being allowed to forget his cow-wrestling feat, and early in the autumn he was repeating. Norman Luxton recalled attending the gymkhana event held in 1892 on the ground which became part of Calgary's Elbow Park district. The Critchleys — horse ranchers Harry and Oswald, ranching north of the Bow and west of Cochrane — were the hosts, and at least 200 people attended. Racing, pole bending and bronco riding were on the program; and if any individual emerged as the athletic star of the day, that one was John Ware. In the bending race his heavy body guided the Molly mare skillfully, and in the bronco riding he laughed boyishly as his fighting horse struggled unsuccessfully to dump him.

The feature of the day's entertainment, however, was John's demonstration of steer wrestling. The four-year-old selected for the test had a span of horns suggesting not more than two generations removed from Texas, and clearly the critter disliked the idea of this contest.

At the end of two lariats the big and irritable brute was brought to the centerfield. Mothers gathered their children together and looked for places of safety in case of trouble. Mildred Ware's expression indicated a wish that her John wouldn't indulge in such rough and dangerous sports.

Bareheaded and barehanded, John walked to the center of the field. While the animal was still held by lariats, he took a position at the left of its head and fixed his grip upon the horns. At once the ropes were removed and the horsemen retired, leaving John and the steer completely alone in the unfenced circle.

For a few minutes the angry longhorn lunged this way and that, trying desperately to free himself so he might dash back to the seclusion of the foothills. But John, like a blood-sucking leech, was sticking with him, more or less riding his position behind the horn. His white teeth could be seen clear across the field, and his smile seemed to match the breadth of horns. Women, increasingly fearful that the big cowboy would be crushed to a gory pulp, looked worried; and Mildred held her breath. Men cheered hopefully, but nobody was sure John could master the steer.

A few minutes went by and the man in the ring ceased to smile. He was working harder now, bearing with all his strength, and twisting the bovine head. The tremendous power in the man's muscles was evident, but power alone wasn't enough; he knew he must gain an advantage by throwing the steer off balance.

Becoming more enraged than ever, the steer plunged forward in one mighty effort to shake the human parasite; but at this moment John's arms twisted the head quickly to the left. The steer staggered; and with an added heave from John, went down on its shoulder and then its side. John threw his body across the beefy neck, keeping the critter immobilized by holding the head at an awkward right angle to the body.

Spectators clapped and roared their approval. John was the victor and no doubt remained. He released the steer and walked away calmly toward the place where Mildred was sitting and worrying.

"Ef that fellah was much biggah, ah don know ef ah coulda handled him," John was mumbling.

From this display Calgary people got the idea of a competition; and at the next summer fair, 1893, there was a scheduled contest in roping and wrestling with three experienced men of the range competing — John Ware, George Lane, and a Montana cowman named Todd. Directors of the fair decided to make this contest a feature and offered as a prize a handmade saddle valued at a hundred dollars.

Each contestant was required to rope a steer, throw it and tie it down. George Lane drew the first steer and took four minutes to complete the tasks. John Ware was next and, riding a horse without bridle, he finished in fifty-one seconds. Spectators recognized his feat as a professional performance and cheered. The third and last performer was Todd, and his time was two minutes and fifty-one seconds. John was the winner by a big margin and accepted the elegant trophy saddle.

By this time, the Lewis family had a house on Stephen Avenue East in Calgary, where Mrs. Lewis was doing a small business in laundry to help buy food and clothing for her family. There in the front window, Mother Lewis proudly placed the handsome saddle for all to see. And by this time, too, she had more than a trophy saddle to bring her pride — there was a granddaughter, Amanda Janet Ware.

John had always considered "9" to be his lucky number, and on the 9th of March in that year of 1893, Mildred presented him with the baby girl who was to be known most widely as Nettie. The wee one was born at the Lewis home in Calgary, and taking a few days away from the ranch, John occupied himself by directing his friends, Indians as well as white, to call and inspect his little wonder.

The name of John Ware was now well-known in Calgary. Only a few people were familiar with the story of his life and progress, but everybody knew him as the winning cowboy performer of 1893. In the next year, however, luck was not with him in the roping and throwing contest at the summer fair. He was still regarded as the best man in the business but he failed to win the competition, the Macleod *Gazette* of July 27, 1894, telling it this way: "John Ware who roped and tied his steer last year in something like 58 seconds, started out with every prospect of lowering his own record. The steer had not made half a dozen jumps before John turned him over. He had him tied in no time but in his anxiety to make time, did the work carelessly . . . and the steer kicked himself free and got on his feet. There was great disappointment among the crowd, having been backed pretty heavily to win."

That convincing fellow Cappy Smart, who was Calgary's fire chief for thirty-five years, saw every local roping and bulldogging contest until organized rodeos became popular, and had no hesitation in pronouncing John Ware the greatest performer of them all. Cappy left a reminder, also, that the steers men worked with in those early competitions were big, fast, powerful and mean.

Because of restrictions in cattle exports in 1891 and '92, many steers which might have been marketed at three years of age were left on the range until they were four or five years old. Of the 6,000 fat cattle bought by the firm of Gordon and Ironside — mostly from the ranges — in the fall of 1893 many weighed 1,800 pounds and some a great deal more.

Big steers felt none of the discrimination which was to come later. On the contrary, size was a mark of superiority. At the Winnipeg Industrial

Exhibition in 1893, the winning three-year-old fat heifer weighed 1,975 pounds; the winning three-year-old steer weighed 2,150 pounds, and the prize winner in four-year-old steers, 2,375 pounds. At Christmas the carcasses of these much-admired cattle were displayed for advertising purposes by the Winnipeg meat firm of Kobold and Company.

And John Ware's ranges had steers to make the Winnipeg specimens appear as dwarfs. The distinguished steer of which the *Nor' West Farmer* of January, 1894, told, paraded past the Lewis home on Stephen Avenue, and John was present to admire. "Hull Brothers, Calgary, lately treated the citizens to a view of a large Northwestern steer which they marched through the streets and afterwards killed as Christmas beef. His live weight was 3,650 lbs., and if allowed time he could have laid on 500 lbs. more. He was led by a 6 ft. cowboy on a good sized horse, but beside the ox they looked rather small. The ox was over 6 ft. at the withers."

If Calgary had the biggest steer, Medicine Hat claimed the fastest. According to another issue of the *Nor' West Farmer* (March, 1893), "Mr. George Nugent, Medicine Hat, is training a fast Mexican steer which may be shown at the World's Fair. He is said to be able at present to trot a mile in three minutes and the only difficulty is about his being safe to drive in such an exciting situation."

The Canadian Cattle Kingdom was still youthful, and both its cattle and its men possessed fascinating distinctiveness. The cattle were big and vigorous; the men were skilful and self-reliant.

CHAPTER 19

THE DRY YEARS

The early 90's were dry — dry as a treasurer's annual report, with the situation becoming most acute in 1894. Crops failed and ranchers found it easy to see the hand of the Almighty working to discourage the sodbuster fellows from settling in the ranch country. A cattleman near Medicine Hat greeted a frosty morning in early June with undisguised enthusiasm: "That's one damn fine morning; should freeze every stem of wheat in this good cow country."

But the grass in that year of 1894 was short too, especially on the plains. When John Ware rode out on the roundup, many sloughs were dry for the first time in white man's memory and ducks were exhausting themselves looking for water. Farmers became discouraged, and some removed the barbed wire from their fence posts and left. Ottawa's politicians, displaying the finest of backsight, revived controversy about the wisdom of opening up the West. Perhaps it was a mistake, they suggested. Perhaps John Palliser was right in questioning the value of prairie lands for cultivation.

The position of ranchers around Medicine Hat was more precarious than that of those in foothills locations. Grazing areas favored with moderately high precipitation were the first to be taken up; but when retired mounties, remittance men, young fellows from the East, and cattlemen who had been "sheeped out" in Montana were searching for grain leases, ranching was bound to expand in all directions.

With 20,000 cattle in the Lethbridge area and nearly as many around Medicine Hat, there was understandable fear that ranges were being overstocked; certainly the figures represented overstocking in a dry year such as was being experienced. Biggest operators in the Lethbridge country were W. G. Conrad with 6,000 cattle; Conrad Brothers with 5,000; Archie McLean's CY outfit with 2,000, and Browning and Maunsell with 2,000.

Around the "Hat," the pioneer herds like those of James Hargrave, James and Robert Mitchell, and the Medicine Hat Ranch had grown bigger, while new ones were being started. Hargrave, taking warning at the first sign of drought, moved his cattle to a place north of Walsh, where an Indian, Little Corn, had pointed out the better than usual supplies of feed and water. J. A. Grant, one of the few to ignore the cattleman's traditional antipathy toward sheep, started the Sarnia Ranch south of

Walsh with "woolies" more than cattle. James Patterson, a Texan who had been foreman for the Walrond, took to the south slope of the Cypress Hills in 1893; and in this summer of extreme drought, Walter Huckvale moved his "fiddleback" cattle to Manyberries Creek, there to become a partner with Sydney Hooper and a prominent member of the Medicine Hat community. In 1912 those two genial Englishmen built the Hooper and Huckvale Block in Medicine Hat; and still later, Huckvale became mayor of the "Hat." Ranch neighbors recalled that only once was the distinguished partnership in danger of rupture. Unwisely, Hooper used Huckvale's very personal tin bathtub to mix some sulphur mange cure. Becoming discolored by sulphur, the tub was never quite the same again; and for a time it seemed as though the human relationship might likewise be permanently damaged.

The dry years were testing years for both farmers and ranchers. Most of the adventurers who settled on the fresh western soil survived. Some didn't. Among those who gave up was Sir John Lister Kaye of the fabulous 76. His boastful stories about bonanza operations on ten ranches had echoed around the world; but now his company was in grave financial trouble. Sir John had refused the advice of men like D. J. "Joe" Wylie, one-time foreman at the Kincorth property, who later organized the Maple Creek Cattle Company to take over the Oxarart Ranch in the Cypress Hills.

Sir John deserved credit for imagination and courage, even though his successes were slight enough. The fact was that no company could prosper while departing so far from reality — trying to irrigate huge prairie wheatfields with watering tanks mounted on wheels, for example; or trying to make dairy queens out of truculent longhorn cows. With the original company failing, Sir John retired. Manager D. H. Andrews went to England in 1895, and with British capital organized the Canadian Land and Ranche Company, and bought the holdings of Sir John's organization. Andrews, an able and practical cattleman, continued as manager until his death in 1906.

But even in that driest year, John Ware had hay because he had followed John Quirk's example and irrigated a big meadow below the buildings. The ditch led from Quirk's main, and Ware built a milkhouse over it to help keep his milk and cream from souring. The grassed-over irrigation ditches can still be detected.

Mildred Ware never trusted herself on a horse. She had a lingering fear of being carried away or trampled; but she did learn to milk cows and bought a lot of the family groceries with money from the sale of butter.

John would milk the cows when he was home, even though anything akin to dairying was generally repulsive to a cowboy. The fact was that he was often absent. He was in demand for horsebreaking, and he continued to participate in the roundups, riding commonly with the Quorn or Bar U wagon. Loyalty to both outfits was unbroken even though faces in the respective crews changed a good deal. E. J. Swann was now the manager of the Quorn, and new men like Douglas Hardwick, destined to become a prominent rancher, were among the riders.

John's loyalty did not go unnoticed. Although there was only one other Negro cowboy in the ranching country, Lige Abels with the Walrond, John was elected to be captain of the roundup several times. As the boss, he directed operations with the friendliness of a mongrel pup and the firmness of a mounted policeman. Inexperienced young fellows, commonly the brunt of jokes, had a friend. John might tease the boys, but he was always ready to assist them — and Heaven help the older cowboy who tried to bully the lads.

A young fellow grabbing for the saving grace of a saddle horn while his horse pitched unmercifully heard John roar, "Ca'efu' yo don pull that thing out." But when the horse continued to give trouble, John mounted it himself and gave the ornery brute a thorough workout.

There was no doubt about it; his compelling way with horses was becoming more and more evident, as an incident at Fort Macleod about this time indicated. He was employed by the day to break horses for the Mounted Police, and while the work was in progress there came an officer from Regina, making inspections. With a display of authority he proceeded to ride one of the recently broken horses; and he was promptly unseated and thrown — to be deposited like a shapeless heap of old clothes on the ground.

Police pride was sorely hurt, and the man protested that the horse wasn't broken at all. John listened in silence, then walked slowly to the horse, removed the saddle, placed a white handkerchief from his pocket on the animal's back and mounted. Spectators, including the police inspector, saw him walk, trot and canter around the parade ground; stop, rein back, and cut a figure eight. Finally, when he dismounted, the handkerchief was exactly where he had placed it and the horse was standing with perfect obedience. Perhaps the self-conscious police officer was not convinced, but every other onlooker recognized the touch of the master hand.

Frank Collicutt, a seventeen-year-old son of the province of New Brunswick, with fame as a breeder of purebred Herefords in his cup, was on the roundup as a horse wrangler in that dry spring of '94 and could tell of John's performances as wagon boss. There was a Saturday night when the roundup crews descended upon High River to celebrate. After spending too long at the bar of the High River Hotel — bought in the next year by Billy Henry at a price of 175 head of cattle — the men became quarrelsome. A fight started; and everybody including Phil Weinard, who was tending bar, wanted to get into it. With cowboys ever ready to bring fists to the aid of friends, there was every prospect of a riot. But at the crucial moment John Ware came upon the scene and undertook to end the brawl: "The way he took a man in each hand and parted the scrappers, you'd think he was separating fighting rabbits."

Out on the plains, drought continued to be the talk of the summer — young ducks never learning to swim, and camels being the proper stock for this country; but in the foothills there was no less interest in the sudden upsurge of coyote and wolf destructiveness. The killers were more numerous than ever before, and bolder. At the Glengarry Ranch it was found necessary to "corral a bunch of thoroughbred cattle every night." (Macleod *Gazette,* July 27, 1894) and on the Hatfield range, "A fat three-year-old steer was pulled down and killed by the wolves," (Macleod *Gazette,* Nov. 15, 1894). The most distressing story of the year came from John Ware's own range: "Wolves have been doing considerable damage through the foothills of late," the Calgary *Herald* of July 13, 1894, reported. "John Ware, near Millarville, lost 24 head of cattle, young and old; and three calves of A. P. Welsh's in the same district are known to have been carried away bodily."

The Government of the Northwest Territories paid bounties, but they were not sufficient to induce trappers and hunters to go after the animals. John's beloved hound pup, Moses, became a big and useful dog and accounted for quite a few coyotes. The wolves, however, were still the bigger problem, and were generally too much for a single dog. John's neighbors recalled an instance of his coming to the hound's assistance when the wolf was too big for Moses. The dog overtook the wolf as the wild creature tried to cross thin ice on the creek, but couldn't hold to the quarry. The two snarling animals rolled over in combat and Moses established a determined grip on the wolf's throat. But the dog was being dragged by superior power. John rode up at a hard gallop; and at a moment when Moses was in urgent need of help, leaped from his horse with knife blade open and fearlessly hamstrung the wolf and stabbed it again and again. That one did not get away.

Neighbor Joe Fisher retained another mental picture of John Ware, the wolf and coyote hunter. It was toward the end of a day spent searching for cattle, and John drew his revolver and shot a coyote. He resolved to take the dead animal home for such reward as might come from skin and bounty. But arriving at Fisher's cabin at sundown, he still had six or seven miles to go and his horse was tired.

"Ah'd like t' bo'ow a f'esh hoss t' get me home," he said to Fisher. "Ah'd leave this done-out nag heah fo' a day."

Fisher didn't have a fresh horse in the stable and said so. "Nothing except that middle-aged stallion, and he's never had a saddle on him. You wouldn't take him!"

"He'll do," John insisted. "Sho, ah'll take him."

The protesting stallion was roped, snubbed and saddled; and Joe shouted, "Say when you're ready and I'll let him go."

But John wasn't ready to mount. "Hold 'im till ah get that wolf on too."

And so the dead coyote, with a hide worth two dollars in trade, was tied behind the saddle and then John mounted and yelled "Let 'im go."

The horse, with saddle, man and coyote on its back, snorted and leaped violently, trying to unload all the strange impediments to its freedom. But John was unworried and merely headed the frantic brute in the proper direction. Fisher watched as the animal, terrified by such unexpected cargo, plunged into Sheep Creek, up the bank on the other side, and disappeared beyond the hill, still bucking furiously.

After two days John returned riding the stallion, now about as amiable as a school pony, and saying: "Thanks fo' the hoss. He sho don lak a cold coyote."

"How are things at home?" Fisher asked.

"Fine," John replied. "No baby yet, but any day now. Gonna be a boy this time, yo know."

At their next meeting John revealed proudly that it was a boy. On November 29, 1894, son Robert was born there beside the creek, and John found it easy to forget that season's worries.

The years 1895 and '96 were dry also — almost as dry as '94. Wheat growers on much of the plains had nothing to sell. But cattlemen, in spite of drought, wolves, storms and rustlers, had a growing number of four-year-old steers worth forty dollars each. Even the editor of the Calgary *Herald* agreed that cattle had more to offer than wheat: "The fact that nearly 20,000 fat cattle averaging $40 a head have been shipped from the western ranges this season establishes cattle raising for the Old Country market as the leading industry of the Territories. Compared with grain growing or any other branch of farming, cattle ranching stands out pre-eminently as the safest, easiest and most profitable thing a man in this country can turn his hand to." (Calgary *Herald*, Nov. 13, 1895).

Cattle exports were increasing again, and so were the cattlemen's problems. The expanding and maturing industry needed better organization; it needed opportunity to speak with strong and united voice on matters of leases, homestead restrictions, wolf bounties, quarantines and so on. In the autumn of 1896, just before the Blood Indian known as Charcoal went on his famous murder spree, stockmen from the mountains to Swift Current received invitations to attend a meeting for the purpose of banding together in an active association.

Previous attempts to organize had met with only medium success. There had been the Southwestern Stock Association, and then the Canadian Northwest Territories Stock Association formed at Fort Macleod in 1886. But not much came of these. Now, while J. T. Gordon of Gordon and Ironside was announcing that his firm expected to export 35,000 ranch cattle in the 1896 season, increased interest and better representation from the stockmen led to the creation at Fort Macleod — still the unofficial capital of the Canadian ranchland — of the Western Stock Growers' Association. D. W. Marsh of Calgary was elected to the office of president, and R. G. Mathews, secretary.

Before the secretary had his minutes written, word went around about a murder on the Blood Reserve, and a police hunt for the heavily armed and dangerous Charcoal was under way. The first murder victim was another Indian suspected of being too familiar with Charcoal's wife; and the last was Sergeant Wilde, who had been trying to effect an arrest. Until the killer was a prisoner in the barracks at Fort Macleod, families as far north as Sheep Creek and beyond lived in fear that the terrible Charcoal might suddenly appear at the kitchen door.

It was understandable that stresses and conflicts and dangers would attend efforts to make a native race renounce its former liberties and adopt a way of life which was an insult to proud, free spirits. Inevitably, there were sleepless nights when armed men with hostility in their hearts and blood on their hands were known to be roaming the country.

But the distractions of murder passed and thoughts returned to the new challenges confronting the Stock Growers' Association in which John Ware was a willing member. In a sense it was a product of drought years with the attendant need for better planning and better order. Necessity is a prolific parent, and the first annual meeting, held at Fort Macleod on April 8 and 9, 1897, proved to be the greatest stockmen's assembly the West had experienced. The secretary reported over a hundred members owning a total of 95,000 cattle and horses.

In the election of officers at that first annual meeting, D. W. Marsh was returned as president; while W. F. Cochrane, Fort Macleod, was named to be first vice-president and F. W. Godsel, Pincher Creek, second vice-president. Directors were chosen to represent the acknowledged ranching districts: William Cowan for Bow River, John Ellis for Medicine Hat, W. H. Andrews for Maple Creek, E. J. Swann for Sheep Creek, Fred Stimson and George Emerson for High River, A. B. McDonald and D. J. Grier for Willow Creek, and C. Kettles and R. Duthie for Pincher Creek.

From that landmark convention there went a request to the CPR for bigger compensation for cattle killed on tracks and further reductions of freight rates on purcbred bulls brought from the East. The Territorial Government was asked to increase the bounty on wolves; and of upper-most importance in the minds of ranchers in 1897, the Federal Government was asked to impose reasonable restrictions upon settlers. Homesteaders should be prevented from cutting and destroying natural shelter along rivers and creeks, and they should be told clearly where they must not squat or settle or hang their terrible barbed wire.

At least the Government would be more likely to listen if the cattlemen were united and spoke with one voice.

"Sho', Sam," John Ware said to his friend, Howe, "sho', oua boys should tell the gove'ment. But ah hope those ol' cowmen nevah get ideas about yappin' t' a gove'ment eve'y time the spwing goes dwy."

"Don't think they'll do that," Sam assured. "A cowman's an inde-pendent critter."

CHAPTER 20

WEATHER AND THE PRICE OF HORSES

"Instead of grousin' about weather and the price of horses in these parts," Sam Howe said to a newcomer, "just smoke a pipeful of tobacco; and by that time, chances are both will be different."

But Sam, in spite of his philosophy, was giving up his ranch on the South Fork of the Sheep. The spring of 1897 seemed to promise another season of drought; and this prospect, after a series of dry years, led many people to quit the land. In Sam's case it was just the restlessness of the old trail rider, one who had run away from his Utah home at the age of fourteen and never settled for long in one place. When a chance came, he sold the ranch and bought the Atlantic Hotel and Livery Stable in Calgary.

Concerning man's frailty in predicting weather in this west country, Sam was positively right, and 1897 turned out to be an excellent year for both grass and grain. Some of those settlers who had abandoned their farms now returned to repair fences and break more sod. With brutal forcefulness, heavy rains in early June signaled the change of weather.

What John Ware and his neighbors living along the Creek saw was rainfall of cloudburst proportions, and overnight the stream was transformed into a raging torrent. Where John's buildings were situated, the swollen river presented no threats of danger; but downstream, where E. D. Adams was living, emergency mounted with the rising water.

Malcolm Millar had warned Adams that Sheep Creek could be wild and that building a log cabin on the flat at the south side of the stream, beside the present Millarville, might prove to be a costly mistake. Now the mistake was apparent. Millar was right; and before Adams realized the full extent of flood danger on that June evening, water was coming through the cabin doorway and covering the floor.

At once the soft-spoken young man prepared to evacuate, knowing that he was now surrounded by water becoming deeper by the minute. Grabbing a loaf of bread and a ham bone to which some meat still clung, he stepped outside into the flood. Sheep Creek by this time was half a mile wide. In escaping to high ground, Adams knew there would be dangers. Before reaching the safety of dry soil, the fleeing man was wading precariously, neck-deep in the flood, and holding bread and ham above his head.

Naturally he was thankful for having escaped with nothing more serious than wet clothes, but he had other worries. Before long the logs of his buildings began floating away; and his cattle, seventy-five head of Galloways, were marooned without feed on a small rise of ground. Nothing, it seemed, could be done about the cattle — not at the moment, at least.

After a night spent at a neighbor's cabin, Adams walked back toward the creek to see how the hungry cattle were surviving. They'd present a dismal picture — he knew it; but just as he came within sight of the herd, whom should he see approaching on a gray mare but John Ware — ten miles from home.

"What in the world are you doing here?" Adams asked. "Haven't you got worries of your own up there?"

"Ah figu'ed yo might be havin' some twouble, Mistah Adams, an' jus' thought ah should come down this way."

Silenced for a moment by the thought of John riding all those miles to offer aid, Adams replied, "Well, I don't suppose anybody can help me, but I'd certainly feel better if those cattle were out of there. However, it's too late; it would be frightfully dangerous to ride through the flood now."

John, still in the saddle, shifted his heavy body slightly to gaze at and study the marooned herd. Making no comment, he handed Adams his precious revolver which should be kept dry, and touched spurs to sensitive equine ribs. The gray mare didn't fancy the plunge, but John insisted and together they advanced slowly into deeper water until, at one point, the animal was obliged to swim.

Nor was it easy to persuade the Galloways to venture from their feed-less island. Their Lowland Scottish spirit rebelled at compulsion, however fine the intent. But John knew something about forcing protesting trail herds to cross unfriendly rivers; and after some minutes of his shouting and maneuvering, the unwilling critters were in the water, swimming to safety.

"That was the reason neighbors loved John Ware," Mr. Adams recalled as he looked back over the associations of many years with the big Negro rancher.

One result of the flood was that Adams chose a better home site, and built next time on higher ground on the north side. Another was that he and Ware saw more of each other. Often when coming home from Calgary at a late hour, John would stop for the night. Together the two men went on the extensive horse roundup of that summer, one which took them as far as Medicine Hat. And now and then they'd trade horses.

"He could do very well in a deal," Adams remarked, recalling one transaction in which he figured he got the worst of the exchange. Adams had been riding a brown horse, sixteen and a half hands, a bit clumsy and with a reputation for bucking and meanness. Already the animal had thrown a Quorn worker and dragged him to his death. But John fancied the big fellow; and while the two men rode together on the roundup of that year, John mentioned again and again that such a big horse should have a big rider.

"Yo too small fo' that big fella. Ah'll buy him. Ah'll give yo seventy-five dollahs fo' him."

Adams countered with an offer to sell for $125. It was perfectly evident from the glint in John's eyes that he wanted the horse. In the best of horse-trading tradition, he was ready with a compromise — match pennies to see if the price would be $75 or $125. Adams agreed. They matched and John won the horse at his price.

Time seemed to remove all doubt — the horse was made for John. Now and then there was some bucking, but that only increased the big cowboy's sense of attachment and man and horse traveled together for thousands of miles in the next few years.

If they were sure of a market, John and other ranchers wanted to raise a lot of horses. Production wasn't difficult, and horses could rustle better than cattle in winter. But the fact remained that cattle, for several years, were easier to sell. Among the incentives to produce cattle were the tycoon buyers, Gordon and Ironside, dominating the export trade; and now, a new and forceful personality in the industry, there was Pat Burns, to whom John sold his steers in 1896.

Burns was the young Irish-Canadian who homesteaded near Minnedosa in 1878 and then seized the opportunity of furnishing beef for crews building railroads. Coming to Calgary in 1890, when the railroad was being constructed between that place and Edmonton, he built a modest slaughter house in East Calgary. But rapidly Burns' livestock and meat business expanded; and by 1897 he was slaughtering 800 head of cattle a month and paying out $55,000 per month for meat animals.

But the horse market, admittedly fickle at the best of times, was looking brighter. Ranchers hardly dared trust their optimism; but the horse roundup of 1897, in which John Ware and E. D. Adams rode together, was an expression of fresh hope after several years of depression. Following the killing winter of 1886-87, ranchers built up their horse numbers at the expense of cattle; but before long, prices dropped so low that bronco stock was scarcely worth rounding up and branding. A decrease in thefts was attributed to the fact rustlers were turning to more profitable loot. Horses simply were not worth stealing.

There were various reasons for the horse depression. Homesteaders needing power were showing strong preference for the more phlegmatic drafters from Eastern Canada — even at considerably higher cost. Coupled with this was the impact of mechanical advances. Gasoline and electricity were growing threats; but the most disturbing force of all was the bicycle, that two-wheeled wonder appearing more commonly on city and country roads.

Editorial writers studied the influence of the bicycle much as they did mechanization of wheatfields at a later date. The editor of the Moose Jaw *Times* (June 7, 1895) was trying to be realistic when he wrote: "How far the bicycle will supersede the horse is hard to say but there is no doubt that it is obtaining a hold in our West that is astonishing. Clergymen make their parish calls on that steed that tires not neither does it consume oats; doctors make sick calls; creditors make the oft-repeated visits and young men and maidens tell the old story during the exhilarating spin in the gloaming on the whirling wheel. The West wants the bicycle. It was built for it. The only hindrance to its general adoption has been the first cost."

An item in the Lethbridge *Herald* about the same time (June 15, 1898) was no more encouraging to the horsemen: "A man who had some horses to sell wrote to a friend in Ottawa asking if they could be sold in that city. The friend replied: 'The people in Ottawa ride bicycles, the wagons are pulled by mules, the street cars are run by electricity and the government is run by jackasses, so there is no demand for horses here.' "

Now, however, in spite of bicycles, gasoline, and Ottawa jesters, interest in range horses was improving. Drafters imported from the East were docile enough to suit the most timid settlers, but they were soft and susceptible to swamp fever. Moreover, contractors undertaking railroad construction in the Crow's Nest Pass needed horses by the hundreds.

All of a sudden there was an upsurge in horse stealing, and ranchers agreed that this was a good sign.

John Ware had sixty or seventy horses and hoped to double the number. They were not superior to the range stock belonging to neighboring ranchers, but when he had handled them they were better broken and more reliable than most broncos. As a horse breaker, nobody was more proficient, and buyers began showing a preference for horses which went through his hands.

When word reached the Creek of Sam Livingstone's death at Calgary in October, 1897, John hitched a pair of half-tamed horses to a buckboard and drove away to attend the funeral. By the time he arrived at Calgary the broncos were well broken, and before leaving the city he contracted to sell them for cash.

"When are you going to buy a bicycle?" Sam Howe asked John.

With a smile on his broad face and unmistakable scorn in his voice, John replied, "When the last hoss is dead."

It was probably the answer hotel-keeper Howe expected, but he was still skeptical. "Weather, women and the price of horses," he repeated; "you can't tell what they'll be tomorrow."

But temporarily, at least, horsemen were optimistic. As evidence of the returning confidence, George Lane, in 1898, made a daring and historic purchase of Percherons from James Maudlin of Dillon, Montana — thirty-five head of purebreds and 1,200 grades, all carrying the Diamond O brand. This notable band was driven over the trails to Lane's Alberta ranch, where the purebreds provided the foundation for what were later the world-famous Bar U Percherons.

And by this time there was still another factor of consequence, a demand for hardy horses to serve the hardy men venturing into the North to search for Klondike gold.

CHAPTER 21

THE ORDER CHANGES

Sure, John was becoming older — just like the business of ranching on Canadian grass. Some of the riders on the Sheep Creek roundup of 1899, at which he was the captain, called him "the old man." Nobody knew exactly how old he was — fifty or fifty-five, but he was now older than most of those with whom he worked in this young man's country. He could still sit a bad horse like nobody else in that area. His nearest rival was his friend Mike Herman. And his strength, like that of Samson's, was undiminished, as some of the young fellows including Jack Dempsey discovered.

Dempsey, a rambunctious youth of sixteen years when he had arrived from his native Ireland in the previous year, was staying with his uncle and aunt, John and Mrs. Quirk. The Quirks by this time had over a thousand cattle, and the Irish nephew took to range life like a cow takes to clover. On the spring roundup he was in the saddle all day, and in one form or another of mischief much of the night.

It happened one evening, as the chuck wagon situated beside Sheep Creek, that two lonely cowhands crossed the stream on a fallen tree to make their way to a ranch home where two pretty daughters resided. It was a perfectly reasonable thing to do; but men with romance in their hearts could expect to be the objects of pranks, and Jack Dempsey had an idea.

Borrowing John Ware's ax, he and three other young cowboy conspirators assaulted the deadfall tree which had served as a footbridge across the creek, cutting it in such a manner that the pieces fell into the stream and floated away. Now the swains, returning late in the evening, would be obliged to ford the stream; and Dempsey and his companions would be in hiding to hear their unholy expressions of anger. The plot worked precisely as anticipated; and the irate victims, after risking their lives against the uncertainties of a fast-running stream in the black of midnight, crept toward their blankets to spend the remaining hours of darkness shivering in wet clothes.

Soon after daybreak, when men were preparing for the day's work, John needed his ax and discovered that the thing had not been returned. Slightly annoyed, he issued a command: "Ah needs ma ax — now. You fellows bettah fetch it, quick."

There was no visible response from those who were confessing as little as possible about the events of the night before, and John spoke again. "Yo fellows who took it, ah'll dump ah of yo in the creek ef yo don get that thing back t' me, fast."

Still there was no evidence that the four who shared the offense were going to act; and John, unwilling to waste precious roundup time, seized one of the young men and literally tossed him into the creek water. Before the victim emerged, John had his hands on Jack Dempsey, six feet, two inches, and hard-muscled like a pugilist. Quite clearly, this wouldn't be as easy; and as the two men grappled, they fell to the ground and rolled down the slight incline which terminated with a sheer drop to the creek. Cowboys saddling for the day's work halted to watch the match between a strong young man and a strong man of more advanced years. But the struggle was brief and ended in a draw as the two antagonists, continuing to roll, went over the edge and fell with a mighty splash in the stream, ten feet below. Both men went under and then reappeared, uninjured. John, grinning as though he enjoyed it all, wiped the free water from his face; and before leaving the creek, seized the Irishman's hand, shaking it to show there was no bitterness. Then, walking back to the higher ground, he said, "They's still two t' go in the creek," and taking the remaining two men who had been party to the ax episode, he picked them up, one in each hand, carried them to the cutbank and simply dropped them into the water.

By this time the ax was back where John could see it, and the big fellow picked it up, saying, "Now, yo fellahs, get into yo saddles an' no mo'e foolin'."

Certainly the experience didn't do the robust young Irishman any harm. A couple of years later he was foreman at the Quirk Ranch, and still later was ranching for himself and distinguishing himself as a foreman at the a7 Ranch. Jack Dempsey died in his native Ireland in 1959. As one of the able cattlemen of his time, he never hesitated to proclaim John Ware as his chief mentor.

No orthodox teacher by any means, John had strong views about most things pertaining to ranching. Dempsey saw him bring a brand-new saddle from Calgary, and forthwith throw it in the creek to remain all night. A new saddle could be stiff and uncomfortable like new boots, John knew. "By tomo'ow mo'nin'," he said "that sadde'll fit ma pony an' ma seat like a buckskin moccasin on a squaw's foot."

And his views about right and wrong were just as strong. Although far removed from the church through most of his life, his moral convictions were like rods of steel. It would have been easy to brand maverick cattle with the four 9's now and then; most cattlemen had done a certain amount of it — but not John Ware. J. C. Stagg, who came to the range in 1898 and worked in that year for Joe Fisher, got to know John well. He recalled John slaughtering a steer he believed to be his own for family beef and then finding another man's brand on the hide after the butchering operation. It would have been easy to shut one's eyes to the indisputable mark of ownership, perhaps even to destroy the evidence. Instead, he sent word to the brand owner, inviting him to come and get the carcass or accept another steer by way of compensation.

Stagg remembered John admonishing Mike Herman for failing to bring in two McLellan heifers encountered in the course of roundup. "Ef anybody is goin' t' be fo' himself only, he might as well pack up an' go home." And not to be forgotten by the younger man were John's words of encouragement at the end of the roundup year when a bottle of whisky was being passed around. The men were jubilant and nearly everybody partook. But Stagg, a nondrinker, refused, and the roundup captain, with the courage of his convictions, came to him, placed a big hand on his shoulder and said, "Good boy; yo' keep it up."

But over the years people had not been easy to convince. John had had to beg for the privilege of demonstrating what he could do on one of Tom Lynch's spirited horses, and only by repeated performances was there recognition of his superior strength and skill.

Good people, with no intention of being unjust or unkind, simply didn't expect a Negro cattleman to be superior in anything. They'd joke with John and enjoy him, but it didn't occur to them to invite his opinions in matters of importance — at least, not for many years. Ultimately, their opinion changed, and they realized that merely because a man was unable to read and write, he was not therefore necessarily mentally immature. The man with all the handicaps of an ex-slave was seen to be growing in stature. Gradually, steadily, John Ware was gaining in reputation for sound judgment, a judgment which he shared willingly with anybody who sought it. His grammar was faulty and his enunciation a little unusual, but his way of analysing the problems of the frontier was practical and people were recognizing this.

"Let's get John's advice," Swann of the Quorn was heard to say again and again when the future of the ranch was in doubt. Sam Howe formed the habit of turning to John for guidance. In 1898 hotelman Sam made a strong plea that he and John go to the Yukon. "Every other son-of-a-gun we know is going." John, looking seriously, inquired: "How'd we get theah?"

Sam explained. They could take the boat from Vancouver to Skagway and go over the Chilkoot Pass and down the rivers. Or they might do as certain of Sam's hotel guests from the East were planning — fit out at Calgary or Edmonton, go overland "and to hell with the obstacles."

"It'd be easy to get rid of my hotel," Sam assured him, "and Pat Burns'll buy your cattle any day. Maybe somebody around Millarville would keep your horses in case you want to start again. You know, John, with farmers coming in it's getting too tough to operate a cow herd out there anyhow. If you're going to stay with cows, you'll have to get more grass somewhere."

John was listening attentively. Sam had been a good friend. Like John, he had never attended school. The two men understood each other, and what Sam said was perfectly true.

"Even some of our cowmen are going north," Sam continued. "A hotel fellow from Maple Creek took a bunch of steers to Dawson last summer and he's just back — Ed Fearon, that is. Says if a man's lucky he could make a fortune. Now Billy Henry is taking steers north for Burns — shipped west with them a few days ago. Billy ran the hotel at High River, you remember. Every good man runs a hotel sometime in his life, but doesn't keep at it too long. Sure, Billy's cattle will go north by boat and then he'll herd them — I don't know how far — to Dawson. Get maybe a dollar a pound for beef after he's taken the critters in there — halfway to North Pole, I suppose. But how about it, John? I'm ready if you'll come."

"Gollyme, Sam, yo wouldn 'spect a man t' sta't gettin' his bag packed without thinkin' bout it."

Flitting through John's mind were thoughts of his growing ranch operations and his home life. Mildred was a splendid wife and mother. She had changed John's life completely. She was a good cook, and a good housekeeper; and being able to read, she patiently read aloud from the *Nor' West Farmer* which came regularly to the home.

"Ah tell yo, Sam," John said, finally, "ah got a family — best any man could have — an' a not-bad bunch of cows. An' yo got a hotel. We bettah look aftah what we got an' let those othah fellahs dig fo' gold. Ah'd sho lak t' be goin someplace with yo but ah saw 'em diggin at Vi'ginie City an' most of those boys didn find nuf gold t' pay fo they pants. If yo sick a sellin booze at a ba', why don' yo go back t' punchin' cows? That's a bettah job fo' a man anyway."

Sam said no more about the Yukon; but months later, after the Boer War broke in South Africa, Sam sought John again. "Let's join up," he suggested. "Let's find out how they fight a war. No work to it. Damn it, they even pay you to shoot and raise hell."

"No, Sam, ah'm stayin'. Ah don want t' shoot anybody. Besides, a man with kids an' cows bettah stay home an' look aftah them. An' look heah Sam, somebody's gotta sta't lookin aftah this good grass befo'e the homestedah fellahs spoil it all. Ah'll find 'nough gwass t' do me fo' ma life but someday they'll wish they didn't exchange so much good gwass land fo' pooah wheat land. But yo Sam, yo bettah go an' see Af'ica. Yo itchin' fo a change, ah know. Yo bettah join that St'athcona a'my an' when yo come back, yo'll be in a mood t' get yoself some cows.''

Sam accepted John's advice, as he usually did; and joining up in early 1900, he went away with the Strathcona Horse under the command of Colonel Sam Steele. And the horse Sam rode through the South African campaign was one of John Ware's raising. Sam said, "It was the best damn horse in the war." And sister Jenny Howe, later known widely in the West as Aunt Jenny, came from Montana to stay with "Ma" Howe while Sam was away.

"The way things are going," Swann of the Quorn said to John, "how long do you figure any of us can run cattle out here?"

Things were changing. Prices were considered fair enough. There at the birth of the new century, a fat four-year-old range steer was selling for three and a half cents a pound; a fat yearling wether might bring $4; a well-broken horse $125, and an uneducated bronco, $24.

Calgary now had the status of a city and was acting smug about it; Stoney Crossing had become Okotoks, the Indian equivalent of the original name; Fort Macleod, Lethbridge, Medicine Hat, and Maple Creek were thriving cowtowns, and High River claimed to be the biggest shipping point in the country for cattle. Even the Sheep Creek district between John Ware's and the Quorn was suddenly transformed into an organized community bearing the name Millarville. Under the direction of Rev. J. Webb-Peploe, an Anglican church of unpeeled spruce logs was built below Malcolm Millar's in 1895; Robert Turner, a settler of 1886 who gave his name to a foothills valley, was winning prizes and fame with Balgreggan Hero and other purebred Clydesdales; and the district polo team was good enough to beat Calgary and hold its own against Pincher Creek.

To the ordinary run of sodbusters, all this represented progress. But as for John Ware and E. J. Swann and their fellow cattlemen, it was a mounting threat to freedom of the grass and the ordinary concept of ranching. Lease tenure was becoming steadily more insecure, with changes nearly always favoring the homesteaders. Back in 1886, rental rates on Crown land had been increased from a cent an acre per year to two cents. Ranchers didn't object strenuously to that, but they protested the mounting invasion by homesteaders — with government sanction — on lands held under twenty-one-year leases.

A few cattlemen still held lands not subject to homestead entry, but they were notified that their leases might be terminated on or after December 31, 1896. The only concession was the right of leaseholders to purchase up to 10 per cent of the land in question at $1.25 per acre. But any way one looked at it, time seemed to be working against the men who lived by grass and had pioneered the range.

There were more cattle than ever — over half a million head in the Territories, compared to 132,000 in 1891 and a mere 13,000 in 1881. Holders of grazing leases were likewise more numerous, but the total grassland held under lease — 610,000 acres — was only a fraction of the four million acres held in 1887. And homestead entries were rising annually — 7,426 in the year 1900.

"They're crowding us right now," Swann added. "And if they put wire around many more quarters on our grass, you can say goodbye to the old Z brand. Directors are worried, I can tell you."

John looked pensive. This menace threatening the security of the people who had struggled to establish themselves on the native grass was serious — no doubt about it.

"It's a big count'y, Mistah Swann," John said, "but theah soon won't be enough fo' eve'ybody an' his cows. Yo boys with the big outfits a' goin' t' be the fi'st t' get h't. We all might as well make up ou' minds weah goin' to' keep cows inside fences if we stay heah. If we don lak that, we bettah sta't lookin' fo some place wheah nobody wants t' plow. Ah'd lak t' find that place. Wouldn't yo, Mistah Swann?"

Sure as the coming of calving time, the old order was changing. Before the end of that year, 1900, the giant Quorn, proudest of pioneer ranches, was being liquidated; and John Ware was resigned to the necessity of moving his cattle to some less popular area. But where would he find it?

CHAPTER 22

CATTLEMEN MOVING

The first months of the twentieth century found the Canadian ranch-land in an unsettled state, like beef calves at weaning time. In the light of changes, adjustment was inevitable; but this was more like reformation or a fresh start. John Ware was moving, and so were a lot of other cattlemen.

Most striking was the new generation of cow-country personalities appearing for the first time. Among the newcomers were Roderick Mac-leay, the Spencers — Sam and John, Walter Ross, James Wallace, Rufus Pope, Raymond Knight, William McIntyre, Tony Day, and others like them. This, to be sure, was no ordinary generation of beginners; it was about as singular as Halley's Comet.

Rod Macleay, from the province of Quebec, abandoned a career in medicine, started ranching modestly on a quarter section southwest of High River, bought the Ware cattle following John's death, and became a Cattle King.

Railroad builder Walter Ross, who had been absent after setting up the Tom Brown Ranching Company north of Cardston about 1885, returned in the year 1900 to pursue the business of beef production on Milk River. In devoting himself to ranching, he brought the same vigor with which he had built ship canals and railroads in many parts of the continent.

It was just before the beginning of the century that J. H. Wallace — Big Jim — along with brothers Steve and Robert, came from Oregon to the Cardston district and operated beside the Brown Ranch. Big Jim was a man of few words but unmistakable purpose. Alberta's Lieutenant-Governor Jack Bowlen delighted to tell of the negotiations leading to the sale of his Q Ranch to Wallace.

"How much do you want for your spread, Jack?" was the first question.

"Fifty cents an acre for the lease land," was the answer.

"I'll give you forty; now, how much for the cattle?"

"Seventy-two dollars and fifty cents a head."

"I'll give you seventy. How many cattle have you got?"

Bowlen said, "Eight hundred and eight head," and Big Jim mumbled, "Call 'em eight hundred and we won't count 'em. I'll give you twenty-five thousand cash and the rest when the lease is transferred."

Thus the transaction was completed, and the only written record was in pencil on the back of a soiled envelope.

Later, Wallace and Ross joined forces and built a cattle empire embracing 10,000 head in Alberta's south-east. Colorful fellows they were, and with a fine sense of integrity. They were John Ware's friends, and in a ranch-country sense, his neighbors.

Another famous family coming shortly before the turn of the century bore that good name, McIntyre. William H., six feet three inches, and a gentleman, was a successful Mormon businessman in Utah. Concluding that Canada offered the best in ranching opportunities, he and son "Billy" bought three townships watered by Milk River and bearing on the Canada-United States border. What the McIntyres acquired was some of the best ranchland in the south; and in the years following, many of the finest beef cattle going to Canadian markets carried the McIntyre brand, IHL.

Following hard upon the heels of the new century was a wave of American cattlemen immigrants, trying eagerly to keep ahead of the homesteaders. In this notable group were the Knights and the Days. Jesse Knight and son Raymond from Salt Lake City acquired land east of Cardston and came in 1900 with a band of sheep which both startled and alarmed the Canadians — 37,000 head of "woolies," to which the Knights soon added 5,000 cattle. Before long, the Knight sheep numbers exceeded 50,000. But even more spectacular was the big and two-fisted cowboy, Ray Knight, becoming one of the best-known figures in the Canadian West. The rodeo he organized and directed at the village of Raymond in 1902 was said to be the first thing of its kind in the entire country, and for years no rodeo was complete without him, either as a producer or participant. The "Knight and Day" Rodeo, distinguished even in name and staged in Lethbridge, was the joint effort of Ray Knight and Ad Day, the latter being the son of Tony Day.

Stocky, jovial "Uncle Tony" Day arrived on the grass south of Medicine Hat and Maple Creek in 1902 with 30,000 Turkey Track cattle and 600 horses. In many ways this was a range landmark.

Oldtimers could never forget that extraordinary, lovable cattleman, born in Texas in 1849. Tony Day was short — five feet, six inches; but in other respects everything a Texas cattleman was expected to be. This was perfectly understandable in one who rode the Panhandle when horns were long, cattle wild, and men with guns made their laws as they needed them. He couldn't imagine a meal in his home without hot bread. "Cold bread," said he, "is just good for stuffing roast chicken."

After ranching in the Texas Panhandle, the Days drove their herds to Nebraska, where there were heavy losses in that killing winter of

1886-87. From Nebraska the trail led to South Dakota; and finally, still pursued by plow-crazy settlers in covered wagons, Day and his cattle swept into the Northwest Territories like flood water over a dam.

The very obvious fact was that cattle were moving more than at any time since the '80's — fanning out, as it were. And right after the roundup in June of 1900, John Ware was leaving the foothills he and Mildred had grown to love, and driving his expanding herd to a range he hoped would offer more grass for his stock and less attraction for homesteaders.

Plans were completed in short order. The 300 or so cattle had been gathered already in the course of roundup operations, and three cowboy friends, including Jim Dowling, agreed to ride with the herd. Household effects were loaded on a wagon. Then at that most opportune moment a stranger came that way offering to buy John's interest in the Sheep Creek place. A deal was made and the purchaser gave a payment. And he gave it more readily than he was to give the second payment after protesting the presence of bedbugs in the log house. John made his position on that future occasion quite clear, however: "Ah jus' want ma money fo' the house an' place; ah'm not cha'ging yo' fo' any bugs."

It was just like a day on the old trail leading from Idaho to the Highwood River. The cattle were started soon after daylight and unhappy cows and calves bawled their objections. But instead of the chuck wagon, there was the ordinary farm wagon loaded with household and ranch equipment, and driven a little awkwardly by Mildred Ware. Beside her on the wagon seat were the two children, and following was the rather usual assortment of dogs which John as a dog lover kept around him — a couple of wolfhounds, a collie, and a few Irish water spaniels. And ahead of them was a journey of at least 150 miles. It would take them between a week and ten days, and the trip would become monotonous and tiresome.

It wasn't easy to leave those pleasant foothills surroundings where the Wares had started their married life and neighbors were good and loyal people. And the countryside had never looked more lovely than on that bright June morning. Foliage was heavy and rich, and little birds argued noisily with crows and magpies coming too close to their nesting premises.

Expertly, John and his helpers guided the cattle toward Millarville and on in the direction of the Quorn headquarters. There was water on that route and lots of grass. Even the cattle seemed to be familiar with it.

The riders figured they had traveled fifteen miles when John called a halt to make camp beside Sheep Creek. That was far enough for the first day, and the cattle were ready to settle quietly without much threat of straying during the night. The Wares made beds on the uneven sod beneath the wagon, and the riders spread their blankets under big trees. Except for shrill howls of coyotes across the creek, and an occasional motherly call from a cow whose udder was becoming painfully full of milk, the night passed peacefully.

The end of the second day found the travelers and their cattle on the Macleod Trail, making a night stop near Midnapore. And early in the afternoon of the third day, they were on the outskirts of Calgary. Driving a herd of cattle through the streets of the old "Cow Town" was not unusual at that time, and it was on the most direct route. Moreover, there were convenient bridges on the Elbow and on the Bow, and they might as well be used. And so, with several hours of daylight ahead of them, John said they should get the herd through Calgary and camp for the night at some point east of the city.

While the men were driving the cattle across the bridges, Mildred and the children drove to the Stephen Avenue home in which her parents resided and had a short visit.

All was going well and the cattle, strung out for 300 yards on the trail, showed little hesitation about continuing along city street and avenues. On Atlantic Avenue leading to the Barracks Bridge across the Elbow, men driving buggies and wagons took to the sides to give the big herd the right of way. And with no interruptions whatever, the cattle entered upon the bridge and galloped over as though it was something they did every day.

No sooner had the cattle crossed, however, than trouble presented itself in a policeman's uniform. Chief English, with shining buttons, waxed mustache and a sergeant-major's look of severity, was on the west side, waiting to inform the man in charge that Calgary bridges were not to be used for cattle drives. "Now get your beasts out of here any way you like, but don't put them over our bridges."

John was taken by surprise, but he was courteous. He said he didn't know there was such a rule and he'd take the herd back across the Barracks Bridge.

"Oh no, you'll do no such thing. You'll not go back over that bridge, or those cattle will go to the pound and you'll land in the cells. Guess you've been there before. Now get your stuff away but stay off our bridges. Understand?"

It was not John's first encounter with Calgary police, and he knew how a uniform makes some men unreasonable, but nothing would be gained by an argument with this man parading his authority. It was now late in the afternoon; and John, not sure how he would get out of this difficulty, decided to seek the nearest secluded place to spend the night. Knowing the district well, he instructed his men to turn the cattle to the left and drive a mile or so upstream to a grassy flat fringed with cottonwood trees. That they did, and then prepared to spend the night in what was later the Calgary district of Elbow Park. They would decide later about their next move.

It was a long evening. Mildred and the children visited the Lewis family, and John rode across the city to study the best exit for a man with 300 unpopular cattle. One might understand the difficulty of driving a herd into a city, but never did he expect to encounter these problems in taking it out.

Presumably, the police expected him to swim the cattle. That could be done; but as John discovered on the evening ride, the Bow was in flood and running very fast. Fording or swimming it in its present state wasn't something anybody would do if he could avoid it.

The more he considered the matter, the more annoyed he became. The Chief had been needlessly surly and officious; the bridges were built to accommodate people, and nobody could blame him for trying to get out of this predicament as quickly as possible.

He had an idea. Instantly, he turned his horse and cantered back to where his friends were watching the cattle in the loop of the Elbow. "That ol Bow is pwetty wild tonight. We could punch these cwitters ovah ef we had t' do it. But we don have t'. They's a bwidge so men an' cows won have t' get wet. Ah think we bettah be up so't of ea'ly in the mo'ning, a little bit befo' daylight. We'll be outa sight befo that sma't police fellow is outa bed."

John didn't sleep. He wasn't taking any chance of oversleeping in early morning. And so, as the first rays of orange color were showing in the eastern sky, he was rousing the other riders and his family. "Gotta get outa heah. Yo can ah sleep tonight. Let's get those cows on theah feet so theah calves can suck an' then they might be quiet when we chase 'em down the stweet. An' no bweakfast fo' anybody until weah outa Calga'y."

Cows and calves were roused; and while calves nursed, horses were saddled or harnessed. The city was still under a blanket of semi-darkness when the herd was started back along the Elbow, then over the hill north-westerly and in a most direct way to the Bow Marsh Bridge. The streets were still deserted, and except for the bawling of a few calves which had not finished their breakfasts, all was quiet. Even for the birds it was too early to sing. And the cattle, overcome by surprise at being driven before sunrise, moved along in an orderly manner.

They were approaching the river. Lead cows shied slightly at the entrance to the wooden bridge and threatened to stampede upstream. But skillful cowboys kept them headed in the proper direction. Once the foremost cattle were on the bridge, others followed readily — if anything, too fast.

Now, however, John Ware had a terrifying thought; what if Chief English had a good and sound reason for denying the right to use the bridge for cattle in large numbers? What if the weight were too much for the bridge timbers and the structure were to give away? What would happen to him and his dear family if this boldness on his part were the means of wrecking a span the young city had worked so hard to get? Perspiration stood out on his forehead, and momentarily he felt sick. But turning back was now impossible; the determined cattle, pressing forward, couldn't be turned.

Cattle crowded onto the span and it swayed dangerously. Cowboys reined in their horses, all of them struck with fear of bridge and cattle crashing into the flooded stream. What a mess that would be! What a tragedy! Cattle might swim to safety; but somebody would go to jail for wrecking the bridge, especially when the crossing was made in direct defiance of the police.

While fear gripped the cowboys and Mildred watched, sharing the anxiety and holding her little ones close to her, there was a mighty crash as though the moment of disaster had struck. It sounded like great timbers being fractured and splintered. John hardly dared to look; but when he did scan the column of cattle filling the bridge, the leaders were running off and up the slope on the opposite side. What the crash meant, nobody ever knew. The bridge, though undoubtedly strained to the limit of its carrying capacity, didn't seem to be broken or damaged in any way, and the cattle were now moving off in a steady and rather orderly stream.

"Thank God that's over," Mildred was saying, knowing how John was worried. "I hope we have no more rivers to cross."

"Golly no! No mo'e wivahs," John repeated, as though partly exhausted, "Ah sho didn lak that. Ah guess ah shouldn have done it. But we'll be ah fine now. No mo'e wivahs an' no police fellahs."

For another week the Wares and their helpers drove for most of each day and camped on strange ground each night. Mildred and the children were sick of it, and didn't even like the open prairie country through which they were traveling. Finally, however, John announced their destination: "Theah it is. We'll stop now."

It was the Red Deer River, flanked by badland formations and not in the least like the picturesque and clear-running Sheep. The spot was twenty miles or so north of Brooks, and there was no store nearer than that place. John saw good grazing, lots of water, and an absence of home-steaders. Mildred saw the necessity of living under the wagon until such time·as the men could build a house; and she saw the weird, hoodoo formations which looked as though they belonged in a bad dream. It seemed a perfect hang-out for ghosts and spooks. She had premonitions of misfortunes but kept them to herself. She might not be happy but she'd try to be cheerful. That she was expecting another baby didn't make things any easier.

John understood; and as soon as he and his friends had completed the construction of a corral to hold the saddle horses, they began a search for logs suitable for building a house or cabin. Before many days, the Wares had a log home with dirt floors and sod roof. It was smaller and less imposing than the one they had left on Sheep Creek, but it would do until they could have a bigger one.

"This is bettah g'ass than we had in the hills," John told Mildred, trying to justify all that had been done. "Doesn look like much but cows do good on it." The point was not fully appreciated — that the prairie grass, less abundant in growth and less luscious in appearance, was higher in feeding value than the rank growth in the hills. This was the observation of one with sharp perception, one able to sense the slightest changes in the way animals reacted to their surroundings. Such astuteness was one of the marks of a great cattleman.

Neighbors? There were some widely scattered cattlemen across the river, but nobody very near on the south side. John Ware was a friendly soul and liked neighbors, but a man with a growing herd of range cattle didn't really want too many of them. Nettie Ware remembered a day when she and her father set out to cross the Red Deer River for a visit with the Eide neighbors on the PK. That ranch was started in the '90's by Prince and Kerr of Eau Claire Lumber; and Pete Eide and family came from Eau Claire, Wisconsin, to run it.

Anyway, a man should know his neighbors; and John, accompanied by his little daughter, drove a single horse and buggy to a point directly opposite the Eide home. He called across, hoping that a rowboat might be sent over for them. There was no response, but John discovered an old and dilapidated boat tied to a tree on his side and resolved to venture forth in it. Although he knew everything about cattle and horses, he knew nothing about rowing and was soon in trouble. The boat drifted downstream, yielding completely to the current. The little girl could do nothing to help, and John's best efforts were clumsy and unavailing. The boat was simply unmanageable and John began to worry for Nettie's safety.

Finally, half a mile lower down, the boat touched the south side again and its occupants were glad to leave it. Father and daughter walked back to the horse left tied in the trees, hitched a lariat to the boat, hauled the craft upstream to where they had found it, and drove home, satisfied to stay with horses as a means of transportation and to leave boats to those who knew something about them.

But in spite of the river barrier, a strong and lasting bond of friendship developed between the Wares and the Eides. When John needed help, he could count on getting it from the Eide boys, Chester and John.

Also on the north side of the river, with headquarters not far away, were the Quail Ranch, the Gordon Ranch, and the V Bar C. The Old Mexico Ranch east of Steveville on the north side was started a short time later — 1903. There were various reasons for the special public interest shown in it. The original owner, D. J. Beresford, was the younger brother of Lord Charles Beresford; and when "D. J." decided to transfer his cattle interests from Mexico to the Northwest Territories, 3,000 critters with Mexican horns and the V Bar C brand were shipped to Brooks.

Even the Old Mexican brand was unusual, inasmuch as the V was on the shoulder, the Bar on the ribs and the C on the hip. And with the cattle came one of Alberta's unforgettable characters, Henry Gordon "Happy Jack" Jackson. At first he was the foreman; but after the owner's death as a result of a train accident in North Dakota, Happy Jack took over completely.

By midsummer John Ware was fully re-established on this more remote grass, but he had worries. There was the matter of the baby. Mildred went to Blairmore, where her parents had recently taken up residence, and there the baby was born; but the wee one lived only briefly and sadness filled the Ware hearts.

And more distressing than the continued influx of homesteaders was the recent spread of an insidious skin disorder in range herds. Mange, it was called. Cattlemen had heard about it in the previous year and one district was declared to be in quarantine. Now, in August of 1900, as authorities confessed that mange had advanced rather than retreated, the entire range country was quarantined. It was extremely awkward for those who wanted to move cattle or sell them; and rangemen, skeptical about the effectiveness of the proposed dipping program, wondered if they would ever see the end of this most recent of cattlemen's plagues.

"Ah nevah saw any of that mange back in the hills," John told Pete Eide. "But, gollyme, ah'm afea'ed some of ma cows have it now. Ah sho' don like it when ma cows a'ent happy. We gotta get busy an' make ouah cows clean again. Ah'll do anything those vet fellahs tell me."

CHAPTER 23

AT WAR WITH MANGE

"Mange" was an ugly word — like "glanders" to the horsemen and "scab" to those whose sheep were affected. Mange was the most hateful thing to strike the Canadian range — and the most costly.

Scurfy and scabby hides were apparent in range herds for several years before the real significance of this parasitic disorder was understood. Even after technical experts expressed fears, wishful-thinking cattlemen argued that it wasn't true mange. "Just buffalo itch," one of them contended; "and it'll disappear after the cattle have been on good grass a while."

But the irritated and itchy skins — sometimes blooding, always unsightly, and usually a forerunner of failing condition — didn't disappear. They spread northward and southward from ranges along the Little Bow where the trouble was first noticed. Presumably, the mange mite was introduced by Circle cattle from south of the boundary. The earliest dipping vats were constructed at Kipp, and treatment proved effective when practiced with thoroughness. By the summer of 1902, battle lines were extended and the main fight had its center right at John Ware's back door.

It was on April 19, 1899, when the Western Stock Growers' Association was holding its third annual convention at Fort Macleod, that the bad news about the presence of genuine parasitic mange was formally announced. Veterinary Inspector Wroughton of the N.W.M.P. reported having found and identified the true mange mite, and he read a letter from a McGill University authority confirming the judgment.

Weeks later, Dr. Duncan McEachern proposed a program of dipping all affected cattle. That was all right, but his further proposal that the Stock Growers' Association should assume the cost of constructing dipping stations proved most unpopular with the cattlemen. In the face of this new emergency, misunderstanding and conflicts developed and there were threats of violence. Feeling ran particularly high when, on July 8, just at the onset of the breeding season, Mounted Police quarantined the entire bull herd belonging to the Medicine Hat community.

Ranchers were furious. The Medicine Hat cattlemen called a meeting and publicly censored the Police for delaying the quarantine order until the usual time for turning bulls out for the breeding season. But before the report of that meeting reached the public, the Mounted Police, upon advice from the Chief Veterinarian, placed a general quarantine on cattle in the country extending from Langevin on the west to Morse on the east and from the South Saskatchewan River to the International Boundary.

Under quarantine regulations, persons known to have mange-infected cattle were obliged to take steps to eradicate, and only by permit from the Mounted Police could cattle be shipped out of the area.

There were lots of complaints and lots of difficulties; but when the cattlemen accepted the necessity of stringent methods, the campaign progressed satisfactorily. Cattle dipped at Kipp in that year totaled 6,860, but too many affected animals escaped the vats. Some longhorn steers, sly enough and fast enough to elude the roundup gangs for several years, were carriers and spreaders of mange; and special effort had to be made to put them through the sulphur solution.

Douglas Hardwick recalled the trials of dipping some of those six- and eight-year-old steers, seventeen hands high and as mean as they were tall. When finally headed for the dipping vat, the outlaw's obvious inclination was to jump over the thing. Falling short of its ambitious purpose, it would land with a great splash in the hot sulphur liquor and roar its bovine anger. "Then," said Hardwick, "when a big fellow like that reached the far side of the vat and got to his feet on firm ground, he'd light out for Mexico at a speed to worry a Thoroughbred."

The need for thoroughness was increasingly evident, and by 1901 the disease was believed to be pretty well stamped out in that area in which it had first appeared. But, undetected, it had spread to the Red Deer River where John Ware was living; and there, in 1902, the battle was renewed.

But before the campaign against mange got under way in that year, John had another problem on his hands. It was a case of conflict between the man and the flooding Red Deer River. Without warning, the stream overflowed its banks and the Ware cabin was inundated.

"We gotta get outa heah—fast," John shouted. Already the water was coming in at the doorway. It was a dismal sight. Passing an ax and some articles of food and clothing for Mildred to carry, John gathered wife and crying children in his arms, walked steadfastly into the cold waters of the flood, and deposited all in a wagon box beside the corral. He then hitched the team to the wagon and drove cautiously to higher ground.

It was good to be out of the water; but the prospect of spending the night on a knoll there in the badlands was not a pleasant one, even if those hoodoo-like formations which appeared usually as symbols of bad luck now seemed repentant and inviting. Allen Robinson, moving a hundred brood mares for Gordon, Ironside and Fares, happened along and witnessed the retreat to dry ground. It was evident to him that Mildred was depressed and the children were upset, but John could still see some humor in the necessity of sleeping in those spooky surroundings. "If they's any ghosts in these valleys," he said, "they'll be comin' up heah t' sleep with us t-night."

A fire would furnish light, warmth and at least a little cheer, and John went about gathering wood for fuel. But troubles come in clusters; and when he was trying to cut some kindling, Mildred walked awkwardly into the path of his swinging ax and sustained a cut on her head.

Blood flowed alarmingly and other members of the family became excited. What could be done where there was no doctor for many miles? Something would have to be done without delay, and John directed her to lie down. Using the extra pieces of clothing, he worked to check the flow and keep the blood out of her eyes. Whatever he did appeared to help, because the bleeding stopped quickly and it was soon apparent that the wound was shallow and probably not very serious.

Beside the fire John spread blankets for his family's bed. He did his best to make them comfortable. As for himself, he did not sleep. He had no intention of sleeping. Instead, he spent the hours of darkness attending to the fire and standing guard over his family. Nor did he forget to offer a prayer of thanks; he and his family were safe from flood, and Mildred's injury was really quite shallow and minor.

When morning came, the Ware cabin was gone—completely. It was as if a badland goblin had whisked it away. Every log floated off and nothing remained. But the water had receded somewhat, and John and his family continued their way southward to select a site for a new home. They didn't go far—five or six miles back from the river, and there they chose a spot beside a little stream, later known as Ware's Creek.

Logs were needed at once. After cutting a few trees, John learned that a boom of logs being held at Red Deer for a sawmill had broken away and good spruce logs were at that moment floating toward his location. They would belong to anybody who could recover them. John had no love for the deep and angry river, but if logs were moving toward him when his need was so great, surely Heaven had something to do with sending them and he'd be an ungrateful scamp if he didn't try to capture them.

Without delay he made his way to the river and stationed himself at a point where the stream was narrow. His only means of recovering logs would be his lariat, the same instrument with which he had faced cattle thieves and a band of hostile Indians. John's lariat was always longer than the average; and on this occasion, using it with customary skill, he caught a good spruce log and then another.

Neighboring cattlemen could use some logs; and they, too, were taking positions beside the stream in the hope of recovering booty. When the Eide boys on the other side caught a log, they used a horse to pull it out. John, having the strength of a horse, pulled each log out single-handed.

The harvest of logs was good, and at the most opportune moment Sam Howe returned from the South African war and went at once to visit his old pal. John was delighted, and together they began building the new house. The drift logs were excellent for the purpose, and John's plan was for a better house—one with three rooms. When additional logs were needed, Sam helped John to get them from a stand of big poplars. In after years, when Sam boasted of cutting the logs in the Ware house, his friends reminded him of at least one he didn't cut, the one with the pointed end showing the unmistakable marks of the Red Deer River beavers which had felled it.

With neighborliness typical of the frontier, people from both sides of the river came to help build the house on a bench overlooking the creek. The work advanced rapidly; and before the last sods were placed on the roof, a strange horse and buggy were seen approaching. Two visitors, a government veterinarian and a representative of the Stock Growers' Association, stopped for dinner and explained their purpose. They had come to propose the construction of a community dipping vat just below the new house.

John offered no objection. Cattlemen had to think of the future of their business. Anything like mange, capable of lasting injury to range and farm cattle, had to be eliminated. Cattlemen had to have vision and faith. Hadn't George Lane, along with Gordon, Ironside and Fares, just bought the Bar U from the North West Cattle Company paying about a quarter of a million dollars for the ranch and some 8,000 cattle and 500 horses? Combining Lane's Flying E and Little Bow with the Bar U would make the new partners the giants in the industry with as many as 30,000 cattle. George Lane was looking to the future.

"Sho, we'll build a dip vat, anywheah yo say," John assured them. "We'ah not goin' t' quit cows o' let the litl mange bugs beat us. We gotta think about next yeah an' the next. That's the weason ah'm wo-ed that people ah'nt goin' t' take good ca'e of this g'ass. Sho, ah'll help ah yo want t' make a vat."

Even before there was time to build a stable or dig a well at the new home site, the vat was constructed — thirty feet long, three feet wide at the top and six feet deep. Supplies of sulphur came on a government order; and for a full month during that summer, mangy cattle were coming and going and the vat beside the house was in constant use, like a merry-go-round at the fair. Cowmen stopped now and then to brand some late calves; and when the workers demanded more in the way of variation, John would undertake to ride a mean horse. Altogether, it was like a month-long rodeo.

Dipping was an unpleasant task, however, The liquid had to be heated and the soupy sulphur solution had a nauseating odor. Clothing was frequently splashed or soaked by the stuff. John, helping every cattleman who came to use the vat, emerged as an authority on dipping. He could even tell exactly how a steer felt when he plunged into the hot brine, having had the experience of one complete immersion. It was when he was pushing calves into the vat that he slipped on the wet ground and went in with a great splash. Onlookers rushed to offer assistance, but help was not needed. John was making his way out in a hurry, spitting and shaking his head. But even an immersion in mange cure failed to rob him of his unfailing good humor. When scrambling out, he was muttering, "Heah's one ol cowman who shouldn't have t' do any mo' scwachin' this summah."

Allen Robinson, who had seen the family made homeless by flood, chanced to pass that way again late in the season. The Wares were then rehabilitated rather completely. The year's dipping program was ended; a log stable had been built and John was back to breaking some lawless horses. Watching the bucking, Mildred called, "You're doing fine, John, You can still show the young ones how to do it."

Fifty years later, John Ware's dipping vat, with sloping cement sides, was still to be seen close to the creek, a stark reminder of the difficult struggle against mange mites, the cattlemen's most trying experience with disease until foot-and-mouth occurred in Saskatchewan in 1951.

CHAPTER 24

THE MAY STORM AND AFTER

Nature seemed to be in a cantankerous mood, that spring of 1903. Warm weather came late and there were floods high enough to put riverside residents to flight. Then, at 4.10 a.m. on April 29, an estimated seventy million tons of limestone fell from Turtle Mountain in the Crow's Nest Pass to entomb part of the town of Frank and kill sixty-six people. It all happened in a matter of seconds: and rock debris — up to a hundred feet in depth lay spread across 3,000 acres.

The Frank Slide produced the most shocking news of that period. All possible relief was provided for the survivors — food, clothing and money; and many ranchers and settlers offered the use of their homes.

The dominant topic of conversation was still the disaster when a spring storm of unusual violence struck the range. Those who saw it and felt it never ceased to tell of the paralyzing blanket of snow and the frosty sting in that "May storm."

It began with rain on May 16 and turned to snow during the night. At first, nobody was concerned except for the survival of a few late calves being born into a snowy world. By the second day, however, there being no relief, fears began to mount. For four days the snow came in on an angry wind; and cattle, cold and cut off from grazing, drifted helplessly. Ultimately, some animals were found fifty miles from where they had been grazing when the storm started. Many other cattle, especially the dogie stock shipped from Manitoba and Ontario, piled in coulees and the corners of the hated fences, and perished.

John Ware was in Calgary and his saddle horse was in the livery stable at Brooks when the weather became rough. Storms had a habit of making special problems for him. Mildred hadn't been well since the last baby was born and John was in the city to get medicine. When the snow started, he longed to be back with his family and took the first train going to Brooks.

The operator of the livery stable advised him against starting from there. "Trails are all blown in, you know. You'll damn well get yourself lost. Don't think of it. Bucking that wind would be like fighting high tide on the Bay of Fundy. Your kids will be orphans if you try it. Now, I'm telling you!"

"But ah gotta go," John replied, tightening the girths of his saddle with clear determination. "Ah got medicine fo' Mild'ed."

John knew his cattle would be in trouble and drifting with the wind; that they would be already scattered widely, and that nothing could be done to help them until the blizzard subsided. Mildred and the children were uppermost in his thoughts as he mounted and turned his horse's head directly into the snow which felt like driven sand.

The horse, normally obedient, was unwilling to face this stinging blast. With head down to protect its face, it resisted, twisted and tried to turn back. Applying his spurs and the loose ends of the reins, John urged the brute on; but it was plain that the animal's fear of the blizzard exceeded its fear of the jabs from spurs. The stableman, still mumbling disapproval and warnings of disaster, watched while horse and rider disappeared at a snail's pace into the swirling snow.

John expected his horse would finally yield to the necessity of facing the storm for the twenty-five-mile trip, but such was not the case. The animal grew more insensitive to the prodding, and before long John realized he could walk through the snow in less time and with less effort to himself. The fact becoming ever more evident was that his horse possessed unusual reactions to the snowstorm. Here was a horse made stupid by the blizzard, and nothing would be gained by punishing or abusing it. After fighting to make a quarter of a mile, John accepted the fact that he could travel faster and easier without the horse. He gave the gelding its head, jogged with the wind and was soon back at the livery stable.

"I knew it," the liveryman shouted. "Nobody but a fool full of booze would travel today. Tie up and you can sleep in the hay tonight. Weather will be better tomorrow — maybe."

John tied the horse in a stall, but he had no intention of sleeping in the hay. He was thinking about the probable situation at home — Mildred feeling poorly, wood to be split and carried to keep the house warm while wind came in at the cracks between logs, a cow to be milked, water to be pumped and so on. He was going home one way or another; and without trying to convert the stableman, he said, "Yo jus' keep that hoss till ah come fo' him. Ah got medicine fo' Mild'ed, yo' know."

Tying binder twine — ever a saving grace in rural Western Canada — around the bottoms of his overalls to keep snow out of his boots, and rolling up the collar of sheepskin coat to protect his face, John struck out with no more fuss than if going a few hundred yards to buy a box of matches. Even under favorable circumstances, it would take six hours or more to walk from Brooks to the cabin beside Ware's Creek, and darkness would be falling before that time elapsed. He was carrying no food; and he had no blankets — and evidently no fears. Inclining his big body against the wind, he walked away at a customary fast and resolute pace.

"Odds are against that fool fellow ever getting through in this weather," the stableman said later in the afternoon. "They'll be finding a frozen Negro piled up with dead cows in one of those draws. But why the hell am I talking? He's big enough to have his own way whatever I think. I'm not going to worry."

John plowed on. As long as the wind didn't shift, he was reasonably sure of his direction. Once he sat in the snow to contemplate; but not for long, because darkness would be settling upon him soon enough; he wanted to reach some familiar landmarks first.

Late in the afternoon he walked directly into strands of barbed wire and believed he recognized them as the fence of a homesteader four miles from his cabin. Without stopping to find the settler's house for purposes of verification, he waded forward with a strength nobody on the frontier could match. Any ordinary mortal would have been at the point of collapse from exhaustion before this. But John Ware was a human powerhouse — never known to have admitted fatigue, illness or despair — and he plodded on, periodically rubbing snow from his face and icicles from short-cropped whiskers.

Meanwhile Mildred was worried, not because she had wood to carry and a cow to milk, but because she knew John well enough to expect his attempt to get home in spite of the most forbidding obstacles. She was sure he'd be making his way from Brooks on horseback, and that would be bad enough. She prayed for his safety and instructed her little ones to do the same; and when darkness came she lit the kerosene lamp and placed it in the window, hoping the light might be seen through the snow.

After seven hours of walking and battling the unrelenting storm, John saw the light in the window and rejoiced. He knew Mildred was anxious. She met him in the doorway, embraced his snow-encrusted figure, and tenderly scolded him for venturing out, with or without a horse.

He was happy to be with his family at any price in human endurance. A man should be at home when weather turns ugly, he was convinced. Mildred took her medicine, confident that it made her feel better even before the bitter-tasting stuff reached her stomach.

Next morning the snow was falling as thickly as ever, but for the benefit of some cattle still huddled in the creekbed, John hauled a load of hay and was sure he had saved a few calves.

After four days of the worst May storm John and his friends remembered, the weather became suddenly clear and calm. John, like ranchers elsewhere, mounted and set out to assess the damage. Everybody knew that losses couldn't be determined accurately until the June roundup, but the evidence was alarming — even sickening. Some Eide cattle were known to have drowned, having drifted aimlessly and blindly into the Red Deer River; and Gordon, Ironside and Fares men estimated their losses in hundreds of head at least. Nobody in the cattle country lying eastward from the foothills escaped.

For "Uncle" Tony Day's 30,000 Turkey Track cattle, recent arrivals on Canadian grass, the storm was a cruel baptism, leaving 2,000 frozen carcasses. Incidentally, while such a reverse appeared terrible, it was small compared with the crushing loss of something over 10,000 Turkey Track cattle in a later winter — the heart-breaking winter of 1906-07, which John Ware didn't live to witness. It was enough to depress the most blithesome spirit, but stout-hearted "Uncle" Tony wasn't giving up.

And as the Knights of Raymond discovered, range sheep suffered about as much as cattle in the memorable blizzard. On account of hardships in the previous winter and their heavy losses in the May storm, the Knights decided to quit sheep and concentrate on other segments of their expanding business. They embarked immediately upon liquidation; and by summer's end, what had been the biggest flock of sheep in the Territories was reduced to less than one-tenth of its former size.

John Ware was never sure how many of his cattle died in the storm but probably the number exceeded a hundred, including calves. Anyway, there were stinking carcasses in every coulee when the spring roundup was started that year. It was depressing, to say the least, and many cattlemen knew their losses could ruin them. But roundups were none the less necessary, and John Ware rode with the two Eide boys and Harry Wagner. Their work lay toward Medicine Hat. John wasn't the captain that year, but he was still the friendly fellow with good judgment and iron muscles. It was to him that men of the range were turning more and more when they needed help.

In the course of that June operation, Harry Wagner's horse stepped in a badger hole; and falling heavily, the rider broke his shoulder. They were working below Brooks at the time, and preparations were made at once to drive the injured man to Medicine Hat. But before such a journey could be undertaken, first aid was needed to give the fractured bones some temporary support.

At the "Hat," when the nurses removed Wagner's shirt, they discovered a most impressive support or splint, bandaged neatly on the injured man's back. It was an iron survey stake, shaped to fit the contour of the human frame. Who had bent the heavy iron shaft? It was John Ware, of course, whose powerful hands had twisted the heavy rod as a more average person would bend barbed wire.

This wasn't Sheep Creek or foothills country; but nevertheless, the cattlemen knew John Ware and respected him. However, there were still some individuals outside the ranks of ranchers who didn't understand, and who lacked the sense of brotherhood which typified the Canadian range more than most communities. It was at the end of the roundup that John and one who was to become a leading breeder of purebred Herefords, seeking rooms for the night, entered a hotel at Medicine Hat. John's request was met with the brusque reply, "No rooms for colored fellows here."

The other cattleman reacted explosively. "What did you say? No room for my friend? Because he's colored? Young fellow, don't you be a fool. This colored man's worth three yellow ones like you. Yes, by George, I said three like you. Now give him a room or you'll have the damndest fight on your hands. Do you get me?"

The hotelman understood well enough and John was given a room — a good one. When he came down in the morning, he was greeted by the man at the desk: "Good morning, sir; how did you enjoy your rest?"

The roundup had served to reduce slightly the estimates of losses from the May storm. It served also to convince any doubters of the changing order of things in ranching. As cowboys who sat to smoke a pipe of tobacco beside the chuck wagon or who met at Medicine Hat agreed, the range was losing a lot of its old character. "Too many farms," they said; "too many people, too much law."

Even before the cattlemen turned toward home, following the roundup, a charge was laid against one of the roundup captains, the outcome of which was to make range history and completely shatter an association's license to dispose of mavericks to its profit. The outcome was almost enough to make men forget about the storm and its high cost. John Ware and fellow cattlemen watched attentively.

Mavericks had been gathered in every roundup herd. It was inevitable. By common consent among big ranch operators both north and south of the international boundary, those unmarked critters became the property of the roundup association and could be butchered to furnish beef for the chuck wagons or sold to pay roundup expenses. Not satisfied with this profitable arrangement, the Stock Growers in annual convention in 1900 went further, and moved to treat cattle with indistinct brands the same way. Ranchers fancied the idea; but farmers and settlers, most of whom did no branding, saw themselves losing cattle.

A. L. Sifton, later Premier of Alberta, became Chief Justice in 1903 and moved boldly. Among his first judgments was one sentencing the notorious Ernest Cashel to be hanged for murder, and then there were several showing a determination to put an end to cattle and horse stealing. Ten-year sentences with hard labor became sufficiently common that no rustler cared to meet Judge Sifton in a courtroom.

But few of Sifton's decisions startled the men of the range more than the one touching upon mavericks, delivered on November 20, 1903. A settler living near Medicine Hat had an unbranded steer which drifted away in the May storm. In due course it was collected by the roundup riders and held by the Association. As chance would have it, the settler recognized his steer and tried to recover it. But the claim was refused by the tradition-bound roundup captain. Along with other mavericks, this one was sold by the Association, bringing nineteen dollars. The unhappy settler notified the Mounted Police, and a charge of theft was laid against the captain, James Crawford. To conduct the defense, the Association engaged P. J. Nolan, to whom, according to Bob Edwards, "all the best murderers go." Everybody expected Nolan to triumph, as he usually did.

The defense lawyer explained that the sale of mavericks was a ranch-land custom in Montana as well as in the Territories, but the learned judge had his own views — and strong ones. The roundup captain, as defendant, was found guilty; and so were other officers of the Association who authorized such a practice knowing they were selling cattle which did not belong to them. To Nolan's contention that unbranded cattle left on the range would be a temptation to rustlers, the judge said organized stockmen were not justified in anticipating prospective stealing on the part of others by stealing such cattle themselves.

Members of the associations were shocked; and as they collected in clusters at Fort Macleod or Lethbridge or Medicine Hat, many were ready to argue that the judge's ruling calling for the return of the maverick steer to the settler was wrong. Certainly it was a new concept; but a few people, including John Ware, short on formal education but long on common decency, said the ruling was entirely right.

"Ah don' love anybody who busts up this good g'ass," John said, "but if people don have t' bwand they cows, nobody — not even an association — should be able to steal 'em. Ah nevah stole a cow an' ah'd sho like t' think none of the cowmen ah know would steal anythin', not even an ol lassoo."

CHAPTER 25

DEATH OF A GENTLEMAN — END OF AN ERA

On September 1, 1905, the two provinces of Alberta and Saskatchewan were created — carved out of the old Northwest Territories — to give most citizens a long-awaited feeling of democratic maturity. A few weeks later John Ware, who had never been thrown from a bad horse, and who laughed boyishly when he rode the rough ones, fell with a quiet one and was killed instantly.

In more than one way the year marked the end of an era. Homestead entries, which totaled 7,426 in the year 1900, soared to 30,891 in 1905. The result John Ware had foreseen was substantially realized. Open range was almost a thing of the past. Barbed wire was becoming as much a part of standard ranch equipment as stock saddles. The CPR was about to irrigate a great tract of dry land east of Calgary, and altogether, the West was emerging with a new face.

Nor were the changes all good. Unfortunately, only a few people were thinking about the evils of poor land use. John Ware had been one of them. "The way they ah plowin up this good g'ass," he had observed, "they must think it aint wo'th much. Some day they'll know they plowed too much — shoulda left mo' of it the way God planted it. Yo know, yo can't plant that kinda g'ass back aftah yo find the land won't do any good fo wheat."

But not many people listened to the warning and fewer were impressed by the philosophy. Breaking plows continued to tear into western sod, regardless of its suitability for cultivated crops.

There was more evidence of transition, lots of it. The Cochrane Ranch, first of the big cattle companies and long symbolic of the enterprise and courage which pioneered the range, was now terminating — selling out. Senator Cochrane, the ranch founder, eighty years of age and with failing eyesight, died on August 12, 1903. In the next year, his half million acres of deeded land was sold to the Mormon Church at $6.25 per acre. Ten thousand cattle remained on the ranch until sold to E. H. Maunsell and John Cowdry of Macleod, the transaction amounting to about $240,000.

Most significant was the fact that this sale marked the end of the first big ranch outfit on the Canadian Prairies. There would be more big beef-making spreads — like the Matador, starting on six townships of lease beside the South Saskatchewan River, north of Swift Current, about the time of the Cochrane Ranch sale, but there'd be no more ranches quite like the Cochrane.

Nor would there be any more cattlemen quite like John Ware, the ex-slave who left a thousand good cattle and the affection of all who knew him. And he left more. This man who had ridden half a million miles in stock saddle left lessons of importance for Canadians.

It was a year of tragedy for the Ware family. Early in the year, Mother Ware became quite sick. There being no doctor within calling distance, John nursed her as well as possible, then insisted she go to a hospital in Calgary. Grandmother Lewis came from Blairmore to care for the five children, Nettie, Robert, William, Mildred and Arthur.

At the breakfast table on an April morning soon after her arrival at the ranch, Grandmother Lewis was telling John about a most disturbing dream; she thought she saw Calgary's Royal Hotel burning. And while she was telling her dream John glanced through the window and remarked, "Somebody on a hoss."

The rider carried a telegram. Mother Ware was dead at Holy Cross Hospital, of typhoid and pneumonia. Sadness settled over the home and over the community along the Red Deer, where Mildred Ware was known as a good cook, a good mother and a good neighbor.

The grandmother took the five children back to Blairmore, and John invited a colored friend, Pete Smith, to stay with him and do the cooking. But John was lonely; and shortly before his tragic accident, his son Bob, then ten years old, returned to the ranch.

It was September 12 and a herd of fat steers was being held near home in anticipation of a visit from a Pat Burns buyer. Mosquitoes made the animals restless; and John, mounted on his gray mare, Flaxie, was turning any cattle showing an interest in heading toward Tilley and Twelve Mile Coulee.

"Yo go on home fo suppah," John instructed son Bob, who had been riding close to his father. "Ah'll stay heah a while and hold these cows till they settle down."

At that instant, as he turned the gray mare, she put a foot in a badger hole and fell awkwardly, with the rider underneath.

The lad saw the mishap and hastened to his father's side. The mare got up and walked away; but the man lying on the ground, was motionless. Bob tried to rouse his father but there was no response. Terrified, he galloped home, told Pete Smith that help was needed, and then continued on to tell the Eides on the PK Ranch.

Pete and John Eide lost no time. They hitched a team to the family democrat, forded the river and drove to where the accident had occurred. The Eides knew little or nothing about medicine or human physiology, but it was perfectly obvious that John Ware was dead. Shocked and saddened to the point of tears, they placed the body on the buckboard and hauled it home. Next day they transported it over the long trail to Brooks.

Some of John Ware's friends, George Lane among them, were loading cattle at Brooks at the time. With emotion in his voice, Lane passed the word to Billy Henry and Sam Howe and the others. "John Ware is dead," he said, then went straightaway and telegraphed liveryman Johnny Hamilton at Calgary to have his hearse meet the train to receive the body.

Sam Howe, working for Billy Henry at the time, asked for time off to attend the funeral of his late great friend. Of course he should be at the funeral. The request was granted. But while Sam waited for the train and minutes seemed like hours, he made the mistake of trying to dull the sorrow by resorting to the contents of a bottle. When it came time to board the westbound train, he was somewhat confused, got on the wrong one and ended up at Medicine Hat instead of Calgary. Sam missed the funeral, and never after wanted to talk about the circumstances of that week.

They brought the body back to Calgary for burial, back to that place where John Ware had experienced so much trouble, where people had allowed the memory of Jesse Williams to becloud their objectivity and sense of justice, where they'd tried to send him to jail for no reason the police could name. But John Ware's character had triumphed over prejudice, as the funeral held at the Baptist Church on September 14 gave the most ample proof. It was the biggest seen in Calgary up to that time. Notwithstanding the primitive state of communications, the sad news reached the foothills and prairie communities; and hours before the service, wagons, buggies, democrats and saddle horses were converging upon the city, bearing men and women in whose hearts pride in knowing John Ware now mingled with sadness.

George Lane, E. D. Adams, Charlie Douglas, Pete Eide and Joe Shannon were pallbearers, and to quote the Calgary *Herald*: "A great many from remote districts as well as townspeople were present to pay their respects to the remains of one of Alberta's pioneers . . . Rev. F. W. Paterson conducted the services. The remains were taken from Smart's undertaking establishment to the Baptist Church and from there to the Union Cemetery."

The tributes written and spoken were many. Stories were told of his generosity, his sense of honor and his strength. Men recalled the day at Medicine Hat when he walked across a corral full of range bulls, stepping from one wild back to another with no other motive than to get to the other side by the shortest route. They talked about the time he pulled a cow out of a bog, single-handed.

A reporter wrote: "He was a man of prodigious strength and with apparent ease could pick up an 18 months old steer and throw him readily for branding. Any person who has tried to throw even a six months old steer will realize that this feat is no small one."

The Ware children had a good home with their grandparents and grew up to be good citizens like their parents.

R. B. Bennett was instructed to settle the John Ware estate, and Sam Howe laughed at a lawyer's professional folly in selling all the horses first, then having to hire saddle horses to round up the cattle.

Rod Macleay, who had taken a lease near Brooks in the previous year, bought the Ware cattle and the brand, and J. T. Bell and Sons bought the hundred or more horses and trailed them to Medicine Hat. They were good cattle and good horses; but in the second year following, ranchers experienced another of those killing winters, and between 75 and 80 per cent of the cattle along the Red Deer River perished. "It's hard to tell how John Ware would have made out if he had been alive," one of his acquaintances remarked; "but John wouldn't have been caught without feed; he was the greatest stockman I ever knew."

As anyone could see, the expressions of admiration and respect were many and they were varied. But the tribute which should have remained in men's minds the longest was from the funeral oration. "John Ware," said the minister, "was a man with a beautiful skin. Every human skin is as beautiful as the character of the person who wears it. To know John Ware was to know a gentleman, one of God's gentlemen. Never again will I see a colored skin as anything but lovely. He leaves me with the thought that black is a beautiful color — one which the Creator must have held in particularly high favor because He gave it to His most cheerful people. Make no mistake about it, black can be beautiful."

Thirty-five years after John Ware's death, a dozen men with the story and spirit of the early West burning in their hearts, sat together in Calgary's Palliser Hotel. It was Stampede Week and everybody in the group was correctly attired in frontier pants, colored shirts and string ties. But these men were together for a purpose — to consider the formation of a society to be dedicated to the preservation of the traditions of the Old West. About the need for such a body there seemed general agreement. But by what name should it be known?

"The Frontier Club" was proposed; also the "Western Society." The suggestions had merit, but enthusiasm was absent until one of those present offered his idea that the organization should be "The John Ware Society."

At once there was agreement. The name conveyed what the prospective members wanted it to convey. These men knew the story about the great colored cowboy — the story of hardships overcome, his success as a rancher, his skill as a rider, the power of his muscles, and the friendly nature which commanded hearts.

The John Ware Society, like many other organizations conceived in enthusiasm, didn't survive very long. That, however, was no fault of its high purpose and the good name which symbolized the spirit of the early range — where pedigree, race, wealth, and color set nobody apart, and where honesty, friendliness, and resourcefulness were the real measures of a man.

GRANT MacEWAN

Grant MacEwan, a native Westerner, has had a long and distinguished career as educator, agriculturalist, author, lecturer, showring judge, politician, and public servant in Western Canada.

The son of pioneers who farmed first in the Brandon district of Manitoba and later in the Melfort district of Saskatchewan, Grant, who was born in 1902, gained firsthand knowledge of the development of prairie agriculture, which he has described in such books as *Harvest of Bread,* 1969 (the story of wheat) and *Power for Prairie Plows,* 1971. Following his boyhood interest in farming, he attended the Ontario College of Agriculture at Guelph, where he received a B.S.A. degree, and he pursued the postgraduate degree of Master of Science at Ames, Iowa.

From 1928 to 1946 he was on the staff of the University of Saskatchewan, in later years as head of the animal husbandry department. In 1946 he was appointed Dean of Agriculture of the University of Manitoba and remained in that post until 1951 when he resigned in order to have more time to follow his many other interests. In that year Calgary became his home, and "Cow Town" later was to know him as its alderman or mayor for many years. He continued to write — books, magazine articles, newspaper columns — and became increasingly in demand as a public speaker and as a livestock and horse show judge in both Eastern and Western Canada.

In 1966 Grant MacEwan was appointed Lieutenant-Governor of Alberta. He has received honorary degrees from the Universities of Alberta, Calgary, Brandon, Guelph, and Saskatchewan. Tall, spare, energetic, Grant MacEwan has astounded and delighted Albertans by his ability to outwalk men a fraction of his age in walkathons designed to raise money for worthy causes, a prowess no doubt inherited from ancestors who developed good leg muscles on the hills of Scotland.